Classroom Management for Elementary Teachers

Classroom Management for Elementary Teachers

SEVENTH EDITION

Carolyn M. Evertson
Peabody College, Vanderbilt University

Edmund T. Emmer
The University of Texas, Austin

Murray E. Worsham
Northeast Independent School District, San Antonio, Texas (retired)

PEARSON

Boston   New York   San Francisco
Mexico City   Montreal   Toronto   London   Madrid   Munich   Paris
Hong Kong   Singapore   Tokyo   Cape Town   Sydney

Senior Editor: *Arnis E. Burvikovs*
Editorial Assistant: *Kelly Hopkins*
Marketing Manager: *Tara Kelly*
Editorial-Production Service: *Matrix Productions Inc.*
Composition and Prepress Buyer: *Linda Cox*
Manufacturing Buyer: *Andrew Turso*
Cover Administrator: *Kristina Mose-Libon*
Interior Designer: *Ellen Pettengell*
Cover Designer: *Suzanne Harbison*
Photo Researcher: *Katharine S. Cook; Larissa Tierney*
Electronic Composition: *Omegatype Typography, Inc.*

Photo Credits: p. 1: Felicia Martinez/PhotoEdit; **p.19:** David Young-Wolff/PhotoEdit; **p. 41:** Getty Images, Inc.-PhotoDisc; **p. 58:** Ariel Skelley/CORBIS-NY; **p. 87:** Mug Shots/ Corbis/Stock Market; **p. 111:** Bob Daemmrich/The Image Works; **p. 132:** LWA-Dann Tardif/CORBIS-NY; **p. 149:** Mary Kate Denny/Getty Images Inc.-Stone Allstock; **p. 170:** Elena Rooraid/PhotoEdit; **p. 194:** Richard Hutchings/Science Source/Photo Researchers, Inc.

Library of Congress Cataloging-in-Publication Data

Evertson, Carolyn M.
    Classroom management for elementary teachers / Carolyn M. Evertson, Edmund T. Emmer, Murray E. Worsham.—7th ed.
        p. cm.
    Includes bibliographical references and index.
    ISBN 0-205-45533-6
    1. Classroom management.   2. Education, Elementary.   I. Emmer, Edmund T.   II. Worsham, Murray E.   III. Title.
LB3013.C528 2005
372.1102'4—dc22

2004062326

Printed in the United States of America

10 9 8 7 6 5 4 3 2 1   HAM   09 08 07 06 05

To the many teachers who have taught us about classroom management

C.M.E.
E.T.E.
M.E.W.

Contents

3

Fostering Student Accountability 41

4

Getting Off to a Good Start 58

5

Planning and Conducting Instruction 87

6

Managing Cooperative Learning Groups 111

9

Managing Problem Behaviors 170

APPENDIX

Appendix: Answer Keys for Chapter Activities 226

Preface

Public scrutiny of our schools has never been more intense than it is today. This attention has placed demands on schools and teachers for accountability and more student testing; it has increased media coverage of school violence at the same time that most scholarly studies report that violence has actually decreased; and it has led to the call for "better schools" as a means of furthering a variety of political agendas. These societal pressures might give the impression that schools and classrooms are fundamentally different and that the task of managing a classroom has changed markedly. In fact, the basic principles for creating an effective learning environment remain the same. What teachers must do is to adapt these core ideas to the settings in which they now teach, a problem that every generation of teachers has had to address and solve as they encounter changing social and demographic conditions.

Students entering the nation's schools come with such widely diverse backgrounds, capabilities, interests, and skills that meeting their needs and finding appropriate learning activities requires a great deal of care and skill. Because one of the first and most basic tasks for the teacher is to develop a smoothly running classroom community where students are highly involved in worthwhile activities that support their learning, establishing an effective classroom management system is a first priority. Teachers who have developed such systems have taught us a great deal about the essential features of their classrooms and how they work to establish them.

What we have learned is that well-managed classrooms exist because teachers have clear ideas of the types of classroom conditions and student behaviors necessary for a healthy learning environment. They not only have clear ideas, but they also work very hard to create these conditions. This book describes what you can do to create a well-managed classroom. The process is described as teachers encounter it: first by planning in several key areas before the school year begins, then by implementing the plan and establishing good management at the beginning of the year, and finally by maintaining the management procedures throughout the year.

We have tried to make the materials useful and practical by providing checklists to help you organize your planning. Several case studies and problem-solving scenarios focus on critical areas for managing students and the curriculum. We hope you will find much here that is helpful as you plan and organize your own classroom.

This edition contains numerous new references and the addition of more than twenty-five websites. Chapter 1 includes more activities for creating workable room arrangements. Chapter 4, "Getting Off to a Good Start," has additional information about creating positive classrooms with an emphasis on building community. To address other issues on planning for instruction in Chapter 5, we have acknowledged the research on learning styles and included a chart on instructional formats that can accommodate different styles. We have added a section in Chapter 9 on bullying and power struggles and have included new references and websites to help educators cope with this serious problem. Throughout the text we have increased our coverage of working with students with diverse backgrounds, needs, and skills.

A classroom management video that illustrates procedures, planning, communication, and managing classroom behavioral issues accompanies this edition. Taken from actual classroom footage, this video shows real teaching examples and challenges new teachers to respond to various problem situations. Also, the My Lab School website available to users of this book contains extensive classroom footage that can be used in class or as homework.

Our own experiences as teachers continue to inform the foundation of this text. However, much of our knowledge about systematic classroom management comes from research and observation, both our own and others'. This text draws on our experiences in providing research-based findings and support to new teachers through COMP: Creating Conditions for Learning at Peabody College, Vanderbilt University (www.comp.org). Data collected in this research are a major source of suggestions, guidelines, vignettes, and case studies in this book. We gratefully acknowledge our debt to the teachers who have allowed us to learn from them.

We are grateful to Margaret Moore, who provided insights and suggestions for this edition and made helpful contributions through her critical analysis and suggestions for revisions. As always, we appreciate the contributions of the many observers, school administrators, and other researchers who have both assisted and enlightened us. We also extend thanks to the following reviewers whose suggestions guided this revision: Judy Bippert, San Diego State University; Sue Evans, California Polytechnic State University; and Diane W. Hudson, Athens State University.

1

Organizing Your Classroom and Supplies

Arranging the physical setting for teaching is a logical starting point for classroom management because it is a task that all teachers face before school begins. Many teachers find it easier to plan other aspects of classroom management once they know how the physical features of the classroom will be organized.

The number of things to consider in arranging the typical elementary school classroom is amazing! Of course, there is furniture—the teacher's and the students' desks, bookcases, filing cabinets, chairs, and a table or two. There also may be audio-visual equipment such as an overhead projector, computer, CD player, VCR, and television. Visual aids such as bulletin boards must be prepared; charts and maps must be displayed; and storage for materials must be provided. Finally, teachers bring personal touches to a classroom—perhaps plants, an aquarium, or cages for pets. When you arrange these features, you must make many decisions. How should desks be arranged? Where should your desk be located? Where will groups meet with you? Where will cooperative groups work? What areas of the room will you use for presentations? How will you and the students obtain materials and supplies?

In this chapter we discuss how to plan for a room arrangement that supports your teaching. You will learn four keys to room arrangement and read numerous suggestions for managing space in your classroom. You will be asked to analyze two room arrangements. This chapter concludes with a checklist for your classroom.

FOR REFLECTION

Before you begin to arrange your classroom, think about the following questions. The answers will help you decide what physical features need special attention. Before you look at your classroom, think about the kinds of learning you would most like to see there:

■ What are your main types of instructional activities (e.g., small groups, whole-class discussions, teacher presentations, student presentations, individual assignments, group projects)? What physical arrangements will best support these activities?

■ Will students be making extensive use of equipment (e.g., microscopes, CD players, computers) or materials (e.g., science or math manipulatives)? Will these be shared among individuals or groups?

■ Does your class include students with special needs that must be considered?

■ Where are the areas of potential distraction (high traffic, animals, group centers)? Which children will need screening or distance from these areas?

■ How much movement around the room will be necessary during the day? What areas of the room will be involved? Will students get their own materials, or will you distribute them?

■ Will students need access to references, research tools, or trade books?

■ How flexible or permanent will the arrangement be? Will you have to change it during a single day, for each new unit, or will it stay the same for months?

Your decisions will have important consequences for the success of your instructional activities. Your room arrangement also affects how smoothly the day can proceed. For example, if areas for storing materials are poorly placed, bottlenecks may occur when students get or return supplies, which could slow down the activities or waste time getting them started. The location for your meetings with individuals and small groups must be chosen carefully, otherwise you may have difficulty watching the rest of the class. The positioning of desks is important because a poor arrangement may interfere with visibility of instructional areas, increase distractions during instruction, or make it difficult for you and your students to move around the room.

Your room arrangement communicates to students how you expect them to participate in your class. Desks arranged in groups imply that interaction and collaboration among students are expected at least for some activities. Desks in rows indicate that the focus of the classroom is the teacher, the board, or some other central point. Your room arrangement should reflect your philosophy of teaching and learning.

This chapter will help you make these and other decisions about room arrangement, equipment, and basic supplies. Each component is described, and guidelines and examples will help you plan. Use Checklist 1 to organize your efforts in this important task and to be certain your classroom is ready for the beginning of school.

Four Keys to Good Room Arrangement

Remember that the classroom is the learning environment for both you and your students. It is not a very large area for up to thirty people interacting for long periods of time—as much as seven hours in a day. Furthermore, you and your students will be engaging in a variety of activities and using different areas of the room.

You will facilitate these activities if you arrange your room to permit orderly movement, keep distractions to a minimum, and make efficient use of available space. Depending on your instructional approach, you may need different arrangements for different activities (e.g., whole-class, small group). Chapter 5 provides more detail about instructional formats. Use the following four keys as guidelines for deciding about your room's arrangements:

1. **Keep high-traffic areas free of congestion.** Areas where many students gather and areas that receive constant use can be sites for distraction and disruption. High-traffic areas include group work areas, pencil sharpener, trash can, water fountain, certain bookshelves and storage areas, computer stations, student desks, and the teacher's desk. These areas should be widely separated from each other, have plenty of space, and be easy to get to. Also, if students will be working at computers or in various parts of the room during a single lesson, make sure they can move easily from place to place.

2. **Be sure students can be seen easily by the teacher.** Careful monitoring of students is a major management task. Your success in monitoring will depend on your ability to see all students at all times. Therefore, be sure there are clear lines of sight between instructional areas, your desk, student desks, and all student work areas. Be especially conscious of the placement of bookcases, file cabinets, and other pieces of furniture and equipment that can block your line of vision. Stand in different parts of the room and check for blind spots.

3. **Keep frequently used teaching materials and student supplies readily accessible.** Keeping materials accessible not only minimizes time spent getting ready and cleaning up, it also helps to avoid distracting slowdowns and breaks in the lesson flow. If you or your students must stop to locate needed materials and supplies, you run the risk of losing student attention and engagement. Time is lost as you must refocus attention to the lesson. (The idea of lesson flow is discussed further in Chapter 5.)

4. **Be certain students can easily see whole-class presentations and displays.** When you plan where you and your students will be for whole-class presentations and discussion, be sure that the seating arrangement will allow students to see the overhead projector screen or board without moving their chairs, turning their desks around, or craning their necks. Also, don't plan to conduct whole-class activities in a far corner of the room away from a substantial number of students. Such conditions do not encourage students to pay attention, and they make it more difficult for you to keep all students involved. Check out how well your students can see by sitting for a moment at desks in different parts of the room.

Applying each of these four keys will help you design workable room arrangements. The specific components that will lead to this goal are described next. By attending to these areas, you will address all of the important aspects of room arrangement.

Suggestions for Arranging Your Classroom

Wall and Ceiling Space

Wall space and bulletin boards provide areas to display student work, instructionally relevant material, decorative items, assignments, rules, schedules, a clock, and other items of interest. Ceiling space can also be used to hang mobiles, decorations, and student work. The following points should be considered when preparing these areas:

1. At the start of school, you should have at least the following displays for walls and boards:
   - Class rules (discussed in Chapter 2)
   - A place for daily assignments or the daily schedule
   - Some decorative display to catch your students' interest, such as a bulletin board with a "Welcome Back to School" motif, or a display that includes the name of each child in the room
   - A calendar
   - If required, emergency escape routes (usually posted near the door)

2. Other displays that teachers find useful include an example of the correct paper heading and a content-relevant display, such as one highlighting a soon-to-be-taught topic. Many teachers also provide posters of useful strategies for content areas such as reading, and informational charts on the steps in writing.

3. Displays may be used to help keep track of your students' locations. You may wish to create a poster with a pocket for each child. These pockets can be made of library cardholders or laminated halves of envelopes. Label each pocket with a child's name. Whenever a child leaves the room, he or she inserts a popsicle stick or construction paper strip labeled with the destination. The same idea can be used to create a record of jobs or privileges, such as being the line leader or materials manager.

4. You will probably want to cover large bulletin board areas with colored paper, burlap, or other fabric. This paper comes on large rolls and is often kept in the school office or a supply room. You can trim the bulletin boards with an edging or border of corrugated paper. If you can't find this item in your supply room, you can find them at a school supply center or other store. You can also find books of bulletin board ideas for sale at such stores. Be sure paper or material on walls or ceiling does not violate safety or fire codes.

5. Don't spend too much time decorating your room. You will have many other important things to do to get ready for the beginning of school. A few bare bulletin boards won't bother anybody. Leave one or two empty and add displays later or allow children to decorate a blank space for an art project or as part of a science or social studies unit. Don't overdecorate. Wall space cluttered with detail can be distracting and make a room seem smaller. Hanging mobiles and decorations from

"Do you sometimes get the feeling that this classroom was designed for older students?"

Cartoon reprinted courtesy of *Phi Delta Kappan* and James Estes.

the ceiling can also be overdone. Your room will seem small enough when your twenty-five to thirty students are in it.

6. If you need ideas for decorating your room or for setting up displays, borrow hints from other teachers or look in some other rooms.

As the cartoon suggests, whatever decorating ideas or displays you use should be age appropriate for your students.

Floor Space

Arrange furniture and equipment so that you can easily observe students from all areas of the room in which you will work. Students should be able to see you, the overhead projector screen, the main board, and any other area to be used for presentations to the whole class. Of course, you will have to adjust to whatever constraints exist in your assigned classroom. Common problems are a classroom that is too small or that has inadequate or poorly placed board space or electrical outlets. Assess your space and determine what changes are feasible within the existing constraints. For example, if the classroom is small, remove unnecessary student desks, other furniture, or equipment; if you have inadequate storage, perhaps you can locate an extra file or supply cabinet.

A good starting point for your floor plan is to determine where you will conduct whole-class instruction. Identify where you will stand or work when you address the entire class to give instructions. You can usually identify this area of the room by the location of a large board or the overhead projector screen. This area should also have room for a table or desk where you can place items needed in presentations and an electrical outlet for the projector. If you prefer to have your students gather on the floor for whole-class instruction, allow adequate space when arranging the classroom furniture. You may also want to provide a large rug for this area.

To plan your floor space, make a scaled drawing of the classroom and templates for various furnishings (e.g., student desks, your desk, bookshelves, computer stations, etc.). This will decrease the number of times you have to move the heavy furniture, and it will be a more efficient use of your planning time. When you start arranging furniture, have extension cords in hand. They are easier to plug in before a heavy bookcase is standing in front of the outlet. Be aware of potential electrical hazards with extension cords.

As you read the following items, refer to Figure 1.1, an example of a workable floor plan for an elementary school classroom. Note how each item has been addressed. Of course, this is just one of many possible alternatives. The location of desks, the small-group area, and other physical features of the classroom will depend on the size and shape of the room and how various parts of the room will be used.

Figure 1.1 An Example of a Workable Room Arrangement

ARRANGEMENT OF STUDENT DESKS

The key to arranging student desks lies in the kinds of activities that will be undertaken in your classroom. If most instruction is whole group, desks should be arranged so that all students can look at the instructional area without having to get out of their seats or having to sit with their backs to the area. If the majority of your instruction is teacher led, you may prefer to arrange the desks in rows. If students will work in small groups frequently, you may want to arrange their desks in groups with students facing one another. If you arrange desks in groups, decide how many students to include in each group. If you have a student with a physical disability or a hyperactivity disorder, you may have to consider special seating.

Determine whether your seating arrangement will vary according to the types of classroom activities or will be permanent. After you have established the seating arrangement, decide whether you will assign students to seats or allow them to choose where they will sit. In Figure 1.1 student desks are arranged in clusters rather than in rows; however, no students are seated with their backs to the major instructional area. If the teacher displays material on the overhead projector screen, all of the students can see it by turning slightly in their seats.

■ It is important to keep high-traffic areas clear, so don't put desks or other furniture in front of doors, water fountains, sinks, the pencil sharpener, or other traffic centers. Also, try to avoid having your whole-class arrangement face potential sources of distraction, such as windows, the small-group area, animals, or other eye-catching displays. Make sure that computer stations are accessible but not distracting.

■ Leave enough room around student desks so that you can move among and monitor the students easily or give them help during seatwork activities.

■ Some classrooms are equipped with tables and chairs for students instead of desks. Table seating presents special problems, especially in grade levels higher than first and second grades. If students are seated on all sides of tables, some will have their backs to instructional areas. If you have enough space and tables, you can avoid this visibility problem by seating students on only three sides of the tables. An additional problem is the storage of student supplies such as paper, notebooks, textbooks, crayons, and scissors. If there are no individual storage spaces under tables, tote trays (boxes or plastic dish tubs) may be used for student materials. These must be stored on easily accessible shelves or carts. If you want to promote sharing among students, "community" tote trays can be shared. This also cuts down on the need for each student to have a full set of supplies. Plan the location of such storage areas carefully, for they will be used frequently and often by many students at once. Give thorough consideration to traffic patterns around and near tote tray storage areas.

■ Count the desks or chairs and make sure you have enough.

■ You may decide to change room arrangements during the year. If you begin the year with desks in rows, switch to a desks touching arrangement later in the year (see Figure 1.2). Changes to routines can stimulate students' interest, and a new arrangement may increase opportunities for social learning.

Figure 1.2 Example of a Double U-shaped Arrangement with Easy Access to Special Topic Areas

SMALL-GROUP INSTRUCTION AREAS

You will need an area where you can meet with small groups of students for brainstorming, helping with a group project, or working with individuals. Arrange this area so that you can observe the rest of the class from your position within the small group. Place your chair so that you face the whole class. Note the position of the small-group area in Figure 1.1. If you are seated facing out toward the room, you can monitor the whole class even when working with the small group. If you are seated in the opposite chair with your back to the class, you cannot see the whole class unless you turn around. Although not required for a reading group, the table allows this area to be used for small-group activities that include writing or working with materials.

When a table or extra chairs are not available, students may be asked to carry their chairs and place them in a circle (or to sit on a rug) for group instruction. An alternative is to assign seats so that students can remain at their desks or tables for small-group instruction while the teacher moves from group to group.

If many small groups will be working in your classroom at once (e.g., cooperative groups, research groups, literature discussion groups, or writing process groups), you will have to provide areas where they can meet. For instance, groups can meet on the floor, at student desks, or at the small-group table. Chapter 6 has additional information on arranging your classroom for cooperative groups.

COMPUTER WORKSTATIONS

Most classrooms are now equipped with computers. This technology can greatly expand the learning opportunities available to students, but it must be managed carefully. Your location choices may be limited because of the need for wall outlets and a phone or cable line, so consider placing the computer workstations first and then arranging other centers and activity areas. Some schools have computers on rolling carts to be shared among classrooms. With this situation, you will have to consider the ease in getting them in and out of the room. Place the computers away from chalk dust, liquids, and magnets.

When arranging your room, make sure that monitors are positioned so that you can quickly scan them to be sure students are on task. This is especially important if students have Internet access. You will probably also need space to store paper, software, ink cartridges, and other supplies.

Large groups of students around a computer can lead to disturbances and off-task behavior. Limit the number of students working on the computer to no more than four. Make sure the children who are using the computers have a purpose and a time limit. Teach students to save their work if they are unable to finish their projects in a given time frame.

THE TEACHER'S DESK, FILING CABINET, OVERHEAD PROJECTOR, AND OTHER EQUIPMENT

Your desk must be placed where it is functional. If you intend to use your desk to store instructional materials, it should be adjacent to the whole-class instructional area and preferably near any other major instructional area. If you plan to work at your desk at any time during the day, position it so you can monitor students. Use the same principle here that you use when arranging the small-group area: Sit facing the students and be sure that you can observe all of them from your seat. It is not necessary that students be able to see you from their seats, and some teachers prefer placing their desks at the back of the room rather than the front. If you plan to confer with individual students at your desk, consider traffic patterns near your desk. For example, student desks should not be so close that students would be distracted by individuals approaching your desk or working with you there.

Consider what access students have to materials on your desk. If they can use materials stored on your desk, such as a stapler or extra crayons, what are the procedures for obtaining these supplies. For example, may students get these supplies whenever necessary, or do they have to ask your permission?

Other furniture items, such as the filing cabinet and storage cabinets, also must be where they are functional. Seldom used supplies can be safely tucked away in a corner or hidden from view. Furniture that contains items that will be used frequently must be near the area in which they will be used. Be sure you can maintain visual contact with your students.

"Miss Marpole, I need to talk to you about your seating arrangement."
Reprinted by permission of George Abbott/*Phi Delta Kappan.*

BOOKCASES

Bookcases should be placed where they will neither hinder your monitoring nor obstruct students' ability to see chalkboards or relevant displays. If the bookcases contain items used frequently, such as dictionaries or the classroom library, they must be convenient and easily monitored. A bookcase for seldom used items should be in an out-of-the-way place. If you have only one bookcase, try to store unneeded items in a cabinet so that the bookcase can be used for the necessary materials. Consider using a rolling cart for materials that may have to be moved from group to group, such as resources for a particular research topic.

CENTERS

A center is an area where students may work on a special activity or study some topic. Often centers have special equipment such as tape recorders with headphones for individual students. Other centers may be built around a thematic study topic in science or social studies or around skill areas in a particular subject such as arithmetic or reading. Examples of types of centers in elementary classrooms include classroom libraries, listening centers, writing centers, science discovery centers, computer workstations, math centers, art centers, and dramatic play areas. The number and type of centers will vary according to grade levels and curriculum.

If you use centers in your classroom, consider carefully the location for each. For instance, if the center is to be a separate area of your room such as the classroom library, consider dividing it from the rest of the class with a low bookshelf or table so you can still monitor students. Also, if you anticipate increased noise or activity at a center, locate it so as not to disturb other students. If any of your centers require electrical outlets or phone lines, arrange them first. Also be certain that all necessary materials and equipment at the center are available and functioning properly. Post instructions for equipment use and cleaning up the center.

Some teachers like to have a more informal area in the classroom, including, for example, an area rug, bookcases, a small table, or some comfortable seating. Such an area can add an inviting, personal touch to the setting. Students might be allowed to use it for special projects, group work, or during free reading activities. (Procedures for use should be developed as described in Chapter 2.) If you use such a center, design its location so that it won't interfere with or distract from other activities. Also, because this type of center requires extensive floor space, weigh its advantages against the loss of space for other activities and the crowding that may result.

PETS, PLANTS, AQUARIUMS, AND SPECIAL ITEMS

These can add a personal touch to a room as well as provide learning experiences for children. However, the first week of school is already quite exciting for students, so it is not necessary to introduce these special features immediately. If you do bring in such items, place them where they won't distract students, especially during whole-class activities. Of course, they should be placed where they will neither impede movement about the room nor interfere with activities of individual students. Check to see whether any students are allergic to pets. You may also want to consider what responsibilities to assign students for the care of classroom pets (e.g., feeding fish).

Storage Space and Supplies

When you have decided on your wall and bulletin board displays and have organized your classroom space, you can concentrate on obtaining supplies and providing for their storage. Some supplies will be used frequently and should be readily accessible. Other items will be seasonal or used infrequently and thus can go into deeper storage.

TEXTBOOKS AND OTHER INSTRUCTIONAL MATERIALS

Identify the textbooks and other materials for use in your class. Other instructional materials may include dictionaries, encyclopedias, magazines, newspapers, maps, globes, and math manipulatives. Determine which books the students are allowed to keep at their desks or take home and which must remain in the room for all students to use. Then find easily accessible shelves in a bookcase for those everyday books and materials that will not be kept in student desks. If you don't know what supplemental materials are available or what the school policies are regarding these items, check with the school principal, media specialist, or another teacher.

STUDENT WORK

If students do not have space to store their folders and journals, or if you prefer to keep them in a central location, make sure this area is easily accessible. For example, if students are seated at tables, place a basket or milk crate in the center of the table. The basket or crate can contain a hanging file for each student at that table. Students can keep their folders, journals, and work in progress in the hanging files. If students are not seated at tables, or the tables are too small for baskets or crates, you can place baskets around the room. Also, if students will be developing portfolios, these must be in a convenient location.

Students' work may also be saved on computer CDs for future use. Frequently, teachers have individual boxes in which students may store their CDs or a class box may be used.

PORTFOLIO FILES

If your students keep portfolios of their work, it may be easier for the students and you to keep up with them if there is a specific storage space for them. Locate this in an area that makes it is easy for students to find their portfolios, place their work in them, and return them to a central spot. Also, think about whether you want to arrange the portfolios in alphabetical order or by tables.

FREQUENTLY USED CLASSROOM MATERIALS

Items included in a basic set of supplies for the children are paper in varying sizes and colors, water-soluble markers, rulers, assorted pens and chalk for art projects, transparent tape and masking tape, a stapler, and glue. These and any other supplies that are used daily—science materials, math manipulatives, calculators—should be kept in a handy place such as on a worktable or shelves. Students are usually expected to supply certain materials such as pencils, erasers, pens, crayons, scissors, and notebook paper or tablets. Because you cannot count on all students to bring these materials at the beginning of the year, make sure you have a supply of these items. Also, give parents a list of supplies each child in your class will need.

TEACHER'S SUPPLIES

You will receive some materials from the school office for your own use. These items may include pencils and pens; paper; a large, lined display tablet; chalk and erasers; overhead transparency sheets; scissors; transparent tape; ruler; stapler; paper clips; and thumbtacks. In addition, you should have a grade book, a lesson plan book, and teachers' editions for all textbooks. Ask about other supplementary books such as thematic resources or math or science standards. These items can usually be stored in your desk. Some schools restrict paper use or other materials for budget purposes. Be sure to note any limitations for the year.

OTHER MATERIALS

If your room does not have a clock and a calendar, obtain these now. Both should be large enough to be seen from all areas of the room. You may wish to buy a desk bell or a timer if you are going to use these as signals for starting or stopping activities. The following items may also come in handy: tissues, rags or paper towels, soap, bandages, plastic gloves, and extra lunch money for emergencies. Some teachers keep a few basic tools such as a hammer, pliers, and screwdriver for minor repairs.

STUDENT BELONGINGS

In addition to supplies that students store in their desks or in tote trays, you need storage available for items such as lunch boxes, book bags, outdoor clothing, lost-and-found items, and show-and-tell materials. Leave spaces for these items as you prepare your classroom. You might prepare signs designating the use to which each space will be put. Planning for storage will help keep your classroom from becoming cluttered and will help avoid the problem of misplaced belongings.

EQUIPMENT

Check all equipment, including the computer, TV, VCR, overhead projector, CD recorder, headphones, and pencil sharpener to make sure they are in working order. Get any necessary extension cords or adapter plugs, and store these with the equipment or in a handy place.

SEASONAL OR INFREQUENTLY USED ITEMS

Holiday and seasonal decorations, bulletin board displays, and special project materials are used only on some occasions, as are calculators, protractors, templates, special art project materials, and science equipment. Because you do not need ready access to these materials, you can store them at the back of closets, in boxes on top of cabinets, or even out of the room if you have access to outside storage space.

To organize and keep track of your activities as you arrange your room and get your equipment and supplies ready, you will find it helpful to use Checklist 1 at the end of this chapter. Each aspect of room arrangement has been listed, and space has been provided for noting what has to be done and for checking off each area.

 ## Further Reading

Butin, D. (2000). *Classrooms.* ERIC Report number ED446421. Washington, D.C.: National Center for Educational Facilities. Available at http://www.edfacilities.org/ir/irpubs.html.

The author discusses classroom design. Trends in classroom design principles and major issues in the use of classroom space are summarized. The website also has articles dealing with classroom design in content areas, as well as links to many related Web sites.

Evertson, C. M., & Poole, I. R. (2004). *Effective room arrangement.* IRIS Center for Faculty Enhancement. Nashville, Tenn.: Peabody College, Vanderbilt University. Available at http://iris.peabody.vanderbilt.edu/casestudies.html.

This website contains activities and case studies for accommodating special needs students in the classroom. Click on "Effective Room Arrangement" for the cases.

Fraser, B. J., & Walberg, H. J. (Eds.) (1991). *Educational environments: Evaluation, antecedents and consequences.* Oxford: Pergamon.

Classroom environments are much more than physical arrangements; they include organizational, instructional, and interpersonal dimensions. Their effects, moreover, depend substantially on how students perceive or experience the environments. This book thoroughly explores many aspects of learning environments, connecting them to a variety of social, institutional, and personal factors.

Jones, R. A. (1995). *The child-school interface: Environment and behavior.* London: Cassell.

Jones presents an analysis of how children's behaviors are influenced by the various environments they encounter at school. The author's point of view is ecological, incorporating the physical setting of the classroom as one of the contributors to children's behavior, along with social and organizational factors.

Meager, J. (1996). Classroom design that works every time. *Instructor, 106,* 70–73.

The author, a veteran classroom teacher, describes a number of charts, bulletin board ideas, and graphs that can be used to feature content and prompt desirable student behavior. Issues of the magazine, Instructor, *are often a good source of ideas and activities for classroom use.*

Schwarz, S., & Pollishuke, M. (1991). *Creating the child-centered classroom.* Katonah, N.Y.: Richard Owen Publishers. Chapter 2: The physical set-up of the classroom.

This book has useful and practical information on room arrangements, planning varied activities, group work, creating learning centers, and creating an effective learning atmosphere. It includes blackline masters for teacher or student use.

Weinstein, C. S., & David, T. G. (Eds.) (1987). *Spaces for children: The built environment and child development.* New York: Plenum Press.

Various chapters address how characteristics of the physical setting influence the behaviors and development of children. Guidelines for constructing and arranging environments are provided based on educational and developmental research. Ideas for including children in planning their spaces are also included.

http://iris.peabody.vanderbilt.edu/casestudies.html

This website contains activities and case studies for accommodating special needs students in the classroom. Click on "Effective Room Arrangement" to read the cases.

http://teacher.scholastic.com

This site includes a classroom set-up tool.

 ## Suggested Activities

The following activities will help you plan and organize your classroom space. Do as many of them as you have time for.

1. Figure 1.3 shows how one teacher arranged a classroom. There are several potential problems with this room arrangement. How many can you find? Suggest one or more ways to correct each problem. (See key for this activity in the Appendix.)

2. a. Examine Figure 1.4. Based on the room arrangement, what activities would you expect to be common in this classroom? What kinds of participation will be expected from students?

Figure 1.3 A Room Arrangement with Potential Problems

Figure 1.4 One Teacher's Planned Room Arrangement

16

b. Picture yourself as a student in the classrooms depicted in Figures 1.3 and 1.4. Place yourself in various areas of the room. Can you see what you need to see? Now place yourself as a teacher in the rooms. Can you see all students? Can you circulate freely among desks and work areas?

c. The teacher whose classroom is depicted in Figure 1.4 has anticipated having twenty-eight students in her class. She has just learned that she will have at least thirty-three at the beginning of the year. How can she rearrange her room to accommodate the five additional students without losing the advantages of the arrangement she has designed?

3. Visit other teachers' classrooms and examine their room arrangements. Use the items in Checklist 1 at the end of the chapter and the four keys to room arrangement (pp. 3–4) to guide your observation and analysis. If you have a specific problem, ask several teachers for suggestions and see how they may have coped with a similar problem.

4. Cheri is a repeating first grader who missed most of her first grade year for medical reasons. She has a syndrome that is characterized by fragile bones, so for Cheri, simple jostling or bumps can result in broken bones. She walks with leg braces and often uses a walker. Cheri is protectively seated beside the teacher's desk separate from the other students. Here Cheri has easy access to her walker. Her academic work shows that she is progressing with her peers, but her social skills are below grade level. From this information, where could you seat Cheri to help her increase positive interaction with peers and maintain safe movement to and from groups and in and out of the classroom? Select A, B, or C in Figure 1.5 and explain your choice.

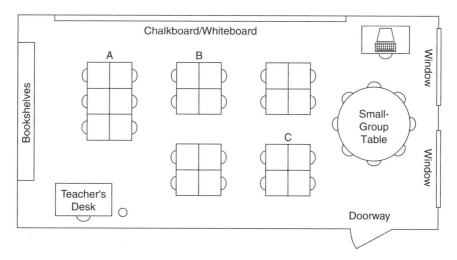

Figure 1.5 A Room Arrangement to Facilitate Access and Interaction for Student with Special Needs

Checklist 1

Room Preparation

Check When Complete	Subject	Notes

Bulletin Boards and Walls

Floor Space

☐   A. Student desks/tables   _____

☐   B. Small-group area   _____

☐   C. Computer workstations   _____

☐   D. Teacher's desk and equipment   _____

☐   E. Bookcases   _____

☐   F. Centers   _____

☐   G. Pets and plants area(s)   _____

☐   H. Traffic patterns   _____

☐   I. Classroom library   _____

Storage Space and Supplies

☐   A. Textbooks and trade books   _____

☐   B. Student work   _____

☐   C. Portfolio files   _____

☐   D. Frequently used instructional materials   _____

☐   E. Teacher's supplies   _____

☐   F. Classroom supplies   _____

☐   G. Student belongings   _____

☐   H. Equipment   _____

☐   I. Seasonal or infrequently used items   _____

2

Establishing Classroom Norms and Expectations

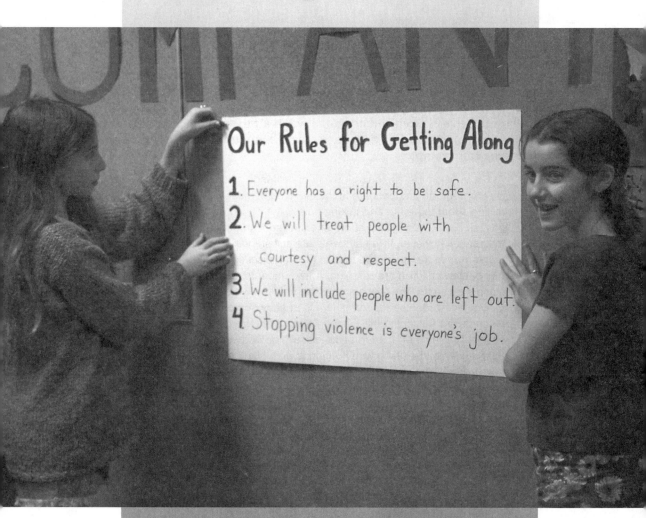

For students to have a successful year in your classroom, they must understand and practice the behaviors you expect of them. Because you will want appropriate and cooperative behavior to become the norm in your classroom, think about how your students will know of these expectations and begin to adopt them consistently.

A carefully planned system of rules and procedures makes it easier for you to communicate your expectations to your students, and it helps ensure that the procedures you set up will be workable and appropriate. Some of the first questions to ask yourself are what are rules and procedures? How do you develop, teach, and reinforce them? The goal of this chapter is to help you answer these questions and develop a sound system of rules and procedures for your class.

What Is an Effectively Managed Classroom?

An effectively managed classroom is one that runs smoothly, with minimal confusion and downtime, and maximizes opportunities for student learning. An effective classroom has patterns and routines in place that make interaction and movement easy to organize and accomplish. It is not possible for a teacher to conduct instruction, or for students to work productively, if they have no guidelines for how to behave, when and how to move about the room, where to sit, when they may or may not interrupt the teacher, or the amount of noise that is acceptable. Consider this example:

> At 8 A.M. when the beginning-of-school bell rings, twenty-one of Ms. Smith's twenty-six fourth-grade students are in the classroom. Most are not at their desks but are milling about the room and talking noisily. Ms. Smith calls out above the din, "Everyone, sit down!" With much effort, she succeeds in getting most of the children in their seats; however, three students are still standing and talking. The teacher goes to the front of the room and tries to begin a discussion of the previous day's field trip, but few children are listening. A few students straggle in at 8:06. Two others leave their seats. The teacher asks the children what they liked about their field trip. Only a few students respond. There is already some evidence of inattention: several students are not facing the teacher, and others are quietly conversing among themselves. The teacher abandons the discussion and asks a girl to pass out papers. At 8:09 students are sitting with nothing to do while the teacher talks with children who have walked up to her desk. At 8:10 the teacher goes to the front of the class and announces that today she will show them something new. Two students are talking loudly, but the teacher ignores them. Three other students leave their seats: one goes to the drinking fountain, one to the pencil sharpener, and one to visit with another student. The teacher tells students to prepare for journal writing. Immediately two students leave their seats to borrow paper, and the noise level in the room increases. About half the students get out notebooks. The students by the far wall are quiet, but they seem to be ignoring the teacher. One student goes to the closet, an-

other to the pencil sharpener. Ms. Smith calls out, "Everyone, be quiet and get out your journals!" Several students call out, "What for?"

Observers of this classroom might criticize Ms. Smith for allowing students to get away with so much misbehavior. "Be stricter," they might say. "Punish the misbehaving students." Or, "Develop more interesting lessons to capture student interest." Some might even suggest that Ms. Smith set up a reward system to encourage good behavior. Although these suggestions could be helpful under some circumstances, they do not address the fundamental problem in this classroom: The students have not learned the behaviors that are expected of them. Furthermore, the teacher has not established procedures to guide student behavior. Problems are evident in several areas: the beginning-of-day routine, bringing materials for class, talking when the teacher is leading the class, out-of-seat behavior, attending to the teacher, and responding to questions.

Of course, even if the students know what is appropriate, they will not necessarily behave as they should. (For that reason, this book will not end with the present chapter!) However, giving the students a clear set of expectations for what is appropriate is a major step toward establishing a positive classroom environment.

Keep in mind that the unique setting created by elementary school organization makes it essential to have a good set of classroom procedures. You will work with twenty-five to thirty students every day. Although your students will leave the room for lunch, recess, and perhaps some instruction, you will generally be confined to a single room with limited space and materials. You will be responsible for teaching many cognitive skills to a diverse population of students, and at the same time you will have to handle administrative tasks, arrange for appropriate materials and supplies, and evaluate students. To do these things well, you and your students need an orderly environment with minimal disruption and wasted time, leaving everyone free to concentrate on the critical tasks of learning. Your expectations and carefully planned procedures help create this environment.

Preliminary Considerations

Definition of Terms

Goals are target aspirations not necessarily attained every day. However, long-term goals determine our daily actions. You should carefully consider your personal goals and the goals you want your students to achieve during the year. Discussing goal setting with your students is an important way to establish common values regarding class activities. Keep in mind that your beliefs and the goals you set will influence the expectations you communicate to your students.

Expectations are desired behaviors or outcomes. Within a classroom, a teacher can make his or her expectations known to students, or the teacher can cause students to guess at the expectations. It is much easier for students to meet a teacher's expectations when they know what these expectations are. Teachers can make their expectations known to students by directly teaching the classroom rules and procedures, providing opportunities for students to practice them, and consistently responding to students' behavior. A teacher's consistent responses can include both positive consequences to reinforce appropriate behavior and negative consequences to deter inappropriate behavior.

Students also have expectations for their behavior with their peers. When the behavior the teacher and students expect and exhibit becomes so routine that it seems to be a consensus, a classroom norm for that behavior has been established. *Norms* are accustomed ways of perceiving, believing, evaluating, and acting in an environment (Goodenough, 1971). They are the familiar ways we interact with each other in a particular setting, in this case, the classroom.

Rules and *procedures* refer to stated expectations regarding behavior. A rule identifies general expectations or standards for behavior. For example, the rule "Respect other persons and their property" covers a large set of behaviors that should always be practiced. Rules may indicate unacceptable behavior as well as expected, appropriate behavior, although teachers sometimes manage to write rules that are only positively stated (for example, "We ask permission before talking in class"). In addition to general rules, many teachers have a rule or two governing a specific behavior that could become an issue or that they want to prevent (for example, "Gum chewing is allowed," or "Gum chewing is not allowed").

Procedures also communicate expectations for behavior. They are usually applied in a specific activity, and they are directed at accomplishing something rather than prohibiting some behavior or defining a general standard. For example, you will set up procedures with your students for collecting assignments, turning in late work, participating in class discussions, using the bathroom, and so on. Some procedures (such as use of equipment at a center) are sufficiently complex or critical that you may want to post guidelines in addition to discussing them with the students. However, many procedures are not written because they are very simple or because their specificity and frequency of use allow students to learn them rapidly.

The rules and procedures you design will depend on the kind of classroom community you want to develop. For example, different rules and, especially, procedures will be necessary in a classroom where most instruction is teacher-led than in one where students work largely independently or in small groups.

Identifying School Rules and Procedures

In most schools teachers are expected to enforce a set of school rules. It is to your advantage to do so. Rules applied consistently in all classes and areas of the building are easy for students to learn. These rules also acquire more legitimacy in the eyes of some students because they are everyone's rules. In addition to rules and procedures that regulate student behavior, all schools have certain administrative procedures that must be followed by every teacher (for example, keeping attendance records). You should know your school's rules and procedures before the year begins so you can incorporate them into your own classroom system. You can find out about school rules for students and administrative procedures for teachers at a school orientation meeting or from a teacher's handbook, a building administrator, or another teacher. Pay careful attention to the following:

1. Behaviors that are specifically forbidden (examples: running in the halls, bringing certain items to school) or required (being in possession of a hall permit when out of the classroom during class time, bringing a note for absence).

2. Consequences for rule violations. In particular, note the responsibility you have for carrying out the consequence, such as reporting the student to the school office. If the school does not have a policy for dealing with certain rule violations, you must decide how to handle them yourself.

3. Administrative procedures that must be handled during class time include beginning-of-year tasks such as assigning textbooks, collecting fees, and checking the class absentees. Money collection (for school lunches, for example) goes on all year, so you will need a record-keeping system and a safe place to keep the money. Some administrative tasks are daily occurrences, including taking and recording class attendance, talking with previously absent students, and filing an attendance report with the office. You will also need a procedure for allowing students to leave the room to go to other parts of the building. Some teachers have an attendance chart for students to indicate their presence each day. At one glance, you can tell who is absent without interrupting ongoing activities.

Frequently, procedures in these areas will already be established and followed throughout the school. If uniform procedures have not been implemented in the school in some area, you may find it helpful to talk with experienced teachers about how they handle it.

Planning Your Classroom Rules

When you have information about school rules and procedures, you will be ready to begin planning for your own classroom. Guidelines for rules will be presented separately from those for procedures.

Many different rules are possible, but a set of four to eight rules should be sufficient to cover most important areas of behavior. Here are four general rules that encompass many classroom behaviors.

RULE 1. RESPECT AND BE POLITE TO ALL PEOPLE. This rule is general; be sure to give sufficient examples and explanation so that both you and your students clearly understand its meaning. You will have to define *polite,* and you may want to extend this definition to include not hitting, fighting, or name-calling. You may also want to emphasize that "all people" includes you, the teacher.

RULE 2. BE PROMPT AND PREPARED. This rule includes guidelines that underscore the importance of schoolwork. Prompt may refer to the beginning of the school day, transition to group work, and moving to individual tasks. Being

CLASSROOM RULES:

NO ANYTHING!

"That's Ms. Clamhouse. She runs a tight ship."
Reprinted by permission of Tony Saltzman.

prepared acknowledges the importance of having the right tools (necessary equipment?), as well as the mental attitude, to be successful in schoolwork.

RULE 3. LISTEN QUIETLY WHILE OTHERS ARE SPEAKING. Use of this rule will prevent call-outs and other interruptions of lessons. You can use the discussion of this rule to teach the students how to comment or ask a question (e.g., raise a hand and wait to be called on).

RULE 4. OBEY ALL SCHOOL RULES. Including this rule gives you an opportunity to discuss whatever school rules are pertinent to your supervision of students outside your classroom (such as on the playground or in the cafeteria). It reminds students that school rules apply in your classroom as well as out of it. It also suggests that you will monitor their behavior in the areas covered by the school rules.

These or similar rules are often found in well-managed classrooms, although they should not be considered a definitive list. You may decide to use other rules (for example, a rule prohibiting a specific behavior) or different wording. Some teachers may find these rules too general, and they might prefer to have more rules with greater specificity.

When presenting general rules, discuss your specific expectations with students. When discussing the rules and related behaviors, emphasize the positive parts of the rules rather than just their negative counterparts. When you do the former, you help students learn how to behave appropriately. You must be explicit about behaviors that are not acceptable when such behaviors might occur frequently (examples: gum chewing, being out of seat, call-outs). These may be incorporated in your set of rules or be discussed when presenting procedures associated with specific activities. Be sure your presentation includes concrete examples and that you explain any terms the children at your grade level might not understand. Role playing situations that model the rules in practice can be helpful.

The rules you choose will be used later in several ways. You will discuss these rules with your students on the first day or two of class. You will also post the rules in the room or make certain that students have their own copies, or both. A posted set of rules allows you to focus attention on and create a strong expectation about behaviors that are important to you. You may send a copy of the rules home for parents' review and signature. Finally, refer to specific rules as needed to remind students of appropriate behavior. Your posted rules need not (and cannot) cover all aspects of behavior in detail. Procedures for specific activities and perhaps some ad hoc rules will be needed. For instance, you may wish to post separately your policies regarding student work.

Student Participation in Rule Setting

Student involvement in rule setting can take many forms. In any classroom, students should discuss the reasons for having rules and clarify the need for and the meaning of particular rules. It is useful for students to generate concrete examples of the kinds of behaviors a particular rule covers. However, teachers must be prepared to supply positive examples ("Respecting property means putting extra supplies away so that others may use them") to supplement the mostly negative examples students tend to give ("Respecting property means not writing on the desk").

Some teachers also involve students in generating the rules to promote ownership and to encourage students to take more responsibility for their own behavior. Many teachers begin developing classroom rules with a whole-class discussion, during which the students and teacher suggest possible rules for the classroom and the teacher records suggestions on an overhead, chalkboard, chart paper, or computer monitor projected onto a TV. After all suggestions have been made, the teacher and students arrange them into broad categories, combining similar ideas and eliminating suggestions that are redundant or unnecessary. After the suggestions have been categorized, the teacher and students develop a title for each category. If everyone agrees, this title becomes a classroom rule. In early elementary classrooms (K–3), this process may take several days. In many classrooms, this activity is followed by role playing each of the rules. Role playing is crucial for students' understanding of rules.

Many effective managers do not allow choice in rule setting. Instead, they clearly present their rules and procedures to students and provide explanations of the need for them. A teacher who establishes reasonable rules and procedures, who provides an understandable rationale for them, and who enforces them consistently will find that the majority of students are willing to abide by them.

As you plan your routines and rules, consider what role students will play in choosing and implementing them. Some teachers prefer that students participate extensively by helping formulate rules, by discussing their rationales, and by offering alternatives in some cases. Other teachers prefer a more traditional, teacher-led system of rules and procedures. Still others prefer a blending of teacher and students working together. Consider which approach you prefer, why you prefer it, and how you would implement it.

Planning Classroom Procedures

If you have never analyzed the specific behaviors required of students in a typical elementary school classroom, you will be surprised by the complexity and detail in this section. Don't hurry through it, even though some of the items may appear trivial. These bits and pieces will combine to form the mosaic of your management system. Six categories are described: procedures for room areas, procedures for seatwork and teacher-led activities, transitions into and out of the room, procedures for small-group work, procedures for cooperative group activities, and general procedures. A seventh area, keeping students accountable for work, is presented in Chapter 3, and additional procedures for cooperative groups are found in Chapter 6.

Remember, procedures may need to be changed, or new ones added, as the year progresses. Procedures always need to be taught and practiced, which is stressed later in the chapter. As you read the discussion in the following sections, note ideas for procedures on Checklist 2.

Procedures for Room Use

Various areas of the room, and furniture and equipment within the room, need procedures to regulate their use.

TEACHER'S DESK AND STORAGE AREAS

The best procedure is that students may not remove anything from your desk or other storage areas without your permission.

STUDENT DESKS AND OTHER STORAGE AREAS

Just as students may not tamper with your desk, they may not bother the desks or storage spaces of other students. You can also help students learn good work habits by setting aside a few minutes each week for them to clean out and organize their desks and materials. This is a good end-of-day activity on Friday.

STORAGE FOR COMMON MATERIALS

Some commonly used supplies (scissors, markers, scrap paper, rulers, etc.) and resources (supplementary books, texts, encyclopedia, dictionaries, etc.) are stored on shelves, in drawers, or in cabinets. Most teachers label these storage areas appropriately and tell students at what times these materials may be used and whether permission is needed to use them.

DRINKING FOUNTAIN, SINK, PENCIL SHARPENER

A common procedure is to allow the use of these facilities by only one student at a time and only when the teacher is not conducting a lesson or talking to the whole class. Some teachers require that students request permission to use the fountain or sink except during specified break times.

RESTROOMS

When restrooms are immediately accessible from or adjacent to the classroom, many teachers allow students to use these facilities one at a time, without asking permission, whenever the teacher is not conducting instruction. Establish a system to let a student know if the restroom is occupied (examples: a reversible sign on the door with a green light and a red light; knocking and waiting). It is also a good idea to go over restroom use procedures, such as flushing toilet, washing hands, wiping off sink area, and disposing of paper towels. When restrooms are separated from the classroom, both group times (before lunch, after recess) and individual procedures should be established.

CENTERS AND EQUIPMENT AREAS

Establish procedures for when the area may be used (perhaps during particular blocks of time only), whether special permission is needed, and how many may use the area at a time. Teachers often allow quiet talking in such areas as long as it does not disturb others. If talking is allowed, the area should be away from areas where students are expected to work quietly. Post rules or instructions for equipment use at each area.

Many teachers also post a number indicating how many students should be at a center at once. You will need procedures for assigning students to centers or, if centers are self-selected, for guiding student movement among centers. Posted instructions for cleaning up centers are also helpful.

COMPUTER STATIONS

Many teachers have one or more computers in their classrooms. Computer stations, while following the general procedures for centers (e.g., may need special permission and only a limited number of students may use them at once), also require unique procedures. Students will need procedures for the following:

- Going to the computer (some teachers identify computers by letters or numbers and then assign students to a particular computer; others randomly choose names to send children to the computer)
- Getting their computer disks or CDs (there may be a central place near the computers where disks and other accessories are stored)
- Using the computer (students may be assigned to sites to visit on the Internet or may be able to access other programs after completing an assignment)
- Sharing a computer (who gets to keyboard and for how long)

Procedures for Individual Work and Teacher-Led Activities

Major concerns include keeping student attention, allowing for participation, and providing assistance when needed. Good procedures prevent or reduce interruptions or distractions that can slow down content development activities or interfere with student learning.

STUDENT ATTENTION DURING PRESENTATIONS

Consider how students should behave when you or a student are presenting information to the class or while you are conducting a discussion or recitation. Typically, students are expected to face the presenter and listen attentively. In fact, teachers often translate this expectation into a general classroom rule such as "Listen carefully when the teacher or another student is talking." Teachers also expect students to remain seated at all times during presentations, to remain quiet, and to have only the books or other materials needed for the lesson on their desks.

STUDENT PARTICIPATION

You must identify ways to allow students to ask questions, contribute to a discussion, or receive help. During presentations and discussions, the simplest procedure is to require that students raise their hands, wait to be called on, and remain in their seats. Some teachers teach students to call on the next speaker to avoid having all interactions channeled through the teacher. In most circumstances, it is not a good idea to allow students to call out answers or comments without raising their hands. Undesirable consequences of allowing call-outs include domination of participation by a few students, frequent inappropriate comments, and interruptions of discussions and presentations. Requiring that students raise their hands gives all students a chance to participate and allows you to call on students who do not have their hands up. Two exceptions to the "no call-out" procedure are sometimes permitted. The first occurs when teachers want students to provide a chorus response; that is, when they want a whole-class response to a question. In this case, tell students at the beginning of the activity that they do not need to raise their hands to respond. Also, children can be taught a signal for a chorus response such as cupping one hand behind an ear or giving a verbal signal or prefacing the question with "everyone." A second exception may occur during activities in which hand raising might slow down or interfere with a discussion. Again, students can be told that it is not necessary to raise hands during that particular activity. Variations from the standard procedure of requiring raised hands usually should not be used early in the school year. Instead, follow a simple routine for several weeks until you are certain that students understand it. Then, if you choose to depart from the procedure, clearly communicate the difference to the students at the beginning of the activity.

TALK AMONG STUDENTS

In many activities, quiet talk is an important part of problem solving. However, students must know when and how loudly they may talk. You must decide what your policy will be and communicate it to the students. The "no talking" rule is an easy rule to break. You must decide whether students may quietly ask a neighbor if they have questions. Then try allowing students to help each other on a trial basis. If you decide to allow students to talk to one another and to work together during individual work activities, you will have to establish specific limitations. For example, you might tell students that during certain activities quiet talking is allowed, but if it gets too loud, the privilege will be lost. It is best to demonstrate what "quiet talking" means and have students practice it to show you they know what is meant. If students work at centers and in groups, you must define with them how much noise is acceptable. Many teachers also find it helpful to have a "zero noise" signal for times when they need to get the whole group's attention. A "zero noise" signal could be your raising your hand or turning off the lights momentarily.

OBTAINING HELP

When students are working at their seats and need help, have them raise their hands. It is not a good idea to allow them to call out or to come up to you whenever they wish as this can distract other students, congest a given area, or prevent you from completing instructional tasks. When they have raised their hands, you may then go to them or have them come to you one at a time. Another procedure is to allow students to come up only if you are seated at your desk (or some other designated place) and not already helping another student. These procedures eliminate long lines of chatty students around your desk. They also allow you to control where you give individual assistance. If you choose to help students at a location other than their desks, choose one that allows you good visibility of the rest of the class. Some teachers help students think about their questions by having students ask themselves, "Can another student answer this?" If the answer is "yes," the student asks another for help.

If students are encouraged to help each other, you will have to establish procedures for how and when. For instance, some teachers establish the "C3B4Me" procedure, which tells students to ask three other students for help before they ask the teacher. Students need guidance in asking appropriate questions and learning how to help peers without merely supplying answers. Chapter 6 has suggestions for teaching these important skills.

WHEN INDIVIDUAL WORK HAS BEEN COMPLETED

When students are assigned work at their desks, some students may finish before the next scheduled activity. This situation is frequently handled either by having students complete an additional enrichment assignment or by allowing these students to use the remaining time for free reading or work at a center or helping with classroom maintenance chores. You may also wish to have students who finish early serve as peer tutors for others. If you have enrichment activities that involve additional materials not in the students' possession, you must specify when these materials may be used, where they will be kept, and what the procedures are for returning the materials to the proper place. If many students frequently complete their work early, maybe assignments are too easy or too much time is being allocated for seatwork activities.

Transitions into and out of the Room

BEGINNING THE SCHOOL DAY

You should establish a routine to open each class day. At the beginning of the year, you should lead this routine so that it is done efficiently and helps students "settle in" to the classroom. During the course of the year, students may begin to take over this routine without your guidance. The routine need not be elaborate or time consuming. Many teachers begin with social items such as a riddle for the day, a discussion of the day's lunch menu, the pledge of allegiance, date and birthdays, discussion of school events, or other items of interest. Some begin each day with a class meeting or a planning session during which students set their goals for the day. Such activities can be important for community-building.

You may also wish to collect money, permission slips, or other items brought from home at this time. If much time is required for morning management tasks, have students begin work on a content-related activity to establish an academic focus, ensuring that students are not in dead time.

LEAVING THE ROOM

Your students will leave the room en masse at several times during the day: at recess and for lunch, for the library, music, computer lab, or perhaps some other instruction. A common technique is to have the children line up after appropriate materials have been put away, with the quietest table or row lining up first. Decide what behaviors are appropriate in line. Some teachers, particularly of younger children, have to specify where hands and feet should be while students are lined up. Some teachers have students clasp their hands behind their backs; others have students keep their hands at their sides. Line leaders can be helpful, and students enjoy the privilege. Because noise disturbs other classes, talking is usually forbidden while the line is passing through the halls. You will also need procedures for helping individual students know when and how to leave the room if they are working with a speech teacher, special education teacher, or peer mentor in another classroom.

RETURNING TO THE ROOM

It is important that procedures be established for this transition, particularly after lunchtime. If students know what to do on returning, they can get started instead of waiting for you to direct them. Common procedures are entering the room quietly, taking their seats, and using the restroom, sink, pencil sharpener, or drinking fountain one at a time in each area. Note that these procedures get students ready for afternoon activities.

When students return from an out-of-room activity that has left them noisy or unusually "chatty," or if they are very excited when returning from recess or lunch, your transition activity should give them time to wind down before you start academic work. For example, you might read aloud as they settle in and get ready for the next activity. Some research has found that students' attention is better after such transitions than when the teacher tries to enforce total silence and an immediate return to academic tasks. However, do not prolong the chatter unnecessarily, and be sure to gain student attention when you begin the next activity. Monitor students so that "wind-down" time doesn't become "wind-up" time.

ENDING THE DAY

An end-of-day routine ensures that student desks and work areas are cleared off, materials to go home are ready, and students leave on time. Planning ahead for the end of the day guards against hurried closings, lost papers, and a feeling of confusion and chaos. Possible routines include feeding room pets, straightening bookshelves, tidying up desks, picking up paper, and stacking chairs on the desks. Other important end-of-day tasks include briefly reviewing important things learned that day, foreshadowing coming events, and checking materials that will be taken home. If you have children who leave early to ride a bus, you may wish to do only the essentials with them and complete the rest of the routine after they leave.

Procedures for Small-Group Instruction

One complication with using small-group instruction is that the teacher is often working with one group while the rest of the class is engaged in individual work. The dual focus complicates monitoring, providing assistance, and dealing with problems that might occur. Well-planned procedures are a must if small-group instruction is to be carried out smoothly.

GETTING THE CLASS READY FOR THE ACTIVITY

Students must know what they are going to do during the time they are not in the group. Therefore, you must post the assignments by group and discuss work requirements beforehand with the whole class. Note any materials that will be needed when students come to the teacher-led group.

STUDENT MOVEMENT INTO AND OUT OF THE GROUP

These transitions must be brief, quiet, and free from disruptions. Describe expected behavior to students: walk, no talking, bring needed materials. Develop a signal to tell students when to come to the group area. They should not automatically come when they see other students leave because you may want to check student progress before working with the next group. Some teachers use a bell or a kitchen timer; others use a verbal signal.

EXPECTED BEHAVIOR OF STUDENTS IN THE GROUP

The rules for attention and hand raising used in the whole class can also be used in the small group. However, with smaller numbers of students, some procedures must change, and these must be taught. For example, some teachers have each student who responds select the next student to participate. Sometimes the exchange between students can be more loosely structured.

EXPECTED BEHAVIOR OF STUDENTS
OUTSIDE THE SMALL GROUP

You will have given instructions to students not in the group and posted their seatwork assignments. However, students may need help as they work. It is not a good idea to allow students to come up to you while you are in the group; therefore, establish a procedure to enable students to get help. One such procedure is to allow students to help each other. Another is to assign certain students the job of monitor. Students can then raise their hands and the monitor can assist them. Permission to interrupt the teacher is given only to the monitors and only when assistance is absolutely necessary. Often students are told that they should skip the part of the assignment they are unable to do and that the teacher will help them later. You should check on their progress even while you are working with the group. Look up frequently to scan the class for signs of difficulty. When you change groups, circulate around the room to help students before you call the next group. Students can raise their hands between groups for help, or they may write their names on the board for assistance when you are available.

USE OF MATERIALS AND SUPPLIES

Small-group activities frequently require the use of materials and equipment. To avoid traffic jams, plan ways to distribute these items and perhaps use more than one distribution place if necessary. Sometimes you can save time by placing needed materials on students' desks or worktables before class starts. Check equipment to make sure it functions and have replacements on hand just in case. Student helpers can be assigned to distribute supplies and materials, to monitor supply areas, and to clean up work areas. If students need to bring special materials for group or project work, let them know far enough in advance so they can get them; you may have to arrange for safe places for their materials to be stored while work is in progress. If any of the equipment you need poses a a potential hazard to students or can be easily damaged by carelessness, identify safety routines and demonstrate proper use.

Procedures for Cooperative Group Activities

Some teachers use groups extensively for a variety of tasks, such as short- or long-term projects, peer coaching and other assistance, and review of content learned in other formats. Other examples include laboratory assignments in science, the preparation of group reports or projects in social studies and reading, and study groups organized to accomplish specific learning objectives. However groups are used, it is important to develop efficient routines that support the learning objectives.

Routines are typically introduced to the students whenever groups are first used, and they are practiced thereafter until the groups are working well. Students need to learn appropriate group behavior, especially if you intend to use groups extensively. Although you can monitor group work, the fact that six or seven groups may be working simultaneously at varying paces, using a variety of resources, precludes your being able to direct all the groups' activities. The procedures implemented for group work must be carefully chosen to encourage students to work more or less independently toward instructional goals, to promote desirable interaction among students in the group, and to support efficient use of time. Detailed procedures that help cooperative group activities proceed smoothly are discussed in Chapter 6.

General Procedures

DISTRIBUTING MATERIALS

At the beginning of the year, books and supplies must be distributed to students. Develop procedures for recording book numbers, noting damage, and handling other details. These are covered in Chapter 4, along with other procedures for beginning the school year. In addition to the beginning-of-year materials distribution, you will have supplies, papers, and books to pass out every day. Unless you establish efficient procedures, much time can be wasted. Many teachers have student helpers pass out materials such as manipulatives, calculators, or graded papers during opening activities. For the distribution of books or supplies, a student helper can be assigned to each group. If you collect papers from assignments by group or by row and preserve the order while you are checking them, you can then redistribute them to the class in the same way. This makes it easy to hand the materials to one student at each table or in each row.

INTERRUPTIONS OR DELAYS

If delays or interruptions occur while students are working, they should be taught to continue their work. Emphasize that they should be courteous and patient if you are interrupted in the middle of a lesson by a visitor or a phone call and that you will return to them as quickly as possible. If you will be detained very long, give the students something to do in case they finish their work before you return. Avoid leaving your classroom unless it is absolutely necessary. In the rare case that you must be away from the room, make sure that a nearby colleague is aware of your absence and can check on your class.

RESTROOMS

If restrooms are located away from your classroom, a hall-pass system may be established to monitor the number of students out of the room and to let students know whether they may leave. You might hang a restroom hall pass next to the hall door to be placed by the student around his or her neck or carried en route to the restroom. See if there is a schoolwide procedure to follow.

LIBRARY, RESOURCE ROOM, SCHOOL OFFICE

When one or a small group of students must go to another area in the school, you will generally remain in the classroom with the rest of the students. For example, small groups doing research may go to the library. Schoolwide procedures are usually established to handle these situations. Find out whether a hall-permit system or some other procedure is used to regulate the movement of students in the halls. Also, review any school rules that govern behavior in transit or at the locations. Make sure your students understand these procedures.

CAFETERIA

Review the school policies for the cafeteria and be ready to explain them to your class before they go to lunch, and after they return, if necessary. If you are planning to (or must) sit with the students, decide ahead of time who will get to sit by you (and whether this will be at random or a privilege) or whether you will use assigned seats. If your students make too much noise or misbehave, you may wish to establish an incentive for good behavior or include lunchroom behavior as part of your in-class reward system.

PLAYGROUND

Safety rules are a must, and you should limit overly aggressive behavior and dangerous play. Also, if any of the equipment on the playground poses a potential hazard, you will have to talk about it with your students. Make clear to your students what part of the school grounds they may use for recess. You also should establish some signal for getting students' attention when it is time for them to line up and return to the classroom; this could be a whistle or a raised hand. If you plan to play a game on the playground, announce this before leaving the room, telling students where they should go when they reach the playground.

FIRE AND DISASTER DRILLS

You need to know what school policies and routines have been established to protect the children and you. Although you may wish to wait awhile before teaching these to your students, you should not wait until you know a drill is imminent. It is better to go over these procedures ahead of time and review them just before the first drill.

CLASSROOM HELPERS

Teachers often use students to help with such chores as erasing the board, passing out materials and supplies, carrying messages to the office, watering the plants, tidying up, and feeding the animals. Students are often chosen to be line leaders. Some teachers use these activities as privileges or rewards for especially good or improved behavior, or they may use them to encourage some students to accept more responsibility. Other teachers make sure that every student has a job each week so that all are contributing to the classroom community.

Some teachers have a chart or bulletin board with slots for the names of students currently serving as monitors or helpers. A card is then made for each child, and this card is placed in the appropriate slot when that child has a particular room helper responsibility. Some teachers ask for volunteers for each job; others appoint students on a rotating basis or use jobs as rewards. Appointment is usually done at the beginning of the week, and the appointments last one or two weeks.

Further Reading

Castle, K., & Rogers, K. (1994). Rule-creating in a constructivist classroom community. *Childhood Education, 70*(2), 77–80.

Creating classroom rules together can be a meaningful experience for children and teachers and can help establish a positive sense of classroom community. Student participation in rule making encourages active involvement, reflection, meaningful connections, respect for rules, sense of community, problem solving through negotiation, cooperation, inductive thinking, and a sense of ownership.

Evertson, C. M., & Poole, I. R. (2004). *Norms and expectations.* IRIS Center for Faculty Enhancement. Nashville, Tenn.: Peabody College, Vanderbilt University. Available at http://iris.peabody.vanderbilt.edu/casestudies.html.

This website contains activities and case studies for accommodating special needs students in the classroom. Click on "Norms and Expectations" to read the cases.

Good, T. L., & Brophy, J. E. (2003). *Looking in classrooms* (9th ed.). Boston: Allyn & Bacon.

This book is an excellent source of ways and means for teachers to develop into successful professionals. It synthesizes the knowledge base about teaching and provides research-based and accessible summaries about effective classroom practices. Particularly helpful are observational tools and rich examples of classroom practices that support teachers' professional development.

Leinhardt, G., Weidman, C., & Hammond, K. M. (1987). Introduction and integration of classroom routines by expert teachers. *Curriculum Inquiry, 17*(2), 135–176.

Data from the classrooms of successful teachers show the importance of establishing and practicing routines from the beginning. Three types of routines are identified: management, instructional support, and teacher-student exchange. The authors point out that teachers build on simple routines to support more elaborate ones.

Short, K. G. (1998). Creating a community of learners. In K. Short & K. M. Pierce (Eds.), *Talking about books: Creating literate communities* (pp. 33–52). Portsmouth, N.H.: Heinemann.

This chapter focuses on the ways in which the author and other teachers have established collaborative social contexts for learning. They believe that a community of learners is formed as learners (1) come to know each other; (2) value what each has to offer; (3) focus on problem solving and inquiry; (4) share responsibility and control; (5) learn through action, reflection, and demonstration; and (6) establish a learning atmosphere that is predictable and yet full of choices.

Suggested Activities

1. Identify the schoolwide rules and procedures you and your students are expected to observe. Be sure these are incorporated into your own classroom rules and procedures where appropriate.

2. Goals represent desired directions of student growth and may be academic, behavioral, or emotional. Write one goal in each area that you would consider appropriate for your students. Write one in each area for yourself.

3. Would you be surprised to know that researchers have determined that a teacher's personality and everyday behavior can be the most powerful motivating tool in the classroom? Think about how your expectations of student behavior or academic ability might influence your actions or responses as a teacher. Will this be important as you begin to establish norms for your classroom?

4. Read Case Study 2.1. It illustrates classroom procedures and rules for most major areas and will help you develop your own system of management. Create a list of reasons Mr. Abrams's class would probably run smoothly.

5. Case Study 2.2 illustrates a more complex classroom organization that involves introducing multiple areas and centers for student activities. List some of the advance planning decisions Ms. Miller has made. What rules and procedures has she developed? How are these taught and monitored?

6. Use Checklist 2 at the end of this chapter to help organize your planning of classroom procedures. Be sure to think through your expectations for behavior in each of the general areas and the instructional areas you will be

using. Then develop a set of procedures that will communicate your expectations to your students.

7. If you have trouble developing procedures in some area or are not sure whether procedures you have identified will work, ask other teachers for their opinions. They are usually more than happy to share "tricks of the trade."

8. Develop a list of four to eight general classroom rules. Be sure these emphasize areas of classroom behavior important to you and to the functioning of your classroom. Review these with an administrator or another teacher.

CASE STUDY 2.1

CLASSROOM PROCEDURES AND RULES IN A SECOND-GRADE CLASS

Mr. Abrams's students follow four rules: We use quiet voices in the classroom. We do our best work. We are polite and helpful. We follow all school rules. At the beginning of the year, Mr. Abrams and his students decided what "quiet voices" meant and practiced using quiet voices in different types of instructional activities. The students also role played situations in which students were and were not using quiet voices. When Mr. Abrams needs to get the attention of the class, he routinely uses a bell as a signal. He practices this signal with the students. When he rings the bell once, they stop talking and look at him. He explains to the class that using the bell is a shortcut to save time, that he will ring the bell only once and not several times, and that he expects students to respond immediately. He uses the bell in a very consistent manner.

The rule "We do our best work" includes listening carefully when the teacher is giving instructions, participating in class discussions, completing all assignments, turning in neat work, and using time wisely.

Behaviors relating to the rule "We are polite and helpful" include listening quietly when the teacher or another student is giving a presentation, cooperating with other students during small-group work, sharing materials and supplies, and respecting others' opinions. Mr. Abrams explains to his students that during some discussions they can raise their hands and wait to be called on to allow everyone a chance to talk and be heard. His signal for this procedure is raising his right hand, and he practices it with his students. At other times, students contribute to a discussion without raising their hands. His signal for this procedure is placing his right hand by his ear. He also practices this signal with the students several times. Consideration and respect for fellow students, the teacher, and other adults in the school are also included under this rule. In addition, the school rules referred to in the fourth classroom rule govern behavior in the halls, cafeteria, and other common areas of the school grounds.

Several other important classroom procedures provide guidelines for behavior in Mr. Abrams's classroom. Students are expected to stay seated at their desks whenever he presents directions or instruction to the class. At other times, they can leave their desks to get supplies, hand in papers, sharpen their pencils, and use the restroom adjacent to the classroom without asking permission, as long as they do not disturb other students. For example, students can sharpen a pencil without permission except when the teacher is talking or when another student is addressing the class. No more than two students can be at the pencil sharpener at one time, one sharpening and one waiting. When the teacher is working with a small group or helping an individual, students may not interrupt him. They stay at their desks and raise their hands to request help. If students finish their work early, they may read books from the classroom library, go to one of the classroom centers, or play an instructional game. They may talk, using their quiet voices, but they cannot disturb anyone still working on the assignment.

CASE STUDY 2.2

USING CENTERS IN A MULTITASK CLASSROOM

Ms. Miller designed her classroom with centers for listening, reading, writing, and creating. Special interest centers on topics the class is studying in science, social studies, or math change every month or so. Although each child has a desk, students are seldom in their seats; instead, they work on a variety of projects individually, in pairs, and in groups. When they meet as a whole class, they gather on a carpet instead of in traditional rows of desks. On any given day in November, a visitor may see an active, busy, somewhat noisy place, but it is easy to discern that there is a sense of order and purpose to the tasks the students are doing.

This classroom didn't get this way all at once. Much of the first six weeks of school was spent preparing students to work independently and collaboratively. On the first day of school, Ms. Miller taught cues for when to gather on the rug and when to return to seats. She explained that there would be times when they could talk to each other, but that during "rug time" they were to raise their hands so only one person would be speaking at once. Ms. Miller prepared a poster with the day's schedule and "center time" clearly marked. She went over it with the students before posting it on a highly visible bulletin board. She referred to the poster during the first weeks of school when giving students instructions for activities, or she asked students to tell her when certain activities were to start or stop.

Centers were introduced one at a time, over several weeks. When each new center became available, Ms. Miller presented it to the whole class, demonstrating the material found there and pointing out times on the day's schedule when it would be available. She also pointed out two signs in each center. One lists the procedures for the center. For example, the sign in the reading center says, "Silent readers may leave the center to find a quiet place to read. Students reading aloud to each other should stay in the center." Every list of procedures ends with instructions for cleanup. The second sign lists the capacity of that center. For example, the listening center has only four sets of earphones, so its capacity is four. Ms. Miller explained to the students that they may sign up for centers each morning when they arrive at school. One period of the day is allotted to "free center time," when students may go to the centers they have chosen. During free center time, students cross their names off the sign-up sheets when they leave the center so other students may enter.

Another period is "assigned center time," when Ms. Miller decides who should be in each center. After each new center was introduced, Ms. Miller saw that every student visited it during assigned center time. She monitored the center's use carefully, making sure that all students understood the use of one center before another center was introduced. Even after all centers have been introduced, Ms. Miller continues to monitor them and brings up problems she sees for discussion during rug time. She balances the available centers so that if activities at one center require her attention, the other centers have more familiar activities available on which students can work independently.

Checklist 2

Norms, Expectations, Rules, and Procedures

Check When Complete	Subject	Procedures or Expectations
☐	What are my short- and long-term goals for myself this year?	_____
☐	What are my short- and long-term goals for my students this year?	_____

Room Use

How will I establish basic procedures in the following areas?

☐	A. Teacher's desk and storage areas	_____
☐	B. Student desks and storage areas	_____
☐	C. Storage for common materials	_____
☐	D. Drinking fountains, sink, pencil sharpener	_____
☐	E. Restrooms	_____
☐	F. Centers or equipment areas	_____
☐	G. Computer stations	_____
☐	H. Board	_____

Individual Work and Teacher-Led Activities

☐	A. Attention during presentations	_____
☐	B. Participation	_____
☐	C. Talk among students	_____
☐	D. Obtaining help	_____
☐	E. When individual work has been completed	_____

Transitions into and out of the Room

☐	A. Beginning the school day	_____
☐	B. Leaving the room	_____

(continued)

Check When Complete	Subject	Procedures or Expectations
☐	C. Returning to the room	_____
☐	D. Ending the day	_____

Procedures for Small-Group Instruction

☐	A. Getting the class ready	_____
☐	B. Student movement	_____
☐	C. Expected behavior in the group	_____
☐	D. Expected behavior of students out of group	_____
☐	E. Materials and supplies	_____

Procedures for Cooperative Group Activities

☐	A. Roles of group members	_____
☐	B. Expected behavior	_____
☐	C. Interaction to include each member	_____
☐	D. Interaction to move toward instructional goals	_____

General Procedures

☐	A. Distributing materials	_____
☐	B. Classroom helpers	_____
☐	C. Interruptions or delays	_____
☐	D. Restrooms	_____
☐	E. Library, resource room, school office	_____
☐	F. Cafeteria	_____
☐	G. Playground	_____
☐	H. Fire and disaster drills	_____
☐	I. Classroom helpers	_____

3

Fostering Student Accountability

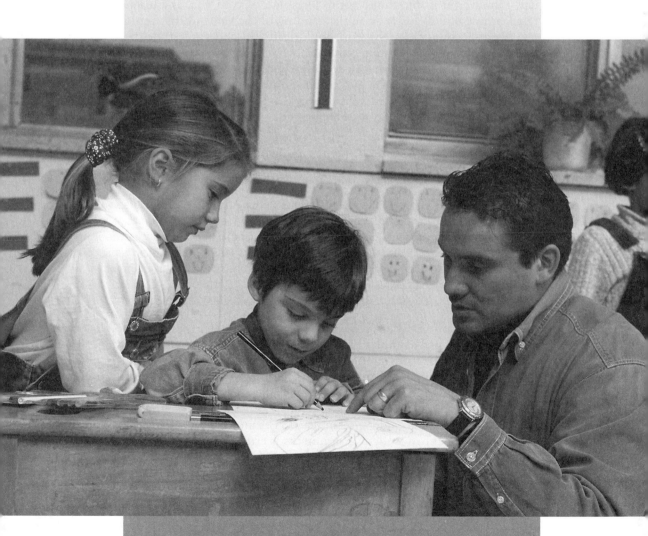

When we presented procedures for establishing an orderly classroom setting in Chapter 2, we indicated that additional procedures would be needed to keep students accountable for their work and learning. In this chapter, we describe additional procedures aimed at encouraging students to complete assignments and to engage in other learning activities. Ultimately, the goal of any accountability system is to help students develop into independent learners; thus, your procedures should give as much responsibility as possible to the students themselves, rather than having the students depend on either you or their parents to see that assignments are completed.

As we discuss student accountability, it is easy to focus on the products students create, such as completed assignments and test scores. After all, these are the tangible, measurable outcomes of the activities you engage in with students each day. However, it is important not to lose sight of your goal as a teacher: to facilitate learning and to foster an understanding of the value of that learning.

Your accountability system should lead you and your students to examine their learning and the learning process in which they are engaged. If you are checking written work daily, but not critically examining what students are learning by doing these assignments, the purposes for doing academic work may be lost. Students may come to see their written work as a task to be completed that doesn't relate to what they learn, in which case your system will not function to support learning as you intend.

FOR REFLECTION

Consider the purposes of accountability systems. As a teacher, of course you need ways to keep yourself from being swamped with paperwork, and you have to provide a fair, documented basis for assessment. But think beyond how just keeping students accountable helps you. What do students learn from an effective accountability system? One example might be organizational skills. List all of the other examples you can think of.

Each day of the school year you will give your students assignments that they will be expected to complete in the classroom or at home. These range from discussion to research to simple recall. Depending on the assignment, they may provide opportunities for exploration, for original thinking, for practice and application, or for repeated exposure to content. Such experiences are crucial for student learning. Thus, your management system should encourage students to become motivated and independent learners. Your support of consistent and successful engagement in student assignments is critical scaffolding toward this end. If students do not care or are not held accountable for their work and learning, many problems can occur. Consider the following example:

It is the second month of school, and Mr. Paul's third-grade class is finishing its fairy tale unit. As a culminating project, five groups of students are creating their own fairy tales. For this assignment, the group members must work together to write and illustrate a fairy tale, and on the last day of this unit they present their fairy tale to the rest of the class.

Mr. Paul is disturbed by the lack of cooperation in all of the groups. He has noticed that many groups have been off-task. Members have also been arguing about story lines, characters, and settings, and these arguments have led some students to work alone. Many of the students have turned to Mr. Paul for answers, whereas he wants them to turn to their peers for help. Mr. Paul has also noticed that some of the groups did not follow the procedures he established for this activity. For instance, he asked them to write and illustrate their books on only one side of their writing paper. Many used both sides of the paper, and their markers and pens bled through the paper, making the story and illustrations difficult to see.

When groups present their fairy tales to the rest of the class, they are very disorganized. Some groups have not decided who will read and show the illustrations. Other groups lack presentation skills, such as clearly displaying their pictures for everyone to see.

After the last group presents, Mr. Paul dismisses the students for recess and sits at his desk. He wonders what he can do to improve the groups' skills. It is clear from their careless manner that the students have not taken responsibility for this project and do not believe it is important.

From this example, it seems that many of Mr. Paul's students do not feel very accountable for their work, nor do they seem to care about what they have found out. It is possible, of course, that the assignment is too difficult or was not explained adequately, but it is also likely that Mr. Paul's procedures are not helping the students develop good work habits or understand the importance of cooperating and effectively presenting information to others.

This chapter focuses on classroom procedures that communicate the importance of assignments, that enable students to understand what is expected of them, and that help students take responsibility for their learning. The critical areas include communicating assignments and requirements, monitoring progress (including self-monitoring), and providing feedback (including self-evaluation and reflection). Checklist 3 will help you organize your planning in these areas, and four case studies of accountability systems for elementary teachers are provided at the end of the chapter.

Clear Communication of Assignments and Work Requirements

Students need a clear idea of what their assignments are and what is expected of them. This means that you must be able to explain all requirements and features of the assignments. You also should provide a reason for doing the assignment or explain what students may gain from the effort: reinforcement, discovery, understanding, challenge, or useable skills. Oral explanation alone is usually not sufficient because students do not all listen carefully, some students may be absent when the assignments and requirements are discussed, and the assignment itself may be complex. In addition, there is often more to completing assignments than doing the work accurately. Accuracy alone may not reflect learning. Additionally, you must consider standards for neatness, legibility, and form. Although you do not want to encourage an overemphasis on form to the detriment of learning, students need to understand what will be expected of them. Consider the following three areas when developing your standards.

Instructions for Assignments

In addition to telling students what the assignment is, post the assignment and important instructions on a board, overhead projector, or chart. Also, teach students to copy the assignment into their notebooks or on the first line of their papers so they will have a record of it if they need it to complete work at home. Go over instructions orally with the class, indicating where the instructions are displayed in the room. Whenever appropriate, use the overhead projector or an example on the board to show students how their papers should look. After giving instructions, check for understanding by asking students to give examples so you know that they understand what to do. One method is to ask a student or students to restate the directions. Another is to ask one group member to share or restate directions for the group.

If you are giving directions for independent work to several groups in preparation for reading group time, be sure the assignment for each group is clearly labeled. For primary grades especially, you might assign a color to each reading group. Use a marker of that color to write the assignments on the board, or use paper of that color when duplicating worksheets. Use the same location for each group's assignment every day so groups will know where to look without your help.

If you are giving directions for group work, move students into their groups first. Make sure you have everyone's attention again before thoroughly explaining your expectations. Check the understanding of at least one member of each group by asking questions such as, "What will your group need to do first?" For older students, provide a set of written instructions to each group, especially if the group task is a complex one. As students become more skilled at group work, they may be able to generate work plans on their own.

Standards for Form, Neatness, and Due Dates

When you have developed a standard set of requirements for written work, students will then learn what is generally expected, and you will have to explain only exceptions or changes as they occur. Students need to know what paper to write on, what heading to use, whether to write on the back of the paper, whether to color any part of it, how to number, whether to use pen or pencil, and whether to erase errors or to draw lines through them.

Decide on a standard but simple heading for papers, and post a sample heading to review with students the first time they are to use it. Remind them of it during the early weeks of school until they use it properly.

Finally, due dates should be reasonable and clear; exceptions should not be made without good cause. Tell students your policy for turning in work on time and follow it consistently. If you regularly extend the due dates for assignments, students may learn that they can negotiate for extra time and may not use their time well. In general, insist that work not done on time be completed at home or after school. This assumes, of course, that students possess the necessary knowledge or skills to do the work on their own.

"Oh no, not homework again."

Procedures for Absent Students

When students are absent, they miss instruction, directions for assignments, and assistance they may need in getting tasks under way. Establishing some routines for handling makeup work is helpful and avoids the interruption of instruction. You may not require that students complete each assignment they missed while they were absent, but students who miss critical assignments may need to make these up. Consider the following ways to help students catch up.

1. Arrange to meet briefly with students who have been absent to discuss makeup assignments. If you post weekly assignment lists for each subject on a bulletin board or in a folder in an easily accessible place, you can point out which of these are to be completed. For young children, you may need a packet of makeup work in a special "makeup folder." Let students know how much time they have to complete it.
2. Establish a regular time, such as fifteen minutes before or after school, when you will be available to assist students with instruction they have missed. In addition, you can designate class helpers to help at particular times of the day (usually during independent activities).
3. Designate a place where students can turn in makeup work and where they can pick it up after it has been checked (for example, baskets or trays labeled "Absent In" and "Absent Out").
4. Determine how students who have missed group work will make it up. Assist groups in planning for the inclusion of absent members and in helping them catch up.
5. For students whose absence you can prepare for in advance (religious holiday, etc.), discuss with the student and parents a plan for completing the work.

Monitoring Progress on and Completion of Assignments

Monitoring Work in Progress

Monitoring student progress helps you identify students who are having difficulty and also enables you to encourage other students to keep working. After you have made an assignment, monitor students carefully. Don't immediately begin working at your desk or become involved with an individual student without first checking to see whether all students are starting and can do the assignment. If you don't check, some students may not even start, and others may begin it incorrectly. Two simple strategies can help to avoid this situation. First, if everyone in the class is doing the same assignment, you can assure a smooth transition into independent work by beginning it as a whole-class activity; that is, have everyone get out paper or other materials and then answer the first question or two, or work the first few problems together as a group, just as you would conduct a recitation. For example, ask the first question, solicit an answer, discuss it, and have students record it on their papers. Not only will this procedure help ensure that all students begin, but any immediate problems with the assignment can be resolved.

A second way to monitor student involvement in the assignment is to circulate around the room and check each student's progress periodically. This way corrective feedback can be given and students can make progress. Note the progress of all students, not just those who raise their hands for help. Check frequently with students who become easily confused or distracted. Also, check in with small groups as they begin working to assure each group is on the right track.

If you are working with reading groups while some students are doing independent work, don't wait until the end of reading time to check on students outside the reading group. Check in with them between meetings with groups to be sure they are doing the work correctly.

Some longer assignments may not be due for several days or even a week or longer. Examples include notebooks, reports, and science or social studies projects. In this case, be especially careful to monitor progress. Define substages in the project or assignment. Then set deadlines and goals for each of these parts, or have students or groups develop work plans on which they report daily. Collect and check assignments at each of these stages and provide feedback. This helps students learn to organize their time and makes it easier for you to monitor and evaluate their progress. If students engage in long-term projects often, support them in developing their own subgoals and deadlines, first as a whole group and later individually.

Monitoring the Completion of Assignments

Monitoring the completion of assignments has several components. First, establish regular procedures for turning in completed work. Second, note whose papers have been turned in. Many different systems are possible. For example, you might have students put completed work in individual "mailboxes"; you can determine at a glance whose boxes are filled and whose are not. Or you might have students put completed papers on a certain corner of their desks so you can spot them as you move around the room. This procedure is useful when you do not intend to collect the papers. Another procedure is to have students put their work in different baskets for each subject. You must find time to check each basket frequently and record each completed assignment in your grade book. As an additional help, you may also give students individual checklists to help them keep track of their own assignments.

Some teachers teach students to keep an assignment notebook for homework. Each day students copy homework assignments into the notebook, and each evening parents initial the notebook after the assignment is completed. Teachers can also use the notebooks to communicate with parents about upcoming events or projects, and parents can write comments or questions to teachers in the notebooks.

Consider also how you will collect work. When all students are turning in materials at the same time, one efficient procedure is to have papers passed in a given direction until you have all papers in your hands. Materials such as notebooks or journals that are bulky might be collected by designated helpers and stacked in a particular spot. Papers or assignments turned in by students at varying times can be placed in labeled baskets, trays, or plastic containers. Locate these drop-off spots away from congested areas or where they might be distracting to students. Let students know the procedure you expect them to use. Following it consistently saves time and prevents confusion.

Maintaining Records of Student Work

An important part of your monitoring system is your record of work completed or skills mastered. Because these records are a part of your grade book, you should have a place for recording the names of students who are absent each day; for example, by putting an *a* in the corner of the appropriate space. When setting up your grade book, you can devote several lines per student and record grades and scores for each subject on a separate line, or you can use a different page for each major subject. If you record grades for different subjects on the same line, you might use a color code to distinguish them. Or you can write in subject headings at the top of the page, separate them with heavy red vertical lines, and then write the name of the assignment and its date above each entry in your grade book.

If you have students from another teacher's class for instruction in a subject, leave space for those additional students on the page for that subject in your grade book. You will need to supply the other teacher with report card evaluations, and it will be helpful to have all of the information in one place.

Many schools provide the teacher with a computer to use for communication and research and for administrative tasks. Teachers often find spreadsheet and gradebook software programs invaluable in tracking and organizing student grades. These programs have the additional advantage of creating progress reports quickly for every student.

Record grades or other evaluations (e.g., E, S+, S, U) for major assignments and test results in your grade book. You may also want to evaluate other classwork such as worksheets or workbook pages. This practice is not as common in the primary grades as in the intermediate grades, where more emphasis is placed on grading and a more complete record of daily work in major subjects is useful. However, some primary grades also maintain a checklist of mastered skills that are part of the school district's grade level or subject area standards. If students will be accountable for mastery of these standards, create a space for this in your grade book.

Managing Student Portfolios

Teaching students to keep portfolios of their work has become a standard practice in many elementary classrooms. For example, students may keep a writing portfolio that shows the progress of their writing from first to final drafts. Helping students create portfolios can be an effective way of showing a student's progress, teaching students to self-assess by selecting and reflecting on their work.

Portfolios also provide teachers with a useful tool for parent conferences and holistic grading. Depending on the purpose of a portfolio, students may have more or less input into the selection of portfolio entries and the eventual evaluation of the complete portfolio. However, over time children should be supported to make more choices about what to include and why. Several good sources are available for teachers who use portfolios in their classrooms. We suggest *Portfolio Assessment: A Handbook for Educators,* edited by James Barton and Angelo Collins, and for young children, *The Portfolio Book: A Step-by-Step Guide for Teachers* by Elizabeth Shores and Cathy Grace.

Managing the Paperwork

Keeping up with all of the papers can be overwhelming. One way to avoid mountains of "back papers" is to look over, grade, record, and return assignments quickly. Not only is this timely feedback for your students, it also helps you to spot students who are "fading" or to diagnose areas needing whole-class remediation. Be realistic about your grading capabilities. If you are behind in grading six sets of papers and are planning to assign essays due in two days, rethink your plans. Allow yourself enough grading time to do the job well—on the last paper as well as the first. Try making a grading schedule to distribute a huge task into manageable segments rather than plowing through until you are exhausted. Instead of collecting, checking, grading, and returning each assignment, try another routine: Go around the room to check each student's work. You can record a grade at the same time if you wish. If you are fortunate enough to have a personal digital assistant (PDA), you can record grades as you move to each student's desk. This type of checking is fast, personal, and efficient and is especially effective for written assignments that require holistic assessment.

To collect papers, some teachers use a separate basket labeled for each subject and have students place papers in the appropriate basket at a designated time. Others have students pass papers up in a designated pattern, clip papers together with a color-coded clip, and place the papers in an "in" basket. If you plan to have students pass papers up, you can prevent "straggler" papers by describing, modeling, and practicing how it is to be done.

Returning papers is simplified if they are already filed together, labeled by subject, and even possibly organized by rows or groups. Papers may be distributed by students; consider using weekly "assistant teachers."

Feedback to Students

Good monitoring procedures are essential for providing quality feedback to students, and frequent and regular feedback is more desirable than sporadic appraisal because it reduces the amount of time students spend making errors. Appropriate times for feedback will occur as you monitor work in progress and after it is completed. Try to give students immediate and specific feedback: Tell them what they need to do to correct errors, and then check their corrections.

Although feedback about completed work cannot occur until after an assignment has been checked, checking should be done within a day of work completion so that students can benefit from the feedback. If you find yourself bogged down with work to check, have your students help you. At most grade levels, students can check their own work occasionally. Use this strategy only for assignments they are capable of checking accurately, such as arithmetic worksheets or spelling quizzes that have specified right answers. Teach them a consistent system for marking right or wrong answers. Displaying correct answers with the overhead projector can make checking work in class proceed smoothly and accurately.

Remember that student checking is not done for a grade. It only provides students with some quick feedback so they may know what they did correctly and you may know what help they may need. Papers that require a recorded grade should be checked and graded by you.

In the primary grades particularly, assignments are often short and easy to check quickly. Rather than collecting the work and checking it later, you can check each child's work as it is completed. If you have students bring their work to you, try to avoid the formation of long lines that distract others and waste time.

Pay attention at the beginning of the year to the completion of assignments. The first time a student fails to turn in an assignment without an apparent reason,

Reprinted with special permission of King Features Syndicate.

talk with the student about it. If the student needs help, provide it, but require that the student do the work. If the student neglects two assignments consecutively or begins a pattern of skipping occasional assignments, call the parent(s) or send a note home. Be friendly and encouraging, but insist that the work be done. Don't wait until the grading period is over to note problems with assignment completion or assume that the report card grade will communicate this information effectively. The parent or parents can be the teacher's strongest ally in ensuring that the child takes schoolwork seriously, so do not hesitate to contact parents. Most parents will appreciate your concern and provide you with support from home. Many parents now have home computers and e-mail accounts. Your school may have a policy regarding contacting parents by e-mail. In addition to personal messages about the progress of an individual student, this is an opportunity to alert parents to new topics to be studied, homework assignments, special equipment required, or other material that you may be sending home for them.

You also may want to communicate with parents by having students take checked assignments home regularly. Be sure that this includes good work, not just poor work. You can occasionally have parents sign and return the papers as a way of rewarding and motivating students to "keep up the good work." Use a large envelope or a folder with two ends taped to convey the materials home rather than leaving them loose. This envelope or folder also is a convenient holder for other important documents that go home for signing or for the parents' information. Be sure that the child's name is on the folder or envelope. Taping a signature sheet on the front that has a place for the date and the number of papers included can ensure that parents see all of the student's work. Keep the returned, signed papers until the end of the marking period in case questions arise. Students can then select portfolio entries from this completed work.

Another means of giving the children feedback is to display good work. Do not make standards for "good" so stringent that some children can never meet them. Effort and progress may be more appropriate criteria.

Finally, teach students how to reflect on and record their own progress. Older children can keep a sheet with test scores or assignment grades. Steps on a ladder, circles on a caterpillar to color in for each completed assignment, or some other similar visual device can be a good motivator for younger students. Students who select their own portfolio entries can write about the learning each piece represents or about why they included particular material. Remember your ultimate goal is to help students develop into lifelong, independent learners.

Further Reading

Burns, M. (1995). The 8 most important lessons I've learned about organizing my teaching year. *Instructor, 105*(2), 86–88.

Many of the ideas in this article focus on planning for instruction. Their implementation would be a big step toward managing student academic work, and they are well worth considering by new or experienced teachers.

Evertson, C. M., & Poole, I. R. (2004). *Fostering accountability for classroom work.* IRIS Center for Faculty Enhancement. Nashville, Tenn.: Peabody College, Vanderbilt University. Available at http://iris.peabody.vanderbilt.edu/casestudies.html.

This website contains activities and case studies for accommodating special needs students in the classroom. Click on "Fostering Accountability for Classroom Work" for the cases.

Guskey, T. R. (Ed.). (1996). *Communicating student learning, ASCD yearbook, 1996.* Alexandria, Va.: Association for Supervision and Curriculum Development.

This ASCD yearbook explores the issues involved in communicating and reporting student learning. The history of grading, the difficulties of communication, the role of assessment, the varieties of student abilities, and the role of technology in reporting are some of the issues explored in this collection of articles.

www.atozteacherstuff.com

Includes tips for teachers, including sections on managing papers, morning work, and learning centers.

www.lburkhart.com

Includes tips for technology integration in elementary, middle school, and special needs classrooms.

Suggested Activities

1. Case Studies 3.1 to 3.3 illustrate accountability procedures that encourage student responsibility. Create a list of those you can incorporate into your classroom.

2. Case Study 3.4 illustrates problems that can occur if certain accountability procedures are not in place. Use the information in this and in previous chapters to diagnose Mr. Ambrose's problems. Compare your ideas with the keys in the Appendix. What steps could Mr. Ambrose take to improve the situation in his class?

3. Use Checklist 3 at the end of the chapter to organize your planning as you develop an accountability system. Can you think of any additional accountability procedures you will need?

4. Go to the Internet site www.atozteacherstuff.com/Tips, then click on "managing papers." What tips can you find that would prevent the student protest, "I know I turned it in"?

CASE STUDY 3.1

MANAGING STUDENT WORK

To help students check their homework and to encourage them to help each other, Ms. Alvarez's fourth-grade students work in teams of four and go over the homework problems together. Ms. Alvarez has taught her students how to take turns reading the problems, answering the questions, and encouraging and helping one another. Each team member takes a turn reading the problem aloud and then gives his or her answer to the problem. Team members rotate leading the discussion of the questions until all questions have been answered. From time to time, Ms. Alvarez plans activities and conversations that reinforce the collaborative environment she strives for in her classroom as well as reviewing procedures for her "group check."

The students use the "group check" process when checking their homework. When a team member reads the answer, the other members give a "thumbs up" if they had the same answer. If someone's answer differs, the student quietly says, "I disagree." Each team member talks through the problem and reworks it to see where the error might be. This process continues until each team comes to consensus about the homework problem.

On one question involving the area of a circle, Jake did not draw his circle the same size as his team members did. When Anita gave her solution, Jake said, "I disagree. I think!" Jake and his team members discussed the sizes of the circles and what they would need to do to draw to scale. They used their compasses and redrew the circle, being careful to note the radius given in the problem. As it turned out, Jake's answer was correct; he had drawn his circle to the correct scale. Jake and his team members marked the problems that were difficult for them on their papers. When Ms. Alvarez brought the class back together, she discussed problems that were difficult for the team to agree on and what questions they still had.

Ms. Alvarez uses this information as a cue for the problems that were difficult for the majority of the class. She plans additional class instruction to clarify these problems. Having the team members first check their work together frees Ms. Alvarez to move around the room and help teams that need assistance. Her "group check" system helps her avoid standing at the front of the room and calling out answers.

At the end of the morning activity, one person from each team collects the team's homework folders and files them in the team members' portfolios, stored on a nearby shelf. When Ms. Alvarez has a conference once a week with her students, their portfolios are within reach. Ms. Alvarez also returns the portfolios at a later time and checks the comments the students recorded on the assignment to be sure the students understand the concepts. If she notes that students need additional support, she works with them individually or in small groups.

CASE STUDY 3.2

KEEPING STUDENTS INVOLVED DURING CENTER ACTIVITIES

Ms. Avery designates a section of the chalkboard for listing the daily schedule for centers. Today's schedule consists of the following activities and times:

	Reading Group	**Research**	**Math**	**Science**
9:00–9:20	Spotted Owl	Gorilla	Panda	Panther
9:25–9:45	Panther	Spotted Owl	Gorilla	Panda
9:50–10:10	Panda	Panther	Spotted Owl	Gorilla
10:15–10:35	Gorilla	Panda	Panther	Spotted Owl

Center time typically consists of four stations, one of which is teacher-directed. At the beginning of center time, Ms. Avery presents directions and shows the students the necessary materials for each station.

The reading groups in Ms. Avery's class are flexible. Sometimes they are created around the students' interests; sometimes they are formed to practice certain skills such as learning about main ideas, cause and effect, and inferring. Presently, the students have selected four endangered animals for in-depth study (spotted owl, panther, panda, gorilla), and the reading groups were formed to study each animal. In addition to their reading groups, small groups of students are developing research projects on their chosen animals.

During today's center activities, the students will meet with Ms. Avery for their reading groups. They will also continue with their research projects, using Internet and print resources the teacher and students have found. At the math center, they will complete a practice sheet on long division. Manipulatives and other aids are also provided for the students at this station. For science, the students will observe the animals in the class terrarium and record their observations in their science logs.

When Ms. Avery meets with each reading group, she sits where she can see the entire class. She scans the class frequently and signals children when necessary to keep them engaged. She does so by making eye contact or sometimes calling individuals' names softly to prevent or stop inappropriate behavior. Because Ms. Avery does not want interruptions while she is in the reading circle, she has assigned one helper for each group. To prevent overreliance on the helpers, Ms. Avery has taught the children to request assistance only for situations that prevent them from doing any work at all. If they can skip the problem or question and move on, they are to do so and wait for help from her.

When the timer rings, she dismisses the reading group, and the other groups clean up their stations, place their writing, practice sheets, and journals in appropriate baskets, and move to their next stations. Ms. Avery circulates around the room checking on student progress, answering questions, and helping students. Between groups, checks usually take no longer than five minutes, after which she is ready to call the next group. Ms. Avery has made sure that this monitoring time is built into her schedule.

CASE STUDY 3.3

USING TECHNOLOGY IN AN UPPER ELEMENTARY GRADE

Ms. Curry's sixth-grade science class has been learning to do research on the computer using Web-based resources. Later they will present their projects using software designed for school-age students that accommodates short videos and other graphics. Students are to complete two multimedia research projects during the year, but Ms. Curry decides to limit the choices for the first project to make it easier for students to begin quickly and to focus on learning the content. This also allows her to adjust the assignment for student ability levels. When she introduces the first research project on cells, Ms. Curry provides two handouts describing requirements: (1) a description of the topic and a list of cards or slide categories the computer presentation should include, and (2) a general outline of requirements for the project, a calendar of checkpoints, a due date for the assignment, and information about how the project will be graded.

Ms. Curry does an initial multimedia presentation for the class as an example and goes over all directions step-by-step. She emphasizes two main requirements: appearance and sources to be included. To illustrate guidelines for appearance, she provides examples of color selections for backgrounds and text to show which color combinations can be easily read and which cannot. She also includes appearance standards such as size and clarity of fonts defined in detail. The second main requirement concerns appropriate sources such as references and the bibliography for which she gives a model for citations for both text and Web-based versions and the inclusion of graphics or video. At least one of the cards or slides has to include a sound or video file rather than written text. Ms. Curry provides a print-out of her sample presentation to each student and posts one copy on the bulletin board. She also indicates the days the class will be scheduled to work in the library and computer lab and provides a sign-up sheet for using the classroom computers during class work time or study hall.

Before the first multimedia project is due, students receive a check-off sheet that they use to determine whether they have met all of the requirements before submitting their disks. She uses this to evaluate their work and to record grades for each presentation, which she discusses with each student.

CASE STUDY 3.4

POOR WORK AND STUDY HABITS IN A FOURTH-GRADE CLASS

Mr. Ambrose's fourth-grade class has been fairly well behaved, with little disruptive behavior. Most students follow his procedures, such as those for staying in their seats during whole-class presentations; raising hands during discussions; and using the pencil sharpener, restroom, and other areas of the room appropriately. Some social talk occurs during independent work activities, but it does not escalate into chaos, and students usually settle down when requested. However, students have been less task engaged lately, and many students have been tardy turning in assignments. They complain that they don't know when assignments are due, and some don't turn in their work at all. To make assignments very explicit, Mr. Ambrose has begun to record the daily assignments on the side chalkboard. Because some assignments are not due until the following day, he leaves the previous day's assignments on that chalkboard also, so students will know when each subject's assignment is due for both days.

Today, during a one-hour period of individual and group work, several students asked what they were supposed to do despite the fact that Mr. Ambrose had listed the morning assignments on the board and repeatedly pointed out where they could be found. After several students turned in papers before they were called for, Mr. Ambrose explained, "Remember that class assignments not finished during class time are supposed to be kept until the next day, even if you get them done later in the day, unless I call for them. If you finish the homework during independent work time, it can be placed in the turn-in box then." Students continued to act confused, not only about when assignments were due but also about how to do the work.

Mr. Ambrose frequently works at his desk during independent work time, but he allows students to come up one at a time if they need assistance. They follow this procedure well, although some of the lowest-achieving students seldom come up. Quiet socializing and other off-task activity go on among students whose seats are located away from the teacher.

Mr. Ambrose has ample activities for students. For example, during a recent one-hour segment, he gave students an assignment and then a quiz (students were told to hold their papers until after the quiz was completed). An extra-credit assignment was listed on the board for students who finished the regular work early. As he handed out the quiz and gave instructions, some students continued to work on the assignment. Later they had to go to Mr. Ambrose to find the instructions for the test, and several did not have enough time to complete the test. Mr. Ambrose has told students that they must work harder and do their best or their grades will suffer, but this seems to have had impact on only the most motivated students in the class.

What steps could Mr. Ambrose take to improve the situation in his class?

 ## Checklist 3

Accountability Procedures

Check When Complete	Area	Notes
	Communicating Assignments and Work Requirements	
☐	A. Where and how will you post assignments?	_____
☐	B. What will be your standards for form and neatness?	_____
	—Pencil, color of pen, typed or on disk	
	—Type of paper	
	—Heading	
	—Due dates	
	—Erasures	
☐	C. How will absent students know what assignments to make up?	_____
☐	D. What will be the consequences of late or incomplete work?	_____
	Monitoring Progress on and Completion of Assignments	
☐	A. What procedures will you use to monitor work in progress?	_____

Check When Complete	Area	Notes
☐	B. When and how will you monitor projects or longer assignments?	_____
☐	C. How will you determine whether students are completing assignments?	_____
☐	D. How will you collect completed assignments?	_____
☐	E. What records of student work will you retain?	_____
☐	F. How will you encourage students to monitor themselves?	_____
	Feedback	
☐	A. What are your school's grading policies and procedures?	_____
☐	B. What kinds of feedback will you provide, and when?	_____
☐	C. How will you encourage students to reflect on their own progress?	_____
☐	D. What will you do when a student stops doing assignments?	_____
☐	E. What procedure will you follow to send materials home to parents?	_____
☐	F. Where will you display student work?	_____
☐	G. What records, if any, of their own work will the students maintain?	_____
☐	H. Will students keep portfolios? If so, how will entries be selected, and how will students reflect on them?	
☐	I. How will you handle grading disputes?	_____

4
Getting Off to a Good Start

The beginning of school is an important time for classroom management because your students will learn attitudes, behavior, and work habits that will affect the rest of the year. It is in the first few weeks of school that students learn the behaviors expected of them and how to accomplish school tasks successfully. They also learn in what ways these tasks are meaningful to them and why success is worth pursuing. Much of this is communicated simply by how you treat your students and what you expect of them from the very first day. Careful planning for the beginning of school sets the stage for the rest of the year.

Your major goal for the beginning of the year, then, is to strengthen each student's belief that school tasks are worth doing. To accomplish this, you must obtain student cooperation in two key areas: following your rules and procedures and successfully engaging in all learning experiences. Attaining this goal will make it possible for you to create a positive climate for learning during the rest of the year.

A concern for establishing appropriate behavior does not imply a lack of concern for student feelings and attitudes. Instead, the intent is to create a classroom climate that helps children feel secure and confident and keeps preventable problems from occurring. Therefore, some of the suggestions in this chapter focus directly on cognitive goals, whereas others incorporate student concerns and other affective considerations.

The major topics in this chapter are creating a positive climate, teaching rules and procedures to the students, and deciding on the classroom activities you will use during the first week of school. Communicating with parents, special problems, and preparing for a substitute are also discussed. A checklist is available to help organize your planning, and two case studies of the beginning of the year will give you many ideas about how to begin.

FOR REFLECTION

Can you remember what it was like to start school when you were attending elementary school? When adults are asked to recall school beginnings, they can rarely remember much detail about what teachers did, but they often remember their own personal experiences, problems, or concerns. Do you remember a year when you felt especially welcomed? Was there a year when you felt left out or unexcited about your new class? How should you attempt to take your students' concerns into account at the beginning of the year? Because your personal concerns and anxieties also may be heightened during those critical days, how can you deal with your own feelings and accommodate student concerns at the same time?

CREATING A POSITIVE CLIMATE IN YOUR CLASSROOM

Having a good management plan before the school year begins is essential, but its effectiveness in building community will depend on the presence of a positive classroom environment. The goal is not to be the ruler of your classroom kingdom but to be the designer and facilitator of an interactive classroom community. The foundation of a positive climate is positive interactions between the teacher and students and among students. A positive environment encourages students to be excited about their school experience and about learning.

Students are with their teachers almost 50 percent of their waking hours, so it is easy to see how teachers are major influences in young people's lives. This large investment of time, plus teachers' influences on students, requires the creation of a positive and safe environment in which students can be challenged, feel free to explore, support one another, and engage in constructing their own knowledge.

Like all human beings, children have a strong need to belong to a group. You can promote that sense of belonging in a number of ways: (Erwin, 2003; Evertson & Harris, 2003).

1. **Speak courteously and calmly.** Students need to hear teachers saying "please," "thank you," and "excuse me." These courtesies become expected and are modeled by the students. A calm voice indicates acceptance and self-control. If children feel threatened or frustrated, knowing that the teacher is not upset is reassuring.
2. **Share information.** Learn each student's name as soon as possible and engage in activities that help students learn more about each other. Introduce yourself and share something about your outside interests. Speak personally with your students to get to know them individually.
3. **Use positive statements as often as possible.** Often negative behavior is more noticeable than positive; therefore, we tend to comment on it more often. Perhaps we also feel compelled to mention negative behavior because we believe it will improve students' behavior. The opposite is usually true. Not only do negative statements cause a student to feel negative, but they also tend to create a negative environment that affects everyone.
4. **Establish a feeling of community.** Teach students to work cooperatively (see Chapter 6) and give them regular opportunities to learn in structured cooperative activities. Conduct class meetings on a regular basis for class-building, problem-solving, and content-related discussions. One of your first meetings can be on establishing class rules and procedures (Chapter 3).

While building a positive relationship with individual students is seen as one of the most critical predictors of student success (Brophy, Good, Payne), understanding the concept of authority is also important to the health of the community. To feel safe, children need to know that there is a source of authority within the classroom (Brophy, 2004; Hoy & Weinstein, in press). The power of authority naturally lies with the teacher, but how that power is used is a critical influence in the learning community.

◎ Teaching Rules and Procedures

One of the surest ways to communicate your expectations for student behavior is through a planned system of classroom rules and procedures. How best to teach this system to your students is an important consideration. The term *teach* is used purposely; you will not communicate your expectations adequately if you only tell students about rules and procedures.

Here are three important aspects of the teaching process:

1. **Describing and demonstrating the desired behavior.** Use words and actions to convey what behavior is acceptable or desirable. Be as specific as possible. For example, do not simply tell students you expect good behavior while you are out of the room; tell them what "good behavior" means—staying in seats, no talking, keep working. Demonstrate desired behavior whenever possible. For example, if you allow "quiet talking" or "classroom voices" during center time, show what this means. If the procedure is complex, present it step-by-step. For example, lining up requires that students know when to line up (the teacher gives permission by tables or rows), where and how to go (push chairs under tables and then walk without talking), expected behavior in line (hands off others, no talking in halls, walk—don't run). You do not have to do all of the demonstrating; students enjoy showing the class the correct procedure.

2. **Rehearsal.** This means practicing the behaviors. Rehearsal serves two purposes: It helps children learn the appropriate behavior, and it provides you with an opportunity to determine whether they understand and can follow a procedure correctly. Complex procedures may have to be rehearsed several times. Practice is especially helpful for primary-grade children; however, older elementary school children can also benefit from rehearsal when procedures are complex or unfamiliar.

3. **Feedback.** After you have asked students to follow a procedure for the first time, tell them whether they did it properly. If they need to improve, tell them that too. Be specific in your feedback—for example, "I liked how quickly you put your materials away, but I did not like the talking at Table Two." If many students do not follow a procedure correctly, repeat one or more of the steps listed here. If only a few students are off track, ask them to describe what they are supposed to do so that you can see whether they understand your directions. Finally, the fact that students follow the procedure correctly once does not mean they will do so consistently. Watch carefully and be prepared to give reminders and feedback as appropriate.

Following is an example that illustrates how to teach procedures. It shows how a complex transition procedure was taught to a second-grade class. The teacher in this example teaches students to respond to a signal, put away their materials, and move to a rug area.

> Ms. Stevens explains to her students that she expects them to move quickly and quietly from one activity to another so they will have time to do all the things planned. She shows them the kitchen timer and makes it ring. When they hear this bell, they should put away the materials they are using and move to the next activity as quickly as possible. She says, "After reading, I will ring the bell, and you are to put your reading materials in your desk as quickly as possible. You should then get up from your desk and walk quietly to the rug so we can begin our Spanish lesson.

Are there any questions?" A student asks if she will always ring the bell for Spanish, and Ms. Stevens says she will.

Ms. Stevens then tells the class that she would like them to practice. "You have paper and pencil on your desk for story writing. I will give you time to finish the story later in the day. Right now, when I ring the bell, put your materials in your desk and come quickly and quietly to the rug." At this point, Ms. Stevens rings the bell. Students immediately begin putting away their materials and moving toward the rug. However, several students line up to get drinks of water and one goes to the restroom. When everyone is on the rug in a circle around Ms. Stevens, she refers to the clock on the wall and says, "It took us three minutes to put the materials away and get to the rug. You are second graders now, and I think you can move faster than that. I think you should be seated on the rug in a circle in one minute. Also, it was not time to get a drink of water or to use the restroom unless it is an emergency. Do you all understand?" The students all nod solemnly.

Ms. Stevens tells students to return to their desks, get out their paper and pencils, and get set to practice again. The students go quickly back to their desks and take out their materials. Ms. Stevens rings the bell again, and students go through the routine, this time more quickly. After everyone is settled, Ms. Stevens smiles and thanks the students. "You've done a super job. It only took you one minute to get to the rug. I'm really proud of you."

In the example, Ms. Stevens demonstrated the signal, described the desired behavior, and gave a rationale for it. The students practiced the steps twice, and Ms. Stevens gave them feedback each time.

Planning for a Good Beginning

Planning for a warm and friendly learning environment for your students is a positive first step in starting the year. In the beginning, you also must consider the management strategies of choosing teaching rules and procedures and a system for ensuring student accountability. These are discussed in more detail in Chapters 2 and 3. You now need to plan activities for the first several days of school.

Planning for the First Days of School

Planning activities that will allow all of your students to be successful will make students feel more secure and confident and will encourage good effort. Initial assignments should be easy and should require only simple directions. In this way, the children can learn lesson routines quickly and encounter little difficulty in completing assignments.

For the first few days, limit the lessons to those that can be presented and explained to all students at the same time. Do not try to group students for instruction for at least several days, and if you can, avoid individual testing or activities or assignments that require lengthy work with individual students that keep you from monitoring the whole class. Don't overload yourself or your students with unnecessarily complicated activities. Your students will already be learning many new procedures during the first few days of school. In addition, you will need to be free to watch students to detect problems and take appropriate action. If you are involved with a small group or with an individual, you may not see important behaviors and events that may grow into problems.

Plan your activities to take into account the students' perspectives, concerns, and needs for information about their new and unfamiliar classroom. A variety of activities, including some with physical movement, music, and provision for occasional short breaks, provide the changes of pace that help maintain interest and alertness throughout the day. In addition, you can stimulate interest in the curriculum and its activities if you are excited about the things they will be learning this year. Foreshadow interesting units in science and social studies or tell them about skills they will develop in your class.

Keep in mind that not all of your students may be present the first day of school. Many times, students will enter or leave the school during the first couple of weeks. For record-keeping purposes, create a temporary grade book and attendance sheet.

Some Typical Activities

Activities for the first school day and for several days thereafter are described next. They are not necessarily presented in the sequence you will use, nor will you use each one every day. Examine the two case studies at the end of the chapter to see how different teachers put the pieces together.

GREETING THE STUDENTS

Prepare student name tags ahead of time, but have extra materials on hand for students who are not on your roll. Decide how name tags will be fastened. If you use straight pins, you may be inviting little dueling matches and surprise pricks and pokes. If you intend to use safety pins, be sure your students can fasten them, or else plan to do it for them. Other options are tape, commercial stick-on tags, or a length of yarn so the name tags are worn like necklaces. In addition to name tags, you might also tape a name card to the top of each student's desk.

When students enter the room, greet them warmly, help them get their name tags, and get them seated. If you have taped their names to their desks, the matter of seating is settled. In some cases, the roster of students is not definite, and you may not want to set up a seating chart before the students arrive. In this case, have them find a desk that "fits" them so that they will be comfortable throughout the year. Students may label their desks with removable sticky-backed notes, which are easy to relocate. Explain that seating may change later.

Make a seating chart or label the desks as soon as practicable, making any necessary adjustments later. Some teachers use a grid, putting student names into the boxes in pencil until their classes have stabilized and seating is set. Another strategy involves using sticky notes on a heavy sheet of 8½-x-11-inch paper and keeping it in a plastic sleeve. This allows you to move, add, or subtract students as necessary. An added advantage is the flexibility if you decide to rearrange desks. The sticky notes may be arranged in any configuration. Further, colored dots may be placed on student sticky notes. Make a key to remind yourself to inform a substitute of information about individual students.

Don't allow the students to wander around the room or become noisy. If students straggle in and you cannot start class right away, provide a simple puzzle, a geography mind-bender, or a piece of paper with open-ended questions such as, "I am thinking about . . . ," "I have a question about . . . ," or "I wonder what _____ is like in school" to give students something to do at their desks. As soon as most students are present, begin with the introduction. Remember later in the day to let students talk about how they solved the puzzles or what they wrote on their papers.

INTRODUCTIONS

You will want to tell the students something about yourself; however, an extended autobiography is not necessary. A few personal notes and something about your interests are appropriate. Have students introduce themselves—nothing more than a name is necessary, but some teachers like to use a little more introduction, having the children tell something about themselves. The introductory activity should not take too long, however, as there will be plenty of opportunity later to get acquainted, and you do not want students to become restless.

ROOM DESCRIPTION

Introduce students to their classroom by pointing out and describing areas of the room, particularly areas that they will be using on the first day. As you do so, describe any procedures associated with room use for that day. For example, show students where they may put their coats, lunches, or other items from home; be sure they know where the pencil sharpener is and when they may use it, where frequently used supplies are stored, where the calendar, wastebasket, and clock are, and so on.

GET-ACQUAINTED ACTIVITIES

Teachers frequently include a get-acquainted activity as part of their first-day plan. Such activities can help students feel that the teacher and others know them better and care about them as individuals. Teachers often describe the goal of such an activity as helping students feel more secure and comfortable with their classmates. The activities are also used to foster a greater sense of class cohesiveness. One of these get-acquainted activities can be used early in the first day's plan of activities for a change of pace after the room description or after the initial discussion of rules and major procedures:

- Ask students to introduce themselves and to name a favorite activity or hobby or tell about something they did during the summer. Keep this activity moving briskly because student attention will wane during long introductions.

A variation of this activity is to use reciprocal introductions. Have pairs of students learn each other's names and something about the other person (hobbies, interests). Then have students introduce their partners.

■ Use a name game to help students remember names and to add interest to introductions. For example, have students make up an adjective to go with their own names (e.g., Happy Holly, Curious Carl) or have students think of a game they like (Nintendo Nick). As students introduce themselves, have them name the other students who came before them (or perhaps the last five students) along with their descriptors.

■ Make copies of a line drawing of the school's mascot. Let students sign their own copies and write personal facts (names of brothers or sisters, pets, likes and dislikes, favorite activities, foods, etc.) on the drawings. Post these on a bulletin board so students can read about each other.

■ Ask students to complete a brief questionnaire identifying their interests, favorite subjects, hobbies, and so on. Upper elementary students can complete a series of open-ended statements that reflect their interests or preferences (e.g., "Today I feel. . . ." or "The thing I do best is. . . .").

The activities described next can be used the first day or later in the week, after students are more acquainted with one another or after you have time to prepare for the activity.

■ Make a puzzle with student names. For example, leave out a few letters in each name for students to fill in, or list first and last names in separate columns in scrambled order and let students match names. Students can identify names arranged in a "seek and find" puzzle.

■ Set aside a few minutes before the children leave to review the day's activities and to discuss with the students what they learned, found difficult, liked best, and so forth. Say a few words about upcoming events and activities. Comment on good work and behavior to reinforce your expectations and to keep the tone positive.

■ Have students from last year's class—you'll need to plan this well ahead—write letters to students in this year's class, telling them what to expect, what was fun about the year, suggestions for study, and what they learned during the year. Share these letters with your students.

■ Have students bring a paper bag containing three to five objects, such as books, pictures, or toys, that tell something about themselves. Let students use these props to introduce themselves on the second or third day of school. Split the activity into two segments, if necessary, to maintain attention and interest.

■ Make up a questionnaire in the form of a scavenger hunt; for example, "Name a student who has three brothers and who plays soccer." Let students work in groups to see how many of their classmates they can identify.

■ Have students bring in one item that represents them for a bulletin board. Students will explain the meaning of their items to the class and put them on the bulletin board, forming a collage of student interests and experiences.

PRESENTATION AND DISCUSSION OF RULES, PROCEDURES, AND CONSEQUENCES

Soon after the introductions, usually after the initial room description, present the major rules and procedures. School rules should be covered along with your classroom rules. Major consequences associated with the rules should be described at the same time. Plan to review the rules later, perhaps on the second and third days, to underscore their importance and help students remember them. Some teachers then test students on the rules, documenting each student's knowledge and understanding of them, but posting the rules is a more common way to remind students. You may also have copies made of the rules and procedures and send these home for parent signatures.

Teach important procedures as they are needed, rather than all at once. For example, during this initial discussion, you will probably want to teach procedures for using restrooms and the pencil sharpener, moving about the room, obtaining help, asking questions, and talking. Later in the day, as they are needed, teach other procedures such as those for major transitions (ending the day, leaving and entering the room at lunch time, or before and after recess) as well as procedures associated with cafeteria or other out-of-room areas. Your opening routine (see Chapter 2) will probably be used on the second day of school, so you may wish to wait until then to describe it. Procedures for special equipment such as computers can wait until you're ready to use that equipment, and small-group procedures should not be introduced until those activities begin. The idea is to provide students with the information they need to successfully complete the activities required of them in the first days of school and to help them feel confident in their new classroom environment.

On the second day of school, review the rules and major procedures students need to know. This reinforces your expectations for appropriate behavior and reminds students of rules and procedures they may have forgotten. When correcting student behavior at the beginning of school, remind students of what rule was

"The hardest part about goin' back to school is learning how to whisper again."
Reprinted with special permission of King Features Syndicate.

broken. In the primary grades, particularly, you will have to observe students carefully for several weeks to be sure they are following procedures correctly and to give reminders, cues, and prompts to help them learn class routines.

When you present your class rules and procedures, set a positive tone by emphasizing the benefits to everyone: "These rules are intended to help us have an enjoyable class in which everyone can learn. We all know that our classroom will work better when everyone respects each other's rights," or "When we allow someone to speak without interrupting, we are showing that we are good listeners." If some procedure or rule is difficult to follow, you might acknowledge this as you discuss it: "I know it isn't easy to remember to raise your hand before speaking when we are having an interesting discussion, but doing so will give everyone a chance to participate," or "It will be hard not to start using the equipment right away, but we need to wait for directions so no one is injured." Explanations such as these help students understand and accept what might otherwise be seen as arbitrary rules.

CONTENT ACTIVITIES

Be sure to select activities that are uncomplicated. Assignments should allow for differences in speed of completion; be sure to have backup activities for students who complete work early. Consult your teachers' manuals and curriculum guides and talk with experienced teachers to get ideas about appropriate beginning content activities for the subjects at your grade level.

TIME FILLERS

Periodically, you will have to fill in time between activities or before and after major transitions. For example, students may complete an assignment earlier than you anticipated, but there may not be enough time to finish another activity before starting the next event on the day's schedule. There may also be times when students need a short break after an intensive lesson. Filling these times with constructive activity is better than trying to stretch out an already completed task or just letting students amuse themselves. Ideas include having a good book to read to the children or some simple games that can be played in the classroom (e.g., Seven Up, Name Bingo, Baseball Math, Spelling Bee). Use handouts with puzzles, riddles, or story starters for creative writing. You can also lead the children in group exercises, sing songs, listen to a good children's story, or have a bulletin board of creative writing ideas. You might have a "share and tell" time in which students focus on telling what they know about a particular topic (e.g., pets, hobbies). Ask other teachers for ideas and accumulate a file so you will be ready with a filler when one is needed.

ADMINISTRATIVE ACTIVITIES

If you use textbooks, you will have to distribute them. You may wish to issue only one or two textbooks on the first day; some teachers wait a day or two before distributing textbooks and use handouts for assignments, especially if class enrollment is likely to change. When you do give out books, you may have to record book numbers for each student, perhaps using a standard form. You should also determine school policies in this area. For example, some schools require that books issued to students be kept covered at all times. If so, you will need a supply of covers on hand, and you must teach the children how to cover the books. In lower grades, it might be better to do the job yourself or enlist the help of parents or an aide. Even in higher grades, some students will have forgotten how to cover books. Plan to show the whole class, and schedule plenty of time for this event.

Determine whether there are any materials that students must take home with them on the first day or later in the week (this might include information about the breakfast and lunch program, school policy on attendance, time of arrival and departure for children, etc.). Keep a file of extra copies of these materials for students who enter school later in the year.

Communicating with Parents

It is a good idea to prepare a letter to send home explaining any essential information not already covered in school handouts. Sometimes teachers at one grade level collaborate on the letter. If not, write one of your own and get it ready to be sent home with the children at the end of the first day. Its purpose is to establish a link with parents and to communicate important information to them. The letter should include information on:

- Materials or supplies their child will need
- Your conference times and how parents may contact you
- Curriculum units you will teach or special field trips coming up during the year
- Special events for parents (e.g., back-to-school night, open house)
- Breakfast and lunch programs if not already provided by the school

A cheerful, friendly letter that is neat, legible, grammatically correct, and free of misspellings will create a good impression and communicate a professional image to the parents. It is easy to become extremely rushed at the beginning of the year and to let this letter be slipshod. Have a friend proofread it before you duplicate it to be sure it is clear, correct, and easy to read. A handout describing class rules and major procedures (especially those relating to assignments) might be sent as an enclosure with the letter. Having parents sign and return this handout will provide you with assurance that they received your letter and enclosures.

Special Problems

It is not possible to predict every problem that could occur in the first few days of school, but it is possible to identify several that occur commonly, occasionally, or rarely. If you are prepared for the commonly occurring problems and at least not surprised by the occasional or rare event, you will be able to cope.

"I know I can train them to be thoughtful, productive citizens if I can ever get past 'sit.'"
© Martha F. Campbell. Reprinted by permission of Martha F. Campbell.

INTERRUPTIONS BY OFFICE STAFF, PARENTS, CUSTODIANS, AND OTHERS (COMMON)

If you can manage the interruption without leaving the room, do so. Invite the person into your room and face your students as you talk with the person. If the interruption is likely to last more than a few seconds, or if you must leave the room, give students something to do before continuing the conference. Let the person wait, not your class. Ask your students to continue working if they are already involved in an activity. If not, tell them they can use the time to read a book they have or to rest their heads on their desks. Have materials for one or two planned activities ready for an unforeseen or lengthy interruption.

LATE ARRIVALS ON THE FIRST DAY (COMMON)

Greet late arrivals as warmly as you did the other students. Tell them you will talk to them about what they missed as soon as you can but that for now they must wait in their seats. Show them where to sit. When you have the total class involved in some activity, meet with these children to explain anything they may have missed.

ONE OR MORE CHILDREN ARE ASSIGNED TO YOUR CLASS AFTER THE FIRST DAY (COMMON)

Try to meet with these students before school so that you can explain rules and procedures to them and handle necessary paperwork. If you have already distributed books to the class, make sure these students also get texts. If you can't meet these students ahead of time, use the first available opportunity while the rest of your class is occupied. Be warm and welcoming with these students; you want to communicate that you are pleased that they have joined the class, not that they are inconvenient! Appoint one or more responsible students to be "buddies" with the new students to help familiarize them with the classroom and school procedures and rules. The amount of assistance you can expect from these buddies depends on their grade level. Be sure to monitor new students carefully to help them adjust to your class and to learn appropriate behavior.

A CHILD FORGETS LUNCH MONEY OR SUPPLIES (COMMON)

Be familiar with your school's policies. The principal or school nurse may have an emergency fund for students without lunch money. Some schools allow students to charge a lunch in an emergency. It's a good idea to keep a couple of lunches' worth of small change on hand. Also, have one day's worth of supplies available for students who forget theirs. If a student continues to forget supplies, you may have to check with parents to see that they are aware that the materials are needed. If you suspect that the family cannot afford the supplies, see whether your school or parent-teacher organization has funds for helping such students.

LARGE AMOUNTS OF PAPERWORK DURING THE FIRST WEEK OF SCHOOL (COMMON)

This may be difficult, but try to do as little paperwork as possible during class time. Rather, plan to spend extra time before and after school, and arrange your personal schedule to accommodate it. This will pay off in reduced tension over the long run. If you must do clerical work during class time, do it quickly while the children are engaged in activities. Monitor the class while you work, and avoid losing eye contact with your students for long periods. Create a checklist (a spreadsheet program works well) for all paperwork and money the children will be returning during the first few days of school. A glance at your master checklist will show you which children need reminders.

A CHILD FORGETS BUS NUMBER OR MISSES BUS (OCCASIONAL)

Help to avoid these problems by rehearsing bus procedures with students. Consider putting a sticker or other label on younger students, identifying how they are to get home (car line, bus number, walker). This way you or another adult in the building may assist any confused students quickly. Make certain students are not left alone while waiting for a ride, and reassure them that the parent or person picking them up will arrive soon. Have bus numbers and parents' and emergency phone numbers on hand for when problems do arise.

INSUFFICIENT NUMBERS OF TEXTBOOKS ARE AVAILABLE, OR VITAL EQUIPMENT AND MATERIALS ARE MISSING (OCCASIONAL)

Before school begins, check on the availability of textbooks and your equipment and find out your school's procedures for getting the needed materials into your room. When you discover shortages, report them to the school office. If you must begin the year without enough texts, you may be able to have students share books, or you might arrange to share a class set with another teacher. If you have no texts at all in some subject, you can probably find earlier editions of the text in the book storage room to tide you over. Depending on the subject, teacher-prepared materials may be sufficient.

ONE STUDENT HAS A DISABILITY THAT INTERFERES WITH UNDERSTANDING OR FOLLOWING DIRECTIONS (OCCASIONAL)

Seat the student close to you, and engage the student in simple activities. Work individually with this student only after the rest of the class is busy. As soon as possible, talk to the resource teacher to determine what the student is capable of doing; then plan the student's educational program. If possible, talk to the teacher from the preceding year for suggestions. You will also find it helpful to set up a conference with the parents soon after the year has begun. For further suggestions, see Chapter 10.

CRYING (OCCASIONAL)

Younger children, especially, may cry for no apparent reason early in the school year. Sometimes the crying stops fairly quickly if you can distract the child and engage him or her in some activity. Sometimes it helps to assign a friend to accompany the child to get a drink of water, wash his or her face, and then come back to join the class. Be understanding and try to find out the possible cause for tears, but do not reinforce crying by giving the child excessive attention or sympathy. If the crying is not disruptive, the child can remain in his or her seat until the episode is over. If the crying is disruptive, take the child out of the room or have someone from the office come to get him or her.

WETTING (OCCASIONAL)

Although accidental wetting is more common with younger children, it sometimes occurs even in the upper grades, especially during the first few days of school. This kind of accident is extremely embarrassing to the child, and the teacher should make every effort not to add to the child's discomfort. Have paper towels on hand to facilitate the cleanup, and handle the matter as privately as possible. Arrange to call home or have an office worker phone to bring a change of clothes to school. Later, talk privately with the child to determine why he or she did not go to the restroom in time. With some younger children, you may have to contact the parents and keep a change of clothes at school as a precaution. In general with younger children, the teacher must schedule regular restroom breaks and even remind some children to use the restroom regularly.

A CHILD BECOMES VERY SICK OR IS INJURED (RARE)

If the child has a known medical condition (such as asthma) and you have been previously informed of what to do, follow directions and stay calm. In other cases, phone the office or send a messenger requesting someone to come to get the child. Do not leave the child unattended.

Preparing for a Substitute

During the first weeks of school, create a handbook for the substitutes who may teach in your absence. Always assume that these people have never been to your school before. This handbook should include the following:

- Class roll
- Seating chart
- Copy of your classroom rules and consequences
- Daily schedule
- List of medical alerts and medication times for various students
- Emergency lesson plans (in case you are unable to leave current ones)
- Names of teachers and students who can provide assistance
- Emergency procedures
- Map of the school

Leave this handbook in a prominent place in your classroom or in the school office so that it is immediately available when a substitute arrives. Tape a note permanently to your desk ("Substitute's notebook in bottom drawer").

 ## Further Reading

Brophy, J. E. (2000). Teaching. In H. J. Walberg (Series Ed.) *Educational Practices.* Brussels, Belgium: International Academy of Education.

This booklet, prepared for the International Bureau of Education, synthesizes much of what is known about teaching through contemporary research. As an easy-to-read description of good teaching, this booklet presents overarching themes, research, and classroom descriptions for classroom climate, learning, curriculum, discourse, activities, engagement, and assessment. Reading this publication could easily prompt thoughtful preparation for the start of a school year.

Emmer, E. T., Evertson, C. M., & Anderson, L. M. (1980). Effective classroom management at the beginning of the school year. *The Elementary School Journal, 80*(5), 219–231.

This article traces the means by which routines are established in the beginning of the school year and their relationship to classroom management throughout the year. Observations of elementary school teachers starting the school year distinguish between teachers who maintained higher levels of task engagement and cooperation in classroom tasks and low levels of inappropriate and disruptive behavior and those who did not in the ways they established and reinforced classroom norms, monitored, paced lessons, and prevented misbehavior from occurring.

Erwin, J. C. (2003). Giving students what they need. *Educational Leadership, 61(1),* 19–23.

The article emphasizes the importance of teacher-student relationships as an integral tool of classroom management and the need to create those conditions that encourage internal motivation and student responsibility as opposed to external motivation that gives teachers full responsibility for motivating students.

Randolph, C. H., & Evertson, C. M. (1995). Managing for learning: Rules, roles, and meanings in a writing class. *Journal of Classroom Interaction, 30*(2), 17–25.

The authors argue that management and content are interwoven. As teachers and students negotiate ways of interacting with academic content and with each other, and as they define the roles that each plays, they establish meanings that influence what academic content can be learned and how it is learned.

Wiske, M. S. (1994). How teaching for understanding changes the rules in the classroom. *Educational Leadership, 51*(5), 19–21.

This article discusses how attempting to share authority and responsibility with students violates traditional classroom and school norms. The author implies that teachers must remain open to and accepting of the uneasiness this change causes both in themselves and in their students.

www.proteacher.com

This website for teachers includes tips for planning and message boards on a range of topics in elementary schools.

http://ci.kern.org.tesa

This website for the Teacher Expectations and Student Achievement (TESA) intervention program (Kern County, L.A.) is designed to increase academic performance and diversity and gender awareness, to promote a positive classroom climate, and to reduce discipline problems.

 ## Suggested Activities

1. Read Case Studies 4.1 and 4.2. They describe teachers beginning the year in diverse settings. As you read them, consider the following questions:

   a. *To what extent are the principles described in this and previous chapters in evidence in each case?*

   b. *In spite of subject matter and grade-level differences, there are similarities between the teachers. Identify as many of these as you can.*

   c. *What differences are apparent between the teachers in their beginning-of-year activities? Which one(s) would you use? Why?*

   d. *In Case 4.1 the teacher uses a literature-based approach to frame activities for students. In Case 4.2 the teacher makes extensive use of groups for cooperative learning. How do these approaches affect the way each teacher begins the year?*

2. What do you think your students' goals and concerns will be at the beginning of the year? How can your classroom management plan accommodate them?

3. Use Checklist 4 at the end of the chapter to organize your planning activities for the beginning of school. What others would you add?

4. Talk with teachers who have had several years' experience at the grade level you will be teaching. Ask them what activities they use during the first few days and how they sequence them. Teachers are often willing to share handouts and ideas. You might also ask someone to look over your lesson plan for the first day and give you suggestions.

5. What are some of the ways you can initiate and sustain a positive climate in your classroom? Make a list and interview other teachers for their ideas.

CASE STUDY 4.1

BEGINNING THE YEAR IN A LITERATURE-BASED PRIMARY CLASSROOM

First-Day Activities

Time/Activity	Description
8:00–8:35 Greeting students	Ms. Gonzalez greets the children as they enter, helps them put on their name tags, and checks the pronunciation of their names. She gives the students laminated name strips and tells each one to choose a desk and place the strip on it. She also tells students to put their lunch boxes in the basket, hang their book-bags on their labeled coat hooks, and place their supplies on the round table at the side of the room. As the first students settle at their desks, Ms. Gonzalez lets each one select a piece of construction paper, write his or her name on it, and decorate it. When students have finished, they get to choose a cubby that will hold their personal belongings and tape the construction paper to the back wall of the cubby. She has placed a tape dispenser at each end of the cubbies for the students to use. Ms. Gonzalez also asks these early arriving students to help their later arriving classmates. As the rest of the students arrive, Ms. Gonzalez helps them settle into the classroom, checks supplies, talks with parents, and monitors students' progress.
8:35–8:40 Introducing teacher	After all of the buses have arrived and she feels that her students are settled, Ms. Gonzalez moves to the next activity. She does not call roll because she can tell who is absent by the remaining laminated strips. She fills in her attendance card and places it outside her door. Ms. Gonzalez, who has taught at this school for many years and already knows many of her students, briefly introduces herself and tells the children that she is looking forward to an exciting year with them. She notices that many of the children are curiously looking around the room, so she starts by describing the classroom and a few class procedures.

Time/Activity	Description
8:40–9:00 Describing room	Ms. Gonzalez begins by pointing out the classroom library, and she tells students that they may get books from the library after they have finished assignments. The students may use the bean bags and comfortable pillows while they are in the library, or they may take the books to their desks. She also shows the listening center next to the library and points out that this center can accommodate only two children at a time. She next shows how to operate the tape recorder and notes the four computers next to the listening center. Ms. Gonzalez says they won't be using the computers until next week, but she tells the students what kinds of activities they will learn to do with the computers. She also highlights materials in the science discovery center, gives procedures for this area, and tells the students that four children may work at this center. Ms. Gonzalez also shows the students other interesting areas of the classroom such as a large space entitled "Message Board" where she and the students can display messages to the class. She also points out the student bulletin board, which is divided into twenty-four large rectangles where the students can highlight their interests and achievements. Last, she shows the students their mailboxes.
9:00–9:25 Drawing self-portraits	Ms. Gonzalez holds up her self-portrait, which she drew the previous day, and they discuss what self-portraits are. Ms. Gonzalez then distributes construction paper to the students and asks them to draw their own self-portraits. She also asks them to write two things about themselves on the back of the pictures. As the children begin, Ms. Gonzalez circulates, offers assistance, and monitors their progress. When some children become concerned about their spelling, she tells them to try their best, listen to the sounds in the words, and write what they hear. A few children finish early, so Ms. Gonzalez tells them to select a book from the class library or go to the listening center.
9:25–9:30 Procedures	At 9:25 the timer rings. Ms. Gonzalez tells the children that she uses the timer to signal the end of an activity. When they hear the timer ring, they should look at her for further directions. Ms. Gonzalez sets the timer again, and the students practice this procedure. She tells the children that it is time to go to the playground, so they need to practice lining up to leave the classroom. She says she will dismiss them by tables, and they should push the chairs under their desks. She demonstrates pushing in chairs and asks a student to show how it can be done quietly. She then asks students to line up quietly without crowding the person in front. As she dismisses each table, she compliments students for following directions.
9:30–10:00 Playground	While students are on the playground with another teacher, Ms. Gonzalez writes a message to the students and posts it on the message board.
10:00–10:30 Sharing	When the students return from the playground, several students notice the message. Ms. Gonzalez reads the message to the class and invites students to post notes on the board. After all of the students are at their desks, Ms. Gonzalez sets the timer and reviews the procedures. When all of the students are looking at her, she asks them to bring their self-portraits and quietly form a circle on the floor.

(continued)

First-Day Activities *(continued)*

Time/Activity	Description
	Everyone, including Ms. Gonzalez, shares the self-portraits and two interesting things about themselves.
10:30–11:00 Story and song	Ms. Gonzalez follows this activity by reading a story about self-esteem. She then teaches the students a song called "I Like Me." She has written the words and has drawn several picture cues on a large sheet of chart paper. They practice reading the words several times; then Ms. Gonzalez sings the song. She then repeats the song, and the students join in the singing. As she dismisses the students from the circle, she collects their self-portraits. Ms. Gonzalez chooses this time to review lunch procedures. Students practice getting their lunch boxes and quietly lining up for lunch. Before they leave, Ms. Gonzalez reviews the lunchroom rules.
11:00–11:30	Lunch.
11:30–11:50	Recess.
11:50–12:00	As the students reenter the room, Ms. Gonzalez goes over the restroom procedures. She lets one or two students practice with the restroom passes. She also lets them practice knocking to be sure no one is in the restroom before they open the door. Students then leave their seats to use the restroom and to wash their hands.
12:00–12:20 Reading aloud	Ms. Gonzalez sits in a rocking chair, and the students gather around her on the rug. She reads a story aloud and explains that the twenty minutes after lunch and recess will always be reading aloud time and that the students will select the books that are read.
12:20–12:30 Discussing school rules	The class remains seated around the rocking chair, and Ms. Gonzalez explains the school rules. There are two: (1) Remain quiet in the hallways, and (2) Every student must have a hall pass. After they discuss the rules, Ms. Gonzalez asks two children to repeat them to the rest of the class and explain what they mean.
12:30–1:00 Developing classroom rules	The discussion of school rules leads directly into the development of the classroom rules. The students remain seated on the rug but shift their attention to the board. Ms. Gonzalez moves the overhead projector next to the students and projects it on the board. She asks a student to turn off half of the classroom lights so the class can see the screen. She tells the students they will have to raise their hands and wait to be called on during the discussion because everyone will need to hear all of the suggestions. She asks the students to suggest rules they feel are necessary for their classroom. The students raise their hands. Ms. Gonzalez calls on them and writes their responses on the overhead. At this point, she is careful not to make evaluative comments on the students' ideas. She wants them to brain-

Time/Activity	Description
	storm suggestions. The students discuss their ideas and often expand, connect, or modify them.
1:00–1:35	Ms. Gonzalez ends this activity when she notices the students' attention beginning to fade. She tells them that this is a good start to their classroom rules and that they will continue with them tomorrow. At the end of this activity, the students return to their desks.
Graphing activity	Ms. Gonzalez focuses the students' attention on the dry erase board where she has hung a large graph. The graph is drawn on brightly colored paper and is titled "How I got to school today." The graph is divided into four columns. A picture of a car, a bus, a bicycle, or a pair of shoes is at the bottom of each column. She asks the students how they got to school this morning. Did they come in a car? Did they ride the bus? Did they ride their bikes? Did they walk? As the students raise their hands, Ms. Gonzalez gives them a picture of a car, bus, bike, or shoes. The students write their names on their pictures, color them, and tape them in the appropriate columns on the graph.
	After all of the pictures are placed on the graph, Ms. Gonzalez asks them to count the number of pictures in each row and determine which row has the most and the least. She draws a bar graph that corresponds with the number of pictures in each row. She explains that the class will be learning a lot of new things this year. They will be doing science projects, math, writing, and so on. She asks them to think about things they would like to know.
1:35–2:15 "What do I want to study this year?"	Ms. Gonzalez hangs another large piece of paper next to the pictures. In the middle of the paper is the question, "What do I want want to study this year?" Again, she asks students to raise their hands and wait to be called on because everyone should listen to the topics. Ms. Gonzalez creates a semantic map with all of the suggestions. She knows that many of the topics will be covered because they correspond with her curriculum guide. Other topics will be pursued through individual and small-group projects.
2:15–2:30 Getting ready to go home	Ms. Gonzalez reviews the day's activities by asking, "If your mom or dad asks you what you did today, what will you tell them?" She also asks questions about the procedures and school rules. She reminds the students to check their personal belongings and check their mailboxes for notes to be taken home. She asks them to leave their name tags on their desks so they can use them the next day, and she shows them how to put their chairs on the desks so they won't fall. She checks to see that everyone has the things they need to take home and rehearses with them the proper procedure for being dismissed. They are to leave their desks table-by-table and line up by the door. She asks two students to demonstrate lining up. When the bell rings, she leads the students out the classroom door and down the hall to the proper outside door for dismissal.

Second-Day Activities

Time/Activity	Description
8:00–8:20 Greeting students	The teacher greets the students at the door and asks them to put on their name tags and get their journal notebooks from their cubbies. On the board, she has written the journal topic "What I liked best about my first day of school." She tells the students they may either write or draw a picture. She takes attendance, fills in the lunch count, and assists the students as they write. The timer rings to signal the end of this activity, and the teacher asks everyone to close the journals. She lets them go by tables to put their journals in their cubbies and gather on the floor. She reminds them of the procedures for leaving their desks and gathering on the floor (quickly and quietly).
8:20–8:50 Introducing morning activities	Ms. Gonzalez shows the students the helper chart. Every student has a job, and the jobs rotate daily. She asks the pledge leader to come to the front of the room and lead the class. She helps the pledge leader point to the words as the students repeat the pledge. She then asks the calendar person to add today's date to the calendar and name the month, day, and year. The weather person tells today's forecast and uses the weather section from the newspaper to record today's expected high and low temperature. Ms. Gonzalez guides the weather person through the forecast. The song leader leads the students through the "I Like Me" song they learned the previous day. Again, Ms. Gonzalez helps the student point to the words while the class sings. Three students volunteer to share what they wrote in their journals. While those students get their journals, Ms. Gonzalez tells the class that journal writing will usually be the first activity every morning. After the students share, Ms. Gonzalez tells each student one thing she liked about his or her writing.
8:50–9:25 Developing classroom rules	Ms. Gonzalez then asks the class to look at the dry-erase board. She turns on the overhead projector and reviews the ideas they brainstormed yesterday for classroom rules. She asks the students whether any of the rules are alike. As the students begin to group the similar ideas, Ms. Gonzalez reminds them to raise their hands. She writes their ideas on another overhead transparency. After they develop six broad categories, she asks the students to think about a title for each category. When titles are proposed for each category, she asks the students whether these would be appropriate classroom rules. After some minor rewordings, the students and Ms. Gonzalez are satisfied with the rules.
9:25–9:30 Procedures	The teacher asks the students to line up at the door. Several students use this time to get a drink of water or go to their cubbies. Ms. Gonzalez asks everyone to come back to the rug, and she asks a student to repeat the procedures for lining up. Ms. Gonzalez dismisses the students again and compliments them for remembering the procedure.
9:30–10:00 P.E.	While the students are in physical education, Ms. Gonzalez writes the classroom rules on a piece of chart paper.

Time/Activity	Description
10:00–10:30 Role playing classroom rules	When the students reenter the room from P.E., they go to their seats and the teacher points out the rules and asks each student to sign the chart. She lets each table go to the chart paper in turn. She asks the students where the rules should be posted, and they decide to hang the poster listing rules on the wall by the dry-erase board. Small groups of students volunteer to role play an example of each rule. The small groups practice for ten minutes and present their demonstration. The other members of the class guess which rule the group is presenting.
10:30–11:00 Math activity	The teacher asks the students to return to their seats, and when they are seated, she asks for their attention. She is standing at the front of the room and holding geometric figures (circles, triangles, squares) made from colored construction paper. Magnets are attached to the figures so they will stick on the board. She tells the students they are going to play a guessing game. She is going to make a pattern on the board with these figures, and the students will have to decide which figure goes next in the pattern. After they complete several of these examples, Ms. Gonzalez asks each of them to continue this game with a partner. Because this is the first time the students will be working cooperatively, she lets them begin with partners rather than in groups of three or four. As she passes out the materials, she asks them which classroom rules should apply to this activity. Several respond that they should listen to their partners and not interrupt them. Others say they should help each other. The teacher tells the students they can remain at their seats or move to a spot on the floor. She allows them one minute to move. As the students make patterns for their partners, she circulates throughout the room and offers assistance. She sets the timer to signal the end of the activity. When the timer rings, the majority of the partners stop their patterning activity and turn to the teacher. A few continue to work, so she asks a student to repeat this procedure. Then she sets the timer again. When it rings, everyone turns to her. She asks the partners to put the geometric figures in a storage bag. When she dismisses the students, they give her their bags of figures and quietly line up for lunch.
11:00–11:30	Lunch.
11:30–11:50	Recess.
11:50–12:00	Restroom break.
12:00–12:20 Reading aloud	Ms. Gonzalez sits in the rocking chair, and the students gather around her as she reads a story they have selected.
12:20–1:00 Writing sample	Ms. Gonzalez likes to collect a writing sample from each of her students early in the year. This sample goes in the student's portfolio and serves as a baseline for the student's writing progress. Because the class has been sharing

(continued)

Second-Day Activities *(continued)*

Time/Activity	Description
	about themselves, this writing sample will be part of a book called, *All About Me*. Ms. Gonzalez has prepared a small book with lines at the bottom of the pages for writing and spaces for illustrations. She brainstorms ideas for the book with the students and reminds them to use invented spellings if they need to.
	When the students return to their seats, Ms. Gonzalez monitors their progress and pays close attention to students who are frustrated. Several children are concerned about their writing, so she tells them to draw the pictures first and then write about the pictures. A few students finish before the timer rings, and they go to various centers in the room.
1:00–1:15 Sharing	When the timer rings again, Ms. Gonzalez asks whether anyone wants to share his or her book. She collects the books from the students who do not want to share, and everyone gathers on the rug. Four students share, and everyone listens attentively. Students comment on the books and applaud the volunteers.
1:15–1:55 "Getting to know you"	Ms. Gonzalez had asked each student to bring something to school today to share with classmates. She had suggested that they bring a favorite book, picture, or stuffed animal. As on the previous day, the class forms a circle and everyone, including the teacher, shares.
1:55–2:15 Sustained silent reading	While they are still in the circle, Ms. Gonzalez explains the procedures for sustained silent reading. She says this will be the last activity every day. The students will select one or two books or magazines and find a quiet place to read. After they choose a place, they will remain there until the timer rings. Ms. Gonzalez says she will also be reading during this time.
	She dismisses the students two at a time from the circle. They put away their sharing time objects, select books, and quietly choose a place to read. After they are reading, Ms. Gonzalez reminds a few students to be quiet. She also reads, but she keeps a close eye on the students.
	Even though twenty minutes are set aside for today's silent reading, Ms. Gonzalez knows that after the procedures are taught, the students will read for only seven or eight minutes. This amount of reading time will steadily increase throughout the school year.
2:15–2:30 Getting ready to go home	When the timer rings again, Ms. Gonzalez dismisses the students two at a time to return their books and collect their belongings to go home. When the students are ready to go, Ms. Gonzalez leads a brief review of today's activities and the classroom rules.
2:30 Dismissal	Ms. Gonzalez reminds the students how to line up and calls the bus riders to line up first. She compliments the students on another good day and leads them out of the room.

BEGINNING THE YEAR IN A SIXTH-GRADE
MATH CLASS USING COOPERATIVE LEARNING

Ms. James teaches math in a departmentalized sixth grade. She repeats the same lesson with three groups of sixth graders each day. The following narrative describes the first day of class for the second group of students.

First-Day Activities

Activity	Description
Before the bell	Desks are arranged in seven groups of four or five students each. Ms. James collects a folder from the previous class for each group of desks and replaces it with another folder of a different color, marked with the period and group number. As students enter, Ms. James tells them that they may sit wherever they choose today but that seats will be assigned later in the week.
Initial greeting (4 minutes)	The teacher smiles and introduces herself, telling students about her family and some out-of-school interests. She tells students she is a hard worker, and she also expects them to work hard. She says she will be in her room starting an hour before school, and she will stay in her room until 4:30 each day, so students can come in if they need more explanation or assistance. "The most important thing in this class is trying. We will all make mistakes and get stuck, but by working together we will be able to solve the problems and learn a lot of new things."
Introduction (10 minutes)	Ms. James says that even though students have all studied math for the past five years, she is curious whether they know how important and useful it is. She elicits ideas about how math might be useful, and she asks students to raise their hands and wait to be called on before speaking during this activity. During the discussion, she calls attention to a bulletin board that has several colorful posters highlighting math applications. Ms. James thanks students on several occasions for raising their hands and for listening well. When a couple of students call out, she reminds them to raise hands before she calls on them. Ms. James comments on the grouping of desks. She explains that in her classes students work in groups much of the time and that this can be very helpful in learning. She says they won't always work in groups; they will also keep an individual notebook and take tests by themselves. For many assignments, however, they will be expected to work together and assist each other in understanding the content and solving problems. She comments that students often find this to be not only a good way to learn but an enjoyable one as well. A student asks whether she can choose her group. Ms. James responds that she must reserve the right to arrange the groups. Because group membership will change at times, however, students will have an opportunity

(continued)

First-Day Activities *(continued)*

Activity	Description
	to work with a variety of other students. Ms. James also emphasizes that working in groups with others is a good way to get to know them. "It's important that you be able to work with anyone in school, just as you'll have to outside of school," she comments.
Initial presentation of procedures (6 minutes)	Ms. James thanks the students for raising hands before speaking. She says she has a few other procedures that will be needed for the class to run smoothly and she will go over some of these now and save the others for later, when they start group work. She says that during class, when she is talking or when a student is presenting something to the whole class, they are to remain in their seats. If they wish to comment or ask a question, they should raise hands and wait for their turn. At other times, when they are working in groups or on individual assignments, they may talk if it is to someone in their group and it is about the assignment. If they need to sharpen a pencil or get materials during work times, they may do so without permission as long as they do not disturb others.
Initial group task (8 minutes)	The teacher designates students in each group as Chair #1, Chair #2, Chair #3, and so on. She tells them that when they work in other groups Chairs will have different roles, and that these rotate so that each student gets a chance to do different things. "Chair #1, please open the group folder on the desk and look in the right-hand pocket. Take out a yellow card and a class card for each student." She asks Chair #1 in each group to distribute these items. Ms. James then has students make name cards for their desks and fill out name cards for her. While students work on this task, she returns to her desk for a couple of minutes to attend to some administrative matters, then asks Chair #1 to collect the cards.
Description of procedures (10 minutes)	Ms. James asks Chair #2 to look in the left-hand pocket and get out the blue sheet listing classroom policies and procedures and to give one to each group member. She tells students that everyone will need a three-ring binder for this class, and that this page should be the first one in it. She then reviews the classroom and school policies regarding absence and tardiness, leaving the room, make-up work, tests, and detention for violating rules. She explains that if she gives a warning to a student and it's ignored, she will assign a lunch detention and the student will have to bring lunch to the room at noon and eat it there. She says, "If I have to come find you, it will be doubled."
End of period	Ms. James notes that time is almost up. She says that she'll explain her grading policies and class activities tomorrow. "Chair #3, if there is a new student in class assigned to your group tomorrow, would you please be responsible for helping him or her get a copy of the class policies, name card, and class card?" She asks the students to return their cards to the folder. She asks students to remain in their seats until she dismisses each group, which she does when materials have been returned to the folder and each group is seated and quiet.

Second-Day Activities

Activity	Description
Before the bell	Ms. James collects folders from each group from the preceding period, replacing them with the next period's folders. She greets students as they enter, asking them to take seats with the same group as yesterday. She directs a few new students to join groups.
Opening the period (3 minutes)	Ms. James greets the students warmly as soon as the bell rings. She reminds them that they are in groups and have a designated number that will be the same as yesterday's. She reminds Chairs #3 of their responsibility to help new members of the group.
Diagnostic test (15 minutes)	"Before we get started on today's lesson, I'd like you to answer some questions. This will not be for a grade, but I would like you to do your best. Your answers will help me understand what topics we need to review and also help me make group assignments." Ms. James distributes the diagnostic test and tells students to show their work. She monitors as students complete the test.
Description of procedures and grading policies (8 minutes)	The teacher reviews talk and movement procedures in groups. "Use group voices, please. Talk loudly enough to be heard by others but not so loudly that groups near you will hear. Like this." (She demonstrates.) She gives students a one-page handout describing grading policies. She explains these in detail and asks students to place this handout in their notebooks.
Preparation for group activity (4 minutes)	Ms. James announces an activity for learning about working in groups as well as learning math concepts. She asks students to volunteer ideas about what it takes to be a good group member. Stressing positive examples, she supports especially the ideas of sharing, helping, listening, encouraging, and working hard.
Math lesson (20 minutes)	Ms. James begins by reading an article from *USA Today,* which states that the average sixth grader in the United States watches 1,000 minutes of television a week. She asks the students whether they are surprised by this fact and then asks them to estimate how many hours of television that would be each day. She stresses that they are *estimating* and that *exact* computations are inappropriate. Next, she asks students to share what they think the article means by "the average sixth grader." She then explains that the students will be calculating how many days of television the average sixth grader watches in one year. She asks Chair #4 at each table to open the folders and distribute the materials. She says she will ask someone in each group to report on the group's solution. After the groups have worked for about five or six minutes, Ms. James calls on one person from each group to report on the group's results; she prompts students as needed as they describe the solution process their group used.
Wrap-up (5 minutes)	Ms. James asks students to comment on their roles in their groups. She also asks for suggestions about what works best for various roles. She praises the students for their creativity in developing solutions and for their effort. She dismisses the class as the next group begins to gather at her door.

Third-Day Activities

Activity	Description
Organization (5 minutes)	Ms. James tells students to check the name list at each group of desks to find their groups. She tells students they will stay in their groups for several weeks. She assigns Chair numbers to the group members.
Textbook checkout (12 minutes)	Ms. James asks Chair #4 from each group to get texts from several stacks at the back of the room. While students cover their books, the teacher circulates from group to group and records book numbers.
Content activity and a new teaching strategy (15 minutes)	The teacher reviews concepts from yesterday's lesson. She asks Chair #2 to distribute materials from a box in each group. Students use the materials to work along with the teacher as she demonstrates various ways problems can be solved. She tells students they will now work in pairs, and she writes "Pair Share" on the chalkboard. Students will work in pairs to solve a problem, and then they are expected to take turns explaining the solution or demonstrating the steps to each other. "It is not enough just to work out a solution. Each of you must be able to explain to your partner how you arrived at it." Afterward, Ms. James asks volunteers to demonstrate and explain their solutions.
Group work (17 minutes)	Students are now given problems to solve as a group. These are somewhat more difficult and require several steps. Ms. James asks each group to work together to develop a way to solve each problem. She asks Chair #4 to record the solutions and Chair #5 to be moderator to make certain that everyone contributes. The teacher reviews briefly, based on yesterday's discussion, what these roles entail. As the groups work on the problem, the teacher checks on progress. She has several groups report to the class. Afterward, students are given an assignment, due the next day, which they work on for the remainder of the class. Students may work together on problems, but they are expected to show their own work on the assignment.
Wrap-up (5 minutes)	With about five minutes remaining in the period, the teacher asks students to put away their work. She says that unfinished problems should be completed as homework. Then she begins a short discussion about appropriate helping by asking students what it feels like not to understand something. She also asks about ways they might react if they were in that situation. "Everyone will experience those feelings and do some of those things, especially if they're made to feel unintelligent. In this class, though, we will learn from our mistakes, and no one should be embarrassed by not understanding something. Also, helping other students is a great way to gain in understanding. I certainly understand math much better now that I have taught it than I did when I was a student." Ms. James explains that everyone will have opportunities to explain problems and answer questions in this class, but if there is something they don't understand, they should ask for another explanation. She and the class then discuss how to explain in ways that are most helpful. The class is dismissed.

Checklist 4

Preparation for the Beginning of School

Check When Complete	Item	Notes
☐	A. Are your room and materials ready (see Chapter 1)?	_____
☐	B. Have you decided on your class procedures, rules, and associated consequences (see Chapters 2, 3, and 7)?	_____
☐	C. Are you familiar with the parts of the school that you and your students may use (cafeteria, office and office phone, halls, restroom facilities, computer lab resource room, etc.) and any procedures for their use?	_____
☐	D. Do you have a complete class roster?	_____
☐	E. Do you have file information on your students, including information on reading and math achievement levels from previous teachers, test results, and any other information?	_____
☐	F. Do you know whether you have any students with disabilities who should be accommodated in your room arrangement or in your instruction (see Chapter 10)?	_____
☐	G. Do you have adequate numbers of textbooks, desks, and class materials?	_____
☐	H. Do you have the teachers' editions of your textbooks?	_____
☐	I. Do you know the procedure for the arrival and departure of students on the first day? For every day after that?	_____
☐	J. Are students' name tags ready? Do you have blank ones for unexpected students?	_____
☐	K. Do you have your first day's plan of activities ready?	_____

(continued)

Check When Complete	Item	Notes
☐	L. Does your daily schedule accommodate special classes (e.g., physical education, music) or "pull-out" programs (e.g., Title I reading, resource room students, programs for the gifted)?	_____
☐	M. Do you have time-filler activities prepared?	_____
☐	N. Do you have a letter ready to send home to parents with information about needed school materials?	_____
☐	O. Do you know when and how you can obtain assistance from school staff (e.g., the resource teacher, school nurse, librarian, office personnel, counselor)?	_____

5

Planning and Conducting Instruction

Let's assume that the steps you have taken so far to ensure that your classroom will run smoothly have worked. Your classroom is organized, you have thought about the climate to be established and the expectations you want to communicate, you've developed and taught your rules and procedures, and you have systems in place to manage student learning. Now that your students are attentive and ready to participate, what do you do? Remember, your purpose is not just to have a smoothly running classroom; your purpose is to help students learn, and to help them ultimately take responsibility for their learning.

It is at this point that management and instruction meet. Well-planned lessons with a variety of developmentally appropriate activities support the positive learning environment that your careful management decisions intend to create. Dry lessons with limited opportunities for students to participate are boring and erode students' motivation; this is when management problems begin. Interesting, relevant, well-planned lessons are the key to holding student attention.

As you may have noticed, not all people learn in the same way. These different modes have been called learning styles or learning preferences. These preferences generally consist of four styles: (1) Sensory/Logical, using a step-by-step approach to gather, rehearse, and explain information; (2) Sensory/ Emotional, using interpersonal relationships to help review and master information; (3) Intuitive/Logical, using natural curiosity to solve problems and understand big ideas; (4) Intuitive/Emotional, using opportunities for creative projects to deepen understanding. Because children learn in different ways, by varying the activities and the formats for learning, you will have a better chance of meeting the different learning preferences in your class. You should not think, however, that you have to determine each child's preferred learning style and accommodate that style in every subject. It is just as important for students to understand that they can be successful in instructional formats that may not seem easiest to them (Brophy, 2004).

This chapter describes how to plan and conduct instruction in ways that support the kinds of learning you want for your students regardless of content area. Combining this information with knowledge from your content area will help you teach each subject more effectively. The chapter is divided into three sections. The first part discusses the planning decisions you must make. The second section discusses how to implement those plans as you conduct instruction. The final section discusses common problems such as transitions between activities and clarity of instruction.

FOR REFLECTION

How do you think students learn? How do you know when someone is learning? What is your own preferred style of learning? How will these beliefs affect your choice of teaching strategies? As you read this chapter, consider how each suggestion supports or fails to support the kinds of learning you believe to be most important.

🌀 Planning Instructional Activities

When you choose instructional activities for your classes, consider primarily whether an activity will lead to learning and what kind of learning you want to encourage. Activities that lead to better memorization are different from those that enhance reflective thinking or problem solving. Next, consider whether the activity will maintain student involvement. Also consider the sequence of activities for and the amounts of time spent on the various subjects in the curriculum. Such considerations lead many elementary teachers to plan reading and at least some language arts activities for the first two hours or so of the morning. These activities usually require sustained effort and often involve a combination of small-group, whole-group, and individual work formats. Involvement in these activities is more difficult to maintain later in the day when students are less alert and more fatigued.

Establishing a daily schedule with specific times for various subjects will help you remain conscious of time so that you do not shortchange subjects taught later in the day. Furthermore, students will be better able to pace their own work if they know the schedule. When you plan your schedule, try to arrange change-of-pace activities to follow periods of sustained effort or intense concentration. For example, you might arrange reading or language arts activities so that they come before recess or physical education. If you cannot schedule such activities conveniently, at least give students a brief break and lead them in exercises or a song or two, or give them time to stand and stretch if they have not had the opportunity to move around.

When you plan your daily schedule, you may find that your school district has established guidelines for the amount of time to be allotted to each subject. Also, special teachers may be assigned to teach a particular subject for certain days and times of the week. Thus, you may find that your class will be taught physical education on Tuesdays and Thursdays from 1:30 to 2:00 and will have music on Mondays and Wednesdays from 10:30 to 11:00. Obviously, your schedule will have to be set accordingly.

At the beginning of the school year, good planning requires extra effort. Overplanning (preparing more activities than can be accomplished in a particular time) and underplanning (preparing too little for the amount of time available) can occur, particularly with inexperienced teachers. It is better to overplan, then be flexible in implementing the plan. Activities not completed one day can serve as starters for second and third days.

Types of Planning

You will engage in several levels of planning, both long range (i.e., by the year and by the term) and short range (i.e., by the unit, the week, or the day). These levels of planning should be coordinated. Accomplishing the longer plan requires dividing the work into terms, the terms into units, and the units into weeks and days.

The lesson outcomes you envision will determine your planning goals and objectives, and your plans should reflect these intended outcomes. Many of these outcomes are determined by state or local curriculum guidelines or by mandated testing, but you should keep in mind that you are also teaching for understanding, appreciation, and application. Thus, your plans, provide road maps that help transform the available curriculum into activities, assignments, and learning experiences that are meaningful. In developing your plans, keep two important considerations in mind: first, which skills and concepts students must learn; and second, through which activities can they become interested partners in the learning enterprise.

Types of Instructional Activities

For each subject you teach, you will design activities to help students construct new knowledge, acquire and practice skills, consolidate and extend knowledge, and receive feedback about their learning. The basic steps in teaching are (1) content development, (2) discussion, (3) recitation or reinforcement, and (4) feedback. These steps may be followed by using a variety of instructional formats (see Table 5.1). Chapter 6 is devoted to Cooperative Learning. In the following sections, the most common types of instructional activities are described. These are whole-group instruction, grouped basic skill instruction, individual work, and feedback.

CONTENT DEVELOPMENT
(OR WHOLE-GROUP INSTRUCTION)

Although teachers sometimes present content to students individually or in small groups, whole-class presentation is often the major vehicle for introducing and teaching content activities. During content development, you may present new information, elaborate on or extend a concept or principle, conduct a demonstration, show how to perform a skill, or describe how to solve a problem. Whole-group content development activities are appropriate for learning goals such as exposure and familiarity and for the efficient presentation of new material.

During content development, the teacher takes an active role focused on helping students think about the new content, relate it to what they know, and apply it. One chief management concern is making sure that students are active, not passive. Therefore, you will have to find ways to involve students in the development of the lesson. Teacher questions are also used for this purpose, allowing the teacher to check student understanding, to encourage students to contribute to steps in problem solving, to apply concepts or principles, and to analyze ideas.

In addition to presentations and questions, content development should include sample problems or other demonstrations of understanding of the new content. These not only help students learn the new content but also provide you with information about how well the class is understanding the lesson. Activities and questions should be thoughtfully designed to expose student thinking and understanding. For example, when a student gives a correct answer, you can probe with further questions: "What led you to that answer?" "What do you mean by . . . ?" "What would come next?" "How else could you do that?"

Table 5.1 Formats for Instruction

Format	How Formed	Purpose	Advantages	Disadvantages
Whole Group	Whole group	To deliver information on new content or skill(s) to all at one time	▪ Cover much information in little time ▪ Everyone hears the same information	▪ Does not meet needs of many students when used as the only method of instruction
Small Teacher-Led Group	Teacher formed homogeneous groups using set criteria	To provide activities to meet specific needs, either remedial or enrichment	▪ Able to check more accurately for student understanding	▪ Some students may be engaged in long periods of seatwork without being actively monitored
Small Cooperative Group	Teacher formed equivalent heterogeneous groups based on performance, gender, race, and so forth	To reinforce previously taught content and foster social skills (Note: Individual grades are a *must* to achieve these purposes.)	▪ More opportunity for students to "interact" with material being presented	▪ Sometimes only two or three of the four to five students benefit from doing the work
Small Noncompetitive Group	Random selection with teacher guidance as needed to form hetero-geneous groups	To experience a process or produce a product with no individual or group academic grading involved	▪ Social skills fostered	▪ Difficult to check for individual student's understanding during activity
Student Pairs	Teacher or student selected based on reciprocal learning needs	To enhance collaborative learning through collaborative/reciprocal processes	▪ Can involve both students ▪ Fosters social skills ▪ Facilitates reciprocal learning	▪ One student may do all the work/thinking
Individualized Instruction	One student	To meet individual student needs, (IEPs, absentee makeup work, enrichment, remediation of content or skills)	▪ Teacher-student ratio a plus ▪ Remedial/enrichment help easily given	▪ May be time consuming ▪ Some students may not be actively monitored
Centers and Stations	Teacher created with equitable student access designated in a variety of ways	To enrich, extend, practice, apply new learning, and/or remediate content and/or skills	▪ Enriches student understanding ▪ Students can practice skills ▪ Students can apply new learning	▪ Difficult to manage time at center and problematic for nonreaders ▪ Requires preparation time ▪ Difficult to monitor

Adapted from Evertson & Harris (2003). © Vanderbilt University, reprinted with permission.

Another way to develop content is to help students engage in research and problem solving, individually and in groups. Review Case Study 2.2 and see further information in Chapter 6 about considerations when planning group work.

GROUPED BASIC SKILL INSTRUCTION

In this format, you work with small groups of students, one group at a time, while the rest of the class works independently. This mode of instruction is most commonly used for reading and frequently for mathematics. Its purpose is to accommodate a wide range of achievement levels in basic skill subjects. Because small-group instruction is used so extensively for basic skills, we will describe its features in detail.

A critical aspect of small-group instruction is that at least two different activities occur simultaneously. The teacher leads one group while students outside the group participate in a variety of independent activities. Because the teacher is actively involved with the small group, it is more difficult to monitor the behavior of other students and give them assistance. And because students may work independently for a long period, careful planning and extra effort are required to keep them involved in their work.

The first step in setting up effective small-group instruction is to plan the stage for the out-of-group activities. Give directions to the whole class at once: instructions for each assignment, a description of needed materials, and a suggested time for completing each activity. This list of assignments should also be posted or written on the board. Check whether students understand the directions by asking students in each group to review them before beginning.

Before calling the first group, monitor the beginning of independent work for a short time. After you are certain that students have started, signal the first group. During your work with the small group, monitor out-of-group students by scanning the room frequently. If you observe inappropriate behavior that is interfering with work, try to stop it with eye contact or some nonverbal signal, by calling the student's name once, or by reminding the student of what he or she should be doing. A "time-out" desk near you can also be used for a student who persists

"You mean we have to process all that data?"

in misbehavior: You can signal such a student to go to the desk for a while, without your having to leave the group.

Another consideration is how students needing help on an independent task can obtain it without interrupting you. Some teachers tell students to skip work they cannot do and go on to another activity until the teacher is available. Others allow students to help each other, or they assign a few students (perhaps one for each table or group) the role of helper. This works best if students are seated in mixed-ability groups. Finally, students can sign up on the board or on a clipboard sheet to indicate the need for assistance when it is available. If you must leave the small group to help a student or to deal with a problem, be sure to give students in the group something to do. One student in the group may be able to lead the activity for a short time.

When work with one small group has been completed, the next group should not be called immediately. Instead, take the opportunity to check the progress of the students who will be continuing individual assignments and help them with any problems they may have. Briefly inspect all students' work to determine whether they have requested assistance. Students who were off-task while you were teaching the small group can be given delayed feedback at this time. Be sure to encourage and give positive feedback to students who are participating appropriately. The students who have left the small group and are moving to other activities should also be monitored to be sure they begin their activity promptly. Then signal the next group to come for instruction.

INDIVIDUAL WORK

In this activity, students engage in assignments that build on presented material. In the upper elementary grades, the portion of the assignment not completed in class often becomes a homework assignment unless the materials or resources needed are available only in the classroom. (Procedures for independent work are discussed in Chapter 2.)

Good management of individual activities has several components. First, adequate content development must precede the independent student activity so that students can work productively on their own. Second, you must communicate clearly the requirements and objectives of the students' work and arrange for access to needed materials or resources. A good strategy is to begin the independent work assignment as a whole-class activity (for example, by working several of the exercises, problems, or questions together) before the independent work phase. This gets students started, gives them an opportunity to ask questions, and enables you to observe and correct common problems in a whole-class format rather than having to deal with the same problem with multiple individuals. Third, actively monitor the students' work so that problems are detected early and corrective feedback is provided.

Independent activities are best used for consolidating or extending prior learning rather than for acquiring new content. Therefore, be careful not to overuse independent activities; a rule of thumb is to devote at least as much time to content development as to independent work. Moreover, student engagement is more difficult to maintain in lengthy individual work activities. If you do find yourself assigning long periods of time to individual assignments, try breaking the activity into smaller segments and having a discussion or review between segments. The change in lesson format will help refocus attention, and it will give you an opportunity to check comprehension and clear up problems.

FEEDBACK

Feedback may be provided during discussion, recitation, or checking, and each of these may occur before, during, or after content development. For example, in presenting new material you may build on prior knowledge, and you might want to begin with a group discussion that leads to a new idea or problem to be solved. Also check individual work to be sure that students' levels of understanding allows for the introduction of new content or skill development. Wherever these feedback activities occur in the instructional sequence, planning and management skills can make them more productive.

Discussion

Discussions are helpful in encouraging students to evaluate events, topics, or results; to clarify the basis for their opinions; to help them become aware of other points of view; or to help them improve their oral expression skills. Sometimes discussions start with a recitation activity (described next) in which the facts of the content to be discussed are reviewed. Compared to a recitation, however, discussion questions are more likely to elicit the students' judgments, impressions, ideas, and opinions; also, teachers are less likely to evaluate the responses directly. Instead, students are encouraged to express themselves, to examine their opinions and beliefs, and to understand other perspectives. Students may respond to each other rather than only to the teacher. The teacher's role becomes one of encouraging, clarifying, and using student ideas rather than evaluating their correctness.

Management of a discussion calls for a number of skills, including warmth or friendliness (to promote security), conflict resolution, and encouraging expression of divergent points of view (to foster acceptance and openness). Although it is more common for some students to contribute to a discussion, avoid allowing a few students to monopolize the discourse; less verbal students should be included skillfully. Inviting reticent members to speak from time to time by asking for their opinions or views of what has previously been discussed is a good way to do so. Giving students opportunities to paraphrase, clarify, and elaborate on their own or other students' remarks helps keep a discussion moving and on target; also, transferring some of the responsibility for maintaining the discussion to students can keep the conversation moving. Getting students to listen to each other rather than treating the discussion as a dialogue with the teacher is sometimes difficult. Therefore, it is important to emphasize that students should respond to each other as well as to the teacher's comments or questions.

If you choose to use a whole-group discussion format, you must plan questions in advance. This can keep the discussion focused and productive. However, many teachers encourage students to formulate their own discussion questions, especially if these follow from group or individual research projects. Whether discussions are student-led or teacher-led, ground rules for participation must be clear (e.g., raise hands, listen carefully, respect others' right to speak).

Recitation

Recitation is a question-and-answer sequence in which the teacher asks questions, usually of a factual nature, and accepts, guides, or corrects student responses. The sequence of question/answer/evaluation is repeated frequently, with many students being asked to respond until a body of content has been covered. In effect, a recitation is a form of checking that is done orally. It can be used as a skill drill or to review student understanding of a previous lesson or assigned reading. It can also be used to check spelling, knowledge of vocabulary words, or other factual recall.

When recitation is used to check understanding, it is important to distribute questions to all students, not just to those who are eager to answer. Calling on only those who volunteer can give you an inaccurate impression of what students know. Develop a way to check systematically on which students get a turn to answer. This can be done by using a checklist or a shuffled stack of name cards. Some teachers place a strip of construction paper on each student's desk as a marker. As a student contributes, her or his marker is removed. It is helpful to ask the question, allow time for students to think, and then call on individual students. Limit the time you call on only students who volunteer. Sometimes you can use choral or whole-group responses as a way of keeping everyone alert and active. These kinds of responses are usually helpful only at the beginning of concept development as new material is being introduced and practiced. Sometimes teachers do not allow students enough time to respond, thus reducing opportunities for those who are slow to answer. Some experts recommend a "wait time" of several seconds before giving a prompt or calling on another student.

Checking

In this activity, students check their own classwork or homework. The checking activity is appropriate only when the judgment of correctness can be made easily. Checking provides quick feedback, and it allows the teacher to identify and discuss common errors on assignments. Careful monitoring during checking is important to be sure that students are doing it correctly. Students must be taught to check papers accurately, so it is important to explain the procedures as well as model them and allow students opportunities to practice. When student checking is used, you should collect the papers and examine them to remain aware of progress and problems.

Arranging Activities within a Lesson

In any given subject, lessons usually consist of a series of activities. A common activity sequence in basic skill areas is this:

1. Checking or recitation
2. Content development
3. Classwork
4. Independent work, group work, or discussion

The first activity allows the previous day's assignment or homework to be corrected. If there was no homework, the teacher leads a review of prior content important for the day's lesson. During content development, new content or skills are taught. Following this, a short classwork activity is used to review the new content and to preview the new assignment. Then practice is provided through independent work, group work, or discussion.

The problem with this sequence is that it requires that the presentation of lesson content and the practice period each be handled in two, usually lengthy, segments. A variation of the sequence that accommodates more complex content and that does not demand as much sustained attention is this:

1. Checking or recitation
2. Content development
3. Classwork or independent work, usually brief, with checking
4. Content development
5. Classwork, usually brief
6. Independent work, group work, or discussion

This sequence allows you to divide the lesson content into two parts, with practice and feedback following the first content development activity. Teaching new content in two parts with an intervening practice period helps students consolidate learning from the first part before they are asked to address new learning required in the second part. The sequence also allows you to check student understanding and to provide prompt feedback before moving on to more complex content. Furthermore, when individual activities are divided into shorter segments, student attention is usually easier to maintain. A problem with this sequence is that it produces more transition points and thus greater potential for student disengagement. Usually these transitions can be managed without difficulty, however, because student movement, new materials, or drastically changed lesson focus are not required in the content development-classwork-independent work cycle. Thus, the various activities blend together, usually without conspicuous transitions.

Of course, not all lessons fit either of the activity patterns just described. For instance, a science or social studies lesson may consist of a relatively long period of active student exploration or problem solving in small groups, followed by a whole-class content development discussion. Ongoing projects may entail long segments of individual seatwork or small-group work interspersed with short segments of whole-class or small-group instruction. Nevertheless, the two common patterns described here provide useful frameworks for building most teacher-directed lessons.

Planning for Clear Instruction

When you have an idea of the range and sequence of activities available to you, examine the content, concepts, and goals of the lessons and units that you will be teaching. One way to start is to review the unit and lesson in the teacher's edition of your textbook(s). Pay careful attention to suggestions for lesson development and activities. Study the exercises, questions, problems, and other activities in the textbook and decide which items provide appropriate review of lesson objectives. Note examples, demonstrations, and key questions and activities to use in the development of the main concepts. Put yourself in the lesson. Try to anticipate problems students may encounter in the lesson or assignments. Check for new terms and be ready to define them and present examples.

The textbook suggestions should not be limiting. Remember, you want your students to understand the content, not just retain it. Many educators talk about the importance of constructing knowledge, having students actively involved in making new information relevant to what they already know. This may be as simple as introducing a problem and exploring possible solutions or reframing a lesson through a thoughtful discussion of how it relates to individual experiences. You are targeting understanding, appreciation, and application.

Consider the interest the lesson is likely to have for students. Will you be enthusiastic about teaching this material to your class in this way? Your enthusiasm about the lesson is contagious and signals to students how you feel about its importance. If you find it interesting and exciting and you communicate this excitement to your class, students will probably respond with interest. However, if you find yourself unenthusiastic about a lesson or topic, chances are your students will share your feelings. Consider approaching the lesson in a different way. For example, rather than giving a lecture presentation of material, perhaps you can find ways for students to contribute through large- or small-group discussions that address the same issues.

Finally, organize your lesson parts into a coherent sequence. Write down or outline the main components. Then you will be well prepared for a clear lesson presentation.

PRESENTING NEW CONTENT

If students understand where a lesson is going, they are more likely to be with you at the end. Tell students what the lesson objectives are, either at the beginning of the activity or during it. If the lesson is complex, give them an outline to help them follow its organization. An outline helps organize the content for the students and provides a road map to keep them on course.

If students are to understand content from silent reading or from viewing a video, provide a content outline with a few items filled in and spaces for students to supply the rest. This task focuses attention and helps motivate them to read or watch carefully. Go over these items with the class after the film, especially if the students use the outline for further work or study. Alternatively, use the video as an opportunity to teach note-taking skills. Guide students in determining the questions they need answered by the film, and then help them identify important information as the video progresses.

As you present a lesson, stay with the planned sequence unless an obvious change is needed. Avoid needless digressions, interruptions, or tangential information. Inserting irrelevant information into a lesson only confuses students about what they are expected to learn. Displaying key concepts, new terms, major points, and other critical information on the overhead transparency screen or the board underscores their importance.

Presentations should be as focused and concrete as possible. Use examples, illustrations, demonstrations, props, charts, and any other means of providing substance and dimension to abstractions in the lesson. Avoid the vague expressions and verbal time fillers that, at best, communicate little information and make presentations difficult to follow. Then allow students time and opportunity to process the information you're presenting.

CHECKING FOR UNDERSTANDING

Find out whether students understand a presentation during the lesson; do not wait until the next day. As content development activities unfold, ask students questions to verify their comprehension of main points. You can also ask students to provide a written response to key questions and then check some or all of their answers either orally or by examining the written work. Asking students to demonstrate comprehension at several points during a presentation not only allows you to verify their progress but also keeps students more involved in the lesson.

You can also check student understanding and emphasize main points by conducting an oral recitation after a presentation. Do this by asking a series of questions that recapitulate the lesson sequence and its major concepts. Be sure to involve many students in answering these questions so that you can identify the overall level of understanding in the class and reteach what has not been satisfactorily learned.

Other methods of checking for understanding include having students respond to your questions in these ways:

- Displaying the correct one of two or more possible answers by holding up prepared color-coded cards
- Using designated body movement (e.g., thumbs up or thumbs down, arms crossed or arms uncrossed)
- Folding a piece of notebook paper into fourths, using each of the eight sections to write responses, and holding them up for you to see
- Writing in their own words explanations of the concept studied and turning these in for your inspection

- Pairing with a designated neighbor and quietly explaining a concept or process to the other while you circulate and listen
- Keeping a journal or a learning log that includes entries on each lesson in a particular unit

Technology in the Classroom

Using computers, whether for content development, research, or practice, requires awareness and planning. Few classrooms have as many computers as teachers would like, but almost all have at least one. Develop strategies to make technology a productive tool in helping students reach their academic goals. Unless your school has a computer classroom, you probably will have to devise activities to be carried out at a computer station. As noted in Chapter 4, this requires that procedures for the use of the station be taught and rehearsed. In addition, you may want to appoint one or more student "computer experts" who can assist quietly while you continue with whole- or small-group instruction.

Making the best possible use of shared technology is a challenge. Useful strategies include using CD-ROMs or the Internet for research or setting up specific content software to reinforce skills. E-mail and word processing software may enable students to improve their organizational and writing skills. You may set up your own base of notes, games, and puzzles to engage your students.

Internet access in the classroom makes it possible for students to find information more easily than ever before. Unfortunately, not all of the information available to them is appropriate, and many schools now use Internet filters. Certain precautions must be taken when including Internet use in your lessons. Some school systems require that parents give written permission before their child is allowed on the Internet. The teacher must find alternative ways for students without that permission to gather information. Children should be cautioned not to give their last names or any personal information over the Internet. All teachers should receive written permission before publishing a child's likeness on the Internet. Additionally, you should preview the sites you have assigned so you can easily recognize a screen that does not reflect the assigned task.

To make more efficient use of browsing time while students search for information, you may want to encourage them to print the resources they find. Teach them to skim headings for appropriate material and print it out rather than reading it on line. Even if the material turns out not to be relevant, it saves time, and other uses for the printed pages may be found.

Students should be monitored frequently as they access information on the Web. By giving them specific information to find and a limited time in which to find it, you can avoid many hazards. It is a good idea to set up guidelines for use at the beginning of the year. For example, have the students sign a contract that states, "I will use the Internet for school use only. If I knowingly search for inappropriate materials, I will lose the privilege of using the Internet for the remainder of the year." To eliminate the argument that a site was accidentally found, teach students to click the "back" button on the browser and get your attention immediately if they access an inappropriate site by mistake.

Kounin's Concepts for Managing Whole-Group Instruction

A central theme in managing teacher-led activities well is the idea of activity flow—the degree to which a lesson proceeds smoothly, without digressions, diversions, or interruptions. Lessons with good flow keep student attention and prevent deviation because most of the cues for behavior during the lesson are focused on behaviors appropriate for the lesson. When lesson flow is jerky, with frequent interruptions and side trips, there is more competition for attention from cues external to the focus of the lesson. Therefore, there will be a greater tendency for students to disengage.

A series of classroom research studies by Kounin and his colleagues (Kounin 1970; Kounin & Gump 1974) identified several concepts that contribute to effective management of interactive group activities, leading to smooth activity flow. According to Kounin, activity flow is maintained through three types of teacher practices, summarized in Table 5.2. Within each class of behavior there are two or three related concepts. Look at how each is defined and consider some examples.

Preventing Misbehavior

Classrooms are complex settings. Many events can occur at the same time. One cannot always predict with certainty what will occur when. New teachers run the risk of focusing too closely on single events or on select areas of the classroom and missing the big picture. Understanding two of Kounin's (1970) concepts, withitness and overlapping, helps to prevent this mistake.

Withitness is the degree to which the teacher corrects misbehavior before it intensifies or spreads to more students and also targets the correct student when doing so. A teacher who is not "with it" either will fail to stop the problem until it has escalated and may require a major intervention or else will fail to catch the perpetrator and instead target the wrong student. It is apparent that underlying aspects of withitness include good monitoring and prompt handling of inappropriate behavior, concepts that are discussed in detail in Chapter 7.

Overlapping refers to how the teacher handles two or more simultaneous events. Here are some examples: a visitor comes to the door in the middle of a lesson, a child from out of the group comes up to the teacher during reading group time, or several students get into a squabble while the teacher is busy helping other children across the room. A teacher who has good overlapping skills will handle both events in some way instead of dropping one event to handle the other or else ignoring the second event. To handle an interruption, for example, a teacher might tell the class or group to continue working or to get out some work, and then deal with the interrupter. The squabble taking place away from the teacher might be handled by eye contact or a brief verbal desist while the teacher stays where he or she is.

Notice that a teacher who is with it and exhibits good overlapping skills is able to insulate lessons from the intrusions that student misbehavior or external interruptions might cause. Furthermore, by reacting promptly to problems (but

Table 5.2 How Effective Managers Maintain Activity Flow Kounin (1970)

Issue	Skills	Definition	Example
Preventing misbehavior	Withitness	Communicating general awareness of the classroom to students; identifying and correcting misbehavior promptly and correctly	The teacher makes eye contact with a student who is about to "shoot a basket" with a wad of paper. The student puts the paper away. A student behind him, who has seen the interaction, decides he's not likely to get away with shooting a basket either.
	Overlapping	Attending to two or more simultaneous events	The teacher is leading a class discussion when a student comes in late. The teacher nods to him, continuing the discussion. Later, when students have begun a seat-work assignment, she attends to him and signs his tardy slip.
Managing movement	Momentum	Keeping lessons moving briskly; planning carefully to avoid slowdowns	The teacher notices that the explanation of a relatively minor concept is taking too long and distracting attention from the primary focus of the lesson. The teacher makes a mental note to go more in-depth on this concept in a separate lesson the next day, and moves on.
	Smoothness	Staying on track with the lesson; avoiding digressions and divergences that can lead to confusion	While being responsive to student interests, the teacher avoids comments that tend to draw attention away from the key points of the lesson.
Maintaining group focus	Group alerting	Engage the attention of the whole class while individuals are responding	Each student has a number that was drawn from a hat on the way into class. The teacher draws numbers and uses them to call on students during a fast-paced review.
	Encouraging accountability	Communicating to students that their participation will be observed and evaluated	At the end of discussion and practice of a new skill, students are told to turn to a neighbor and explain the process to him or her.
	High-participation formats	Using lessons that define behavior of students when they are not directly answering a teacher's question	While some students work problems at the board, students at their desks are instructed to check them by working the problems on paper.

not overreacting), the teacher is often able to use simple measures (eye contact, redirection, a quiet desist) that do not interfere with ongoing activities or distract students very much. If a teacher is not with it or does not overlap when needed, lessons may be interrupted by student misbehavior and by the teacher's subsequently more visible and tardy reactions.

Managing Movement

Whereas withitness and overlapping are accomplished by handling external interruptions and student intrusions into the flow of the lesson, movement management is accomplished by avoiding teacher-caused intrusions or delays. Good movement management is achieved through momentum and smoothness.

Momentum refers to pacing and is indicated by lessons that move along briskly. Teachers can cause slowdowns in momentum by dwelling on individual parts of a lesson, direction, or skill and by unnecessarily breaking an activity into too many parts. For example, teachers should provide a standard heading for assignments that can be used routinely rather than altering its form and having to explain it over and over.

Smoothness, as opposed to jerkiness, is epitomized in lesson continuity. A smoothly flowing lesson keeps student attention. If a teacher leaves a topic or activity to do something else or to insert new material, students may be distracted and miss the point of the lesson.

Maintaining Group Focus

Classroom instruction involves teaching children in groups, often a whole class at a time. Doing so means that a teacher must be conscious of the group influence on the instruction. Like a conductor leading an orchestra, the teacher must elicit the performance of the individuals and still provide signals and direction to the whole class. Group focus can be maintained through several techniques.

Group alerting means taking action to engage the attention of the whole class while individuals are responding. It can take the form of creating suspense, telling students they might be called on next, calling on students randomly, asking students not reciting to listen carefully because they might be called on to add to the answer, or using some new visual aid, display, or attention-getting strategy. Engaging in a dialogue with one student or calling on students before asking questions are examples of poor group alerting.

Accountability occurs when the teacher lets students know that their performance will be observed and evaluated in some manner. It does not require a letter grade or a score (although it might); it simply communicates some degree of awareness of how students are performing. For example, the teacher might ask everyone who knows an answer to raise a hand and then call on one or more of those students. The teacher could have all students write answers and circulate to check them. The teacher might also have students keep notebooks and check them from time to time.

High-participation formats are lessons that program the behavior of students when they are not directly involved in answering a teacher's question. Such lessons have a higher built-in rate of participation than do lessons that merely assume that students will sit and watch when other students respond. Higher-participation formats occur when students are expected to write answers, solve problems, read along, manipulate materials, or perform some other concurrent task.

Some activities lend themselves more to one type of group focus than another. When planning instruction, it is helpful to consider which of the three aspects to use. For example, during a demonstration that involves expensive materials, it might be difficult to use a high-participation format, but group alerting might be easy to incorporate.

Kounin's concepts for managing group instruction not only help identify key aspects of effective teaching, but they can also be used to diagnose instructional problems and identify possible solutions. For example, if lessons seem to drag and student response is unenthusiastic, there may be a problem with group focus; a solution may be to work on alerting or accountability or to increase the degree of participation. Activities that take too long and that seem to get off track constantly may have a problem with movement management. Perhaps the teacher should check for slowdowns and jerkiness.

Common Problems in Conducting Instruction

Two areas give many teachers difficulty in conducting instruction: transitions and clarity. This section focuses on common problems in these areas and suggests possible solutions.

Transitions

The interval between any two activities is a transition. Several management problems can occur during transitions, including long delays before starting the next activity, which can contribute to high levels of inappropriate or disruptive behavior. Transition problems can be caused by a lack of readiness by the teacher or the students for the next activity, unclear student expectations about appropriate behavior during transitions, and faulty procedures for transitions. Here are some examples of transition problems, along with suggested ways of correcting them.

Transition Problem	Suggested Solution
Students talk loudly at the beginning of the day. The teacher is interrupted while checking attendance, and the start of content activities is delayed.	Establish a beginning-of-day routine, and clearly state your expectations for behavior at the beginning of the day.
Students talk too much during transitions, especially after an assignment has been given but before they have begun working on it. Many students do not start their work activity for several minutes.	Be sure students know what the assignment is. Post it where they can see it easily. Work as a whole class on the first several exercises so that all students begin the lesson successfully and at the same time. Watch what students do during the transition and urge them along when needed.
Students who go for supplemental instruction stop work early and leave the room noisily while the rest of the class is working. When these students return to the room, they disturb others as they come in and take their seats. They interrupt others by asking for directions and assignments.	Have a designated signal that tells these students when they are to get ready to leave, such as a special time on the clock. Have them practice leaving and returning to the room quietly. Acknowledge appropriate behavior. Leave special instructions in a folder, on the board, or on a special sheet at their desks for what they are to do when they return. Or for younger students, establish a special place (e.g., the reading rug) for returning students to wait and an activity for them to engage in until you can give them personal attention.
During the last afternoon activity, students quit working well before the end; they begin playing around and leave the room in a mess.	Establish an end-of-day routine so that students continue their work until the teacher gives a signal to begin preparations to leave; then instruct students to help straighten the room.
Whenever the teacher attempts to move the students from one activity into another, a number of students don't make the transition but continue working on the preceding activity. This delays the start of the next activity or results in confusion.	Give students a few minutes' notice before an activity is scheduled to end. At the end of the activity, students should put all materials from it away and get out any needed materials for the next activity. Monitor the transition to make sure that all students complete it; do not start the next activity until students are ready.
The teacher delays the beginning of activities to look for materials, finish attendance reporting, pass back or collect papers, or chat with individual students while the rest of the class waits.	Have materials organized ahead of time, and when transitions begin, avoid doing anything that interferes with your ability to monitor and direct students.

The preceding items summarize the major problems that occur in classrooms at and around transition times. If you feel that your class is wasting time or if you are having difficulty keeping control during transitions, the suggested solutions may prove helpful.

Clarity

Communicating information and directions in a clear, comprehensible manner is an important teaching skill. Clear instruction helps students learn faster and more successfully; it also helps students understand your directions and expectations for behavior more readily. Although clarity is important in all classroom activities, it is crucial during content development, when nearly all new subject matter is introduced and taught.

Clear instruction results from several factors: organization of information into a coherent sequence, use of an adequate number of illustrations or examples, precision and concreteness of expression, keeping in touch with student comprehension, and providing enough practice to ensure mastery.

Clarity involves stating goals or major objectives and making sure that students know what they are accountable for knowing or doing; carefully outlining a lesson sequence, moving from simpler to more complex ideas; providing instructions both orally and in writing; checking understanding by asking specific questions or obtaining work samples; and providing for meaningful practice and feedback through classwork or homework assignments that review all lesson skills and content.

Further Reading

Alvermann, D. E., O'Brien, D. G., & Dillon, D. R. (1990). What teachers do when they say they're having discussions of content area reading assignments: A qualitative analysis. *Reading Research Quarterly, 25,* 296–322.

Although teachers often say they utilize discussion activities, this study found that the nature of discussion varies greatly from class to class. Maintaining control was very important to many of the teachers, and the more this dominated their perspective, the more their discussions resembled recitations rather than open forums for expressing views.

Brophy, J. E., & Alleman, J. (1991). Activities as instructional tools: A framework for analysis and evaluation. *Educational Researcher, 20*(4), 9–23.

The authors provide a detailed analysis of the design, selection, and evaluation of activities, with a central concern being how activities contribute to learning. Several major principles underlying activity design are proposed in this comprehensive analysis.

Casey, M. B., & Tucker, E. C. (1994). Problem-centered classrooms: Creating lifelong learners. *Phi Delta Kappan, Oct.,* 139–143.

The authors give guidelines for establishing a problem-centered instructional program. They address the teacher's role in posing open-ended questions, teaching the steps in thinking, and connecting lessons to children's interests. Their summary of strategies at the end of the article is especially useful.

Fuchs, D., Fuchs, L. S., Mathes, P. G., & Simmons, D. G. (1997). Peer-assisted learning strategies: Making classrooms more responsive to diversity. *American Educational Research Journal, 34*(1), 174–206.

Reporting a study on peer tutoring as a portion of planned reading instruction, the authors identify that students at low, average, and high levels of achievement all had achievement gains when involved in peer tutoring in comparison to students who were not part of planned reading instruction involving peer tutoring.

www.lessonplanspage.com

This website for educators, maintained by the University of Scranton, contains more than 2,500 sample lesson plans for all subjects (PreK–12).

www.teachervision.fen.com

This is the website for the Family Education Network; it has tips for teachers and a lesson planning center.

www.lburkhart.com

This website includes useful suggestions about technology integration in the classroom for elementary, middle, secondary, and special needs students.

Suggested Activities

1. Use Checklist 5 at the end of the chapter to plan one or more lessons.

2. Read Problems 5.1 through 5.3, which describe problems three teachers are experiencing with the management of instruction. After reading each paragraph, review this chapter and decide what strategies they might use to help overcome their problems (other chapters may also provide useful suggestions). You might use each problem as a basis for a group discussion and generate a list of many possible solutions or strategies. Then compare your list with the keys in the Appendix.

3. Read Problem 5.4. How many examples of Kounin's concepts noted on page 101 can you identify in this problem? Create a lesson outline that will improve the sequence of Mr. Case's instruction.

4. Case Study 5.1 illustrates problems that can arise in conducting instruction. Use the concepts in this and previous chapters to diagnose Ms. Lake's problems. Compare your list with the keys in the Appendix.

5. Teachers are sometimes caught between the need to cover a broad range of content quickly and the need to develop more specific content to deepen students' understanding. Interview several experienced teachers to get their ideas on how to meet this challenge.

6. Go to either www.lessonplanspage.com or www.teachervision.fen.com and select a few lesson plans. How well are they organized around powerful ideas, long-range goals, and supporting objectives and activities? If you were to teach from one of these plans, what changes would you make? Why?

PROBLEM 5.1

Ms. Kendall is beginning her first year of teaching fourth graders. She is writing out her plans for the first few days of class. She has familiarized herself with the scope and sequence of the fourth-grade curriculum. One of the first decisions she will make is about her class schedule. She must decide how best to organize her students' day. What should she consider as she develops her daily schedule? What long-term plans should she make to ensure that students learn to manage their own academic work and develop good work skills?

PROBLEM 5.2

During reading instruction, Mr. Hart generally works with a small group of students while the remaining students do assigned work. Lately, Mr. Hart has noticed that some students are not following seatwork directions and never finish their work, although he feels he allows appropriate amounts of time for work to be completed and gives thorough instructions before the reading groups start. A few students finish early, turn in their papers, and then wander around, interrupting other students and socializing excessively. Mr. Hart has to stop his work with the group to quiet the students. What can Mr. Hart do to get students to work more productively during seatwork?

PROBLEM 5.3

Ms. Jackson is trying to include more science lessons in her curriculum. She wants to try a discovery approach with her third graders. For a lesson on how sound is made, Ms. Jackson passes out paper cups in two sizes. Her plan is to have the students hum into the cups and feel the different vibrations. However, as soon as students receive their cups, they begin to plop them noisily on the desks. Some students poke holes in the bottoms with pencils. Other students place them over their ears and show their neighbors, while another group tries to figure out how to make the cups stay on their heads as hats. Ms. Jackson cannot get their attention back to the lesson. How could advance planning have helped her to avoid these problems? Use Checklist 5 to help you analyze this lesson.

PROBLEM 5.4

As he is about to begin class after lunch, Mr. Case makes eye contact with two students who are exchanging notes; the students quickly get out their class materials. "Let's begin by working some of the exercises at the end of the chapter; you will need a piece of paper with a heading." As students begin to get out their materials, Mr. Case calls out, "Oops! I forgot to tell you to bring money for tomorrow for the field trip. How many of you will be going?" After a brief discussion, students finish getting out their materials. Mr. Case says, "We'll go through these exercises orally, but I also want you to write the answers on your papers as part of today's classwork. I'll come around later and check your answers. Now, who can answer the first question? Hands please. Tyrone?"

Mr. Case conducts the lesson by calling on various students, some with hands up, others seemingly at random from the nonvolunteers. About halfway through the exercises, a student enters the room and says that he is new to the school and has been assigned to the class. Mr. Case goes to his desk, sits down, and says, "Okay, come here. I'll check out some of your books to you. I wish the school office wouldn't send children in the middle of the day. Where are you from, anyway? That's a nice shirt you are wearing."

After finishing with the student and sending him to a seat, Mr. Case leaves his desk and says to the class, "Now where were we? Oh, yes, question 7. Say, where did Kim and Lee go? I didn't give them permission to leave."

After several more minutes, Mr. Case calls a halt to the activity and says, "Now, I'd like us to discuss the test coming up this Thursday. Let's make sure that you are all clear on what will be on the exam and what you will need to get ready for it." After a pause, he adds, "I almost forgot. Get your questions from before and look at the next to the last one. We have to add an important point that was left out. . . ." After finishing the item, Mr. Case turns the topic back to the upcoming test: "Now, where were we? Oh, yes. I want to show you some items that will be similar to those on the test. Here's one." He writes it on the chalkboard, then pauses: "Well, I don't want to give away the test, do I?"

Without discussing the test further, he turns to another topic: "Just wait until you hear about the videotape we will be viewing tomorrow. I borrowed it from another teacher, and she said that her students thought it was one of the most interesting, exciting stories they had ever seen!"

CASE STUDY 5.1

A SCIENCE LESSON IN A SIXTH-GRADE CLASS

Ms. Lake has been having great difficulty obtaining acceptable or even completed work from many of her sixth-grade students. They never seem to be able to follow instructions or directions, even for assignments in the textbook. Only the most able four or five pupils are actually doing good-quality work. Ms. Lake likes to challenge the students with new ideas to stimulate their curiosity and promote independent thinking. Although much of the class appears to enjoy her presentations, the students don't seem to be able to transfer their enthusiasm to their assignments. For example, in a recent science assignment, students were supposed to draw pictures illustrating stages in the evolution of birds from reptiles; most students did not perform satisfactorily. The lesson preceding this assignment included a five-item test containing questions on birds, reptiles, and vertebrates, reviewing some content covered during the preceding week. Students checked their own answers to this test in class and then passed them in. Although it was not a difficult test, most students got three or fewer items correct. After the checking activity, the teacher began a twenty-minute presentation on the possible evolution of birds from reptiles. The following topics were discussed:

- The meaning of adaptation, with an example supplied by students.
- An example of environmental action in the local community. This topic was introduced by a student, and other students added comments.

- The possibility of life on other planets, including a discussion of the number of solar systems in our galaxy.
- A consideration of the question of why birds might evolve from reptiles, with a student's answer, "To get away from enemies, they would take to the air," as the only reason given.
- The classification system of living organisms: kingdom, phylum, class, order, family, genus, and species.

At this point in the presentation, students were instructed to copy the classification system from the board. Ms. Lake also provided an example of classification, using the lion in the animal kingdom, vertebrate phylum, mammal class, and so on. Two similar examples were also presented and listed on the board. The teacher asked whether students understood and whether they had any questions. No questions were forthcoming, so the teacher gave the assignment of illustrating the stages in the evolution of a reptile to a bird. Students were given twenty-five minutes and told, "Use some color in your picture, make it neat, and use three stages." As was the case with many of the assignments Ms. Lake gave, only a few students completed their work satisfactorily, although most seemed to make an effort to do some drawing, and many students checked frequently with Ms. Lake to see whether their pictures were acceptable.

What problems are evident, and what changes might Ms. Lake make to achieve more success in helping students complete assignments satisfactorily?

 ## Checklist 5

Planning for Instruction

Check When Complete	Before the Lesson Ask Yourself	Notes
☐	A. What are the most important concepts or skills to be learned?	_____
☐	B. What kind of learning is your goal (memorization, application, appreciation)? Have you communicated this to your students?	_____
☐	C. What learning style is targeted by this lesson? Are you varying learning modalities?	_____
☐	D. Are there difficult words or concepts that need extra explanation?	_____
☐	E. How will you help students make connections to previous learning?	_____
☐	F. What activities will you plan to create interest in the lesson?	_____
☐	G. How will you make transitions between activities?	_____

(continued)

Check When Complete	Before the Lesson Ask Yourself	Notes
☐	H. What materials will be needed? Will students need to learn how to use them?	_____
☐	I. What procedures will students need to know to complete the activities?	_____
☐	J. How much time will you allocate for the lesson? For different parts of the lesson?	_____
☐	K. If activities require that students work together, how will groups be formed? How will you encourage productive work in groups?	_____
☐	L. What examples and questioning strategies will you use? Prepare a list of examples for explanations and list higher-order questions.	_____
☐	M. How will you know during and after the lesson what students understand?	_____
☐	N. What are some presentation alternatives if students have trouble with concepts (peer explanation, media, etc.)?	_____
☐	O. Are there extra- or special-help students?	_____
☐	P. How will you make sure that all students participate?	_____
☐	Q. How will you adjust the lesson if time is too short or too long?	_____
☐	R. What kind of product, if any, will you expect from students at the end of the lesson?	_____
☐	S. What will students do when they finish?	_____
☐	T. How will you evaluate students' work and give them feedback?	_____
☐	U. How will the concepts you present be used by students in future lessons?	_____

6

Managing Cooperative Learning Groups

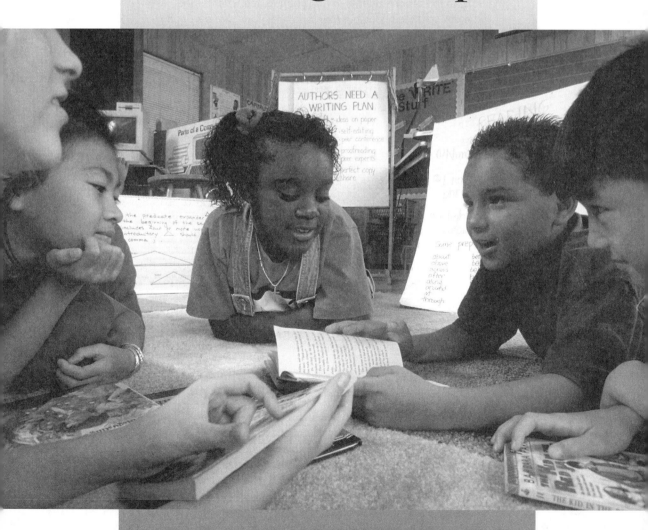

Students in Mr. Stockton's fourth-grade class are seated at small tables in groups of three or four. In previous lessons, each group drew a design for a bridge after studying types of bridges and assembling reports on famous historic bridges around the world. Each group currently is constructing a model of its own design, using materials such as Popsicle sticks and tongue depressors, paper, glue, string, and rubber bands procured from the classroom supply center by the group's "materials manager." The students are very engrossed in the activity and proceed without much direction from their teacher. The teacher circulates among the groups, encouraging, asking questions, and making occasional suggestions.

> When Bryce leaves his group to complain to Mr. Stockton that DaLynn is wasting materials that his group needs to finish the bridge, Mr. Stockton asks Bryce whether he has talked to DaLynn about the problem. He suggests that Bryce bring up the matter with the other students in his group to see whether they can resolve the difficulty before seeking his help. When another group stops working, Mr. Stockton goes to their table and suggests that they review their construction according to a list of criteria developed in an earlier class discussion.

Mr. Stockton is using a form of instruction called *cooperative learning groups*. As the name implies, the method involves organizing students into small groups in which students complete assignments cooperatively, assist each other, solve problems, share materials, and participate in discussions. Teachers who use cooperative learning groups do so because they believe that the method increases learning and involvement. Many teachers also value the increased independence of students from the teacher's direction that results from an emphasis on group planning and decision making. These teachers describe their roles as being more facilitators than directors of group activities. Finally, teachers value the social skills and problem-solving abilities that are learned through frequent group work. These important life skills will serve students well in social settings they encounter in or out of school.

Using cooperative groups requires some modification of traditional managerial routines. A number of the procedures that you developed for managing work and behavior in whole-class and individual formats also apply to cooperative groups, but you will have to modify some of your procedures for talk and movement. In addition, your managerial tasks of pacing activities, monitoring, and giving feedback to students become especially important. Most important, you must teach your students the skills necessary for working effectively in groups.

Research on Cooperative Learning

Substantial research on cooperative learning has focused on its effects on achievement and other outcomes of interest, such as interpersonal relations and student attitudes toward learning (Johnson & Johnson 1994b; Nastasi & Clements 1991; Slavin 1995). Cooperative learning has increased dramatically in classrooms over the past several years. A 1998 survey indicated that 93 percent of elementary teachers use cooperative learning and found academic achievement to be significant. Results for other outcomes, such as motivation, attitudes, and behaviors, often favor cooperative group methods. (See Educational Research Service 1989 and Wade, Abrami, Poulsen, & Chambers 1995 for extensive summaries and reviews of this research literature.)

Explanations of the positive benefits of cooperative groups usually point to the students' increased engagement with the content as an important factor. Compared to large-class or individual seatwork formats, small groups have greater potential for participation, feedback, and mutual construction of meaning among students. The group format encourages students to become active participants rather than passive recipients of information. Other explanations suggest that lower-achieving students profit from their peers' explanations, and high achievers benefit from constructing explanations for other students. All students can develop interpersonal skills through group tasks with a common goal. Furthermore, all can benefit from the support they receive in a cohesive group. Such support can help create positive norms for achievement and learning.

Although cooperative groups can improve learning and other outcomes for students, these results are by no means ensured simply by grouping students. For example, although research has shown that achievement is promoted by helping behaviors such as giving and receiving explanations (Nattiv 1994; Webb & Farivar 1994), such assistance does not occur automatically. Students who need help do not always ask for it, nor do they necessarily receive assistance when they do. Helpers may simply give correct answers or share a solution rather than engaging in constructive dialogue. Without feedback and instruction on how to collaborate, higher-achieving students may retreat to a less advanced level of cognition (Tudge 1992). More frequent use of group activities promotes positive outcomes when the quality of group interaction is high, but when group interactions are of low quality, outcomes are negatively affected (Battistich, Solomon, & Delucchi 1993). Students with disabilities, for example, need supportive, positive partners, and teachers must be proactive about arranging group membership, teaching group behaviors, and monitoring to promote their successful participation in group activities (O'Connor & Jenkins 1996).

Research has identified a number of strategies that you can use to promote the effectiveness of cooperative groups (Cohen 1994b; Emmer & Gerwels 1998; Slavin 1995). Such actions include teaching students how to work in groups, practicing the role of facilitator, carefully choosing and pacing academic activities, and promoting interdependence along with individual responsibility. Characteristics of more effective cooperative group lessons also include some form of daily accountability (versus later or no evaluation of individual or group performance), teacher monitoring of and feedback to groups, and the use of manipulative materials (Emmer & Gerwels 2002).

The importance of these and other skills depends in part on your goals and the nature of group-based academic tasks. Some teachers use groups as the primary means of instruction and develop projects and an integrated curriculum to deliver much of their academic content. Other teachers use groups primarily as a supplement to whole-class and individual instruction in one or a few subject areas, relying on groups during the classwork portion of lessons to provide short practice activities. Whichever approach you adopt, you will find the skills described in the remainder of this chapter to be helpful. You will, however, have to tailor them to your own application.

Examples of Group Activities

In Ms. Liu's second-grade class, students work in pairs with a chart and a bag of plastic coins of various values. The chart has ten rows, with columns headed by "penny," "nickel," "dime," "quarter," and "half-dollar." Ms. Liu asks the groups to fill in the chart with coins to total a particular amount. After about fifteen minutes, Ms. Liu has some of the groups demonstrate their results using the overhead projector.

Mr. Garcia uses groups of three for reading comprehension activities. Students rotate in the roles of reader and questioner, depending on the day. Some days, before the activity begins, Mr. Garcia conducts a short whole-class discussion about how to ask and answer questions in the group. During the twenty-minute activity, the teacher observes each group for two or three minutes, occasionally giving feedback or making a suggestion.

Ms. Dodd's fifth-grade class has been studying the culture and customs of the Quiluit people. During one activity later in the unit, students choose tribal roles to dramatize in a "freeze frame." Each group of four or five students plans the dramatization to depict an important activity, such as whaling, in the Quiluit culture. Ms. Dodd monitors, answers questions, and makes suggestions as she circulates among the groups during a thirty-minute planning and rehearsal period. Afterward, each group enacts the "freeze frame" for the class. A follow-up discussion of each role play is conducted to clarify the depicted concepts.

Ms. Richardson's sixth-grade science class works in groups to build models of a go-cart, using wooden wheels of various sizes, sticks, rubber bands, paper clips, and other materials. In a sequence of three lessons, students explore various constructions to try to create self-propelled models that will travel various distances. Ms. Richardson encourages the groups to discover the effects of friction and various sizes of wheels, how to generate power, and how to transfer motion using an axle. Each student records observations in an individual notebook, but the construction is a group activity.

These examples indicate the range of group activities possible in several content areas of the elementary curriculum. However, getting multiple groups to operate smoothly and productively requires planning by the teacher and preparation of the students. Try to visualize these groups in action and imagine the repertoire of behaviors students need to engage successfully in the activity. Consider also how the physical setting of the classroom must be altered to accommodate group activities. Note that the teacher's role during the group activity is less focused on giving information and more concerned with monitoring and giving feedback. This doesn't mean that teachers who use groups don't engage in teacher-led content development activities or use individual seatwork exercises. Such activities are used, to varying degrees, along with group work.

We turn next to the procedures, routines, and teaching skills that will help you manage group-based activities effectively.

 ## Strategies and Routines That Support Cooperative Learning

Room Arrangement

If you plan to make extensive use of groups, arrange seating in groups rather than have students move to group seating each time the format is used. Some classrooms are equipped with tables; to facilitate monitoring, these should be arranged to permit your unrestricted movement among them. Remember also that groups will be talking among themselves as they complete projects. Try to arrange groups to minimize distraction from other groups' noise. In the absence of tables, desks can be pushed together to form groups. Teachers often begin group activities with pairs of students, rather than larger numbers of students, but seating arrangements can still accommodate larger numbers, for example, table groups of four.

Storage of student materials is an integral part of room arrangement. Individual materials can be kept in desks, of course, but if your room has tables, you will have to decide where the students can keep personal items. One approach is to use plastic dishpans or similar containers, which can be kept under students' chairs or tables. Although this keeps materials accessible, a floor full of plastic dishpans can become very cluttered and impede movement. As an alternative, use open closet shelves or a bookcase to store the individual containers. In the latter case, students must keep smaller containers at their tables for frequently used items such as pencils, erasers, and so on. Some teachers place a small box or bin in the middle of each table for materials to be used by everyone in the group. This eliminates the need for borrowing, and it reduces the need for trips to out-of-group storage areas.

Talk and Movement Procedures

Teachers often report that when they begin using groups they are bothered by the increased noise level. After a while they get used to it and are less anxious when they realize that the noise is coming from engaged, involved students. Nevertheless, to prevent excessive noise you should discuss your expectations about talk with students and give them some guidelines. A common guideline is the use of "six-inch" or "twelve-inch" voices. Another is to speak quietly enough so that students in nearby groups can't hear or aren't distracted. Using "whisper voices" does not work well as a guideline because groups usually can't work efficiently and conduct discussions while whispering. If noise becomes excessive, you can use a group attention signal to decrease noise to an acceptable level. If noise continues to be a problem, groups can work silently (communicating through written notes only) for the remainder of the session.

Movement will not be a major problem if students are already seated in their groups, although it may be useful to provide a guideline such as "Stay with your

"This class will stimulate your ideas and thoughts. And remember—no talking."
Reprinted by permission of James Warren.

group" or "Take care of out-of-group business promptly" to limit unnecessary wandering and visiting. Some movement is needed, of course, when students obtain materials. Assigning a "materials manager" for each group helps take care of such business efficiently.

Some teachers change group composition for various activities, resulting in movement during transitions between the activities. Such transitions can be real time-wasters and make it difficult to start the next activity. An efficient routine is to announce the beginning of the transition, state the expectation, and tell students how much time they have to get ready ("All of you must bring your materials and be in your group in one minute.") Continue to monitor throughout the transition to cut down on stragglers. You can also give the students an expectation about what they are to do when they arrive at their group's location ("Sit in your seat and put your supplies—book, paper, pencil, and so on—on the table," or "Start work on your project right away").

In some classrooms, it is necessary to move from whole-class arrangements to small groups. Plan ahead to speed these transitions. Mark the location of tables or desks in each arrangement on the floor with masking tape. Teach and practice movement into groups as you would any other procedure. Many teachers have found that putting slit tennis balls on the bottoms of the chair and table legs makes for quieter, quicker movement. Teachers can also mark the location of groups by hanging symbols or signs over their sites in the classrooms.

Group Attention Signals

When your students work in groups, you may have to stop their work to provide additional directions or to make a transition to another activity or task. You may also have to provide feedback to the whole class, modify some aspect of the assignment, or provide additional instruction. Also, noise may rise to unacceptable levels, requiring that you intervene. In all of these cases, you must interrupt students who are already engaged in a task or who are interacting with each other, making it difficult to gain their attention. The solution to this problem is to use a signal.

Efficient signals for group attention require that the students make an overt response, which interrupts whatever else they may be doing:

> The teacher says, "One, two, three," clapping as she does so. Students respond, "Eyes on me," and "Look at the teacher."
> The teacher says, "Thumbs up if you can hear me," "Fold your hands if you can hear me," or "Clap if you can hear me."

Each of these signals gains student attention by requiring that they substitute a behavior, thus effectively stopping the prior activity. These are especially useful when students are working with manipulatives, which might distract them from attending.

Sometimes a signal may be used to pace students through a transition between activities. A signal is especially helpful when the transition involves the movement of students from one location to another. The following signals may be used for such transitions, as well as to gain student attention:

> The teacher claps rhythmically, first twice, then three times. Students pick up the clapping rhythm: after the teacher claps twice, they clap in unison three times.
> The teacher flips the overhead projector light (or the room lights) on and off twice, then begins clapping and counting, "Ten, nine, eight, seven, six, . . . one, zip." Students pick up the count as they complete the prior activity, clap, and repeat "zip" in unison with the teacher, "zipping" their lips at the end.

Bell ringing and a simple oral direction such as "Stop, look, listen" are useful signals when students are not as interactively engaged and thus require a less dramatic or intrusive stimulus to get their attention. Teach several signals to avoid overworking one of them and to give you some options. Finally, avoid interrupting students unnecessarily. Present information or directions ahead of time, or post them on a chalkboard or overhead to minimize the need to break into ongoing student activities. When appropriate, give reminders to individual groups rather than to the whole class.

Promoting Interdependence within the Group

Positive interdependence has occurred when either the group's product or the individual's performance is enhanced by the actions of the group members. In addition to improving performance, interdependence builds group cohesion and helps create group norms that support learning. Interdependence can be fostered in a number of ways:

- Each student can be responsible for contributing a unique component to the group's product. For example, students might do research on different aspects of a topic for a group report.
- Each student chooses a specific part of a topic to teach to the rest of the group. Or, in groups of four students, pairs work together to prepare information for the other two students in the group.
- In groups of two, students work as drill partners to help each other learn.
- The teacher assigns roles to students (e.g., reader, checker, recorder, materials manager) to ensure that each student makes a contribution to the group's activity.
- Group assignments (e.g., projects, reports, performances, constructions, oral group presentations) can be given a group grade, recognition, points, or some other reward.

Individual Accountability

Although interdependence is important, students must also feel individually responsible for their learning. This is not much of a problem when they complete the assignments as individuals, but with group support. When group assignments are the outcome, however, establishing group accountability—for example, by giving the group's product a grade or by asking the group to report orally—may not be sufficient for some students, who may be content to loaf or ride other students' coattails. Individual accountability in the context of a group-based assignment may be increased in several ways, as noted in the following examples:

- Require that individual students perform an identifiable portion of the group assignment.
- Ask groups to turn in a list of each student's contribution to the final product.
- Ask students to record observations in individual notebooks that you will collect and grade at various times.
- Have students turn in individual work along with the group's product.
- Require that students keep a daily record of their individual work in spiral notebooks.
- Let students know that when their group reports to the class, each student should be ready to explain his or her work.
- Have selected students report individually on their group work.
- Give students a quiz based on the group assignment.

You can foster individual responsibility when you set expectations: Stress to students that even though they are working on a group assignment, each member is responsible for learning the material. Tell them that it's important for all members of a group to help each other understand what they are learning, and for each person to contribute. Finally, when you monitor group work, note participation by individual students. If some are not contributing, try to determine why not; then take corrective measures such as redirecting the student. When simple interventions don't work, teachers often ask the group to help solve the problem, or they may have a conference with the student to try to assess the situation and to work out a solution.

Maintaining individual responsibility in a group setting is not easy. Adding individual assessments on top of group assessments may increase the amount of time the teacher must spend on planning and preparation, as well as evaluation. Moreover, focusing on individual accountability may deflect attention from group outcomes. Procedures for accountability, therefore, should be planned carefully and amended as necessary until you develop a balance between accountability needs and available time and energy.

Monitoring Student Work and Behavior

Good monitoring of group work requires that you be on your feet and walking among the groups, scanning the rest of the class, just as you do when monitoring any classroom activities. Try not to spend too much time with any one group at the expense of another. Goals for monitoring include keeping track of individual performance and growth in academic areas, group skills, and individual behaviors. A complicating factor is the extent to which individual versus group performance must be distinguished. Students sometimes complain about group grades because they feel that they have contributed more than other group members to the group's product. At the beginning of each group assignment, spend time explaining to the class how individual and group progress will be assessed, and structure and monitor group tasks carefully to see that all students are participating.

The way teachers keep track of student work in groups depends on the nature of the group activity. When individual assignments are used and the group's function is to support individual learning, monitoring academic performance is not much different from monitoring in classrooms in which whole-class and individual seatwork are the primary formats. You can circulate among the groups and note individual performance, and you can also collect the individual assignments and check them. Critical to the effective utilization of groups for the support of individual learning is the quality of interaction among students. It's important to note the degree to which students provide explanations and demonstrations for each other rather than simply give answers or ignore peers' questions. Remember that the best way to teach appropriate helping behaviors is to model them yourself.

An effective monitoring technique is the use of a clipboard or PDA that contains student names and space to record ratings or notes about performance and behavior during group activities. When this technique is used, it encourages teachers to obtain information about all students, not just the active, visible ones. The information can be used later to give feedback to groups and individuals or to add to performance evaluations. The use of this strategy as seldom as once or twice a week can add important information about individuals and supplement other types of monitoring.

With group assignments, the focus of monitoring shifts to the group's collective progress, along with individual performance. If you provide checkpoints and time limits, you will not only give yourself monitoring milestones, but you will help students self-monitor. Asking groups to report to you on their progress, plans, or difficulties also provides information about comprehension that you might not obtain through observation alone. As noted in the previous section on individual accountability, it may be beneficial to include an individual component in a collective assignment. For example, ask students to record individual observations, solve a problem, or write a summary of their contribution to the group's project. Not only do such data increase your information about each student's achievement, but the procedure also improves individual accountability.

Group skills are also an important concern when monitoring (for examples, see the section on social skills in this chapter). As is the case with academic skills, students vary in their understanding and use of cooperative behaviors. Posted checklists and a careful program of teaching students important group skills go a long way toward helping the students self-monitor, but you should also pay attention to the extent to which individuals and groups operate appropriately.

Teachers use various indicators to determine satisfactory group functioning. Because students usually have a specific task to perform in the group, it is not difficult to determine whether they are engaged in a suitable activity. When students are talking with each other about the task and performing behaviors needed to complete an assignment such as writing, assembling materials, practicing, or constructing, teachers can easily identify appropriate, on-task behavior. Teachers also watch for signs that individual students may be uninvolved or disengaged. Momentary off-task behavior usually can be ignored, but if it is prolonged, intervention may be needed. Another indicator is the level and nature of emotionality exhibited by students. Teachers notice students in a group when they exhibit tense, angry, or hostile behaviors. Such emotional reactions suggest frustration or potential conflicts that could escalate and therefore call for early intervention to prevent the development of more serious problems.

Interventions for Groups

Interventions for groups are closely tied to the monitoring features described previously. The most common interventions are simple, easy to use, and brief. Individual students and groups who are off-task may be orally redirected to the task. Students who persist in inappropriate behaviors may be given a short time-out (such as one or two minutes, initially) or sent to work alone for a longer time if they don't respond to milder interventions. Other interventions for individuals are described in detail in Chapter 9.

Conferences with students can be used more readily during group work than during whole-class activities. The teacher can meet individually with one student or a group because other students are engaged in the group activity. Such conferences typically last for a short time—less than a minute—and consist of feedback to the student or group, along with redirection and a plan for changing the behavior. Such an approach is more effective than simple reprimands because it offers an alternative behavior. A brief conference also allows the teacher to provide feedback on the spot, rather than delaying it so long that it would prove ineffective.

Teachers engage groups in a conference when a group process has broken down. Examples include groups in which students don't ask or give assistance constructively, make poor progress toward the group's goal, or encounter a problem that they aren't able to overcome. Teachers often describe their role as that of facilitator or mediator in this type of conference. Although the teacher may provide feedback about the problem and a reality check for the group's perceptions, students are encouraged to solve the problem themselves. Strategies teachers use to facilitate a solution include asking them to identify the problem, asking them to suggest alternatives, asking for reactions and comments, and calling for the group to select one different approach to try. As a last resort, teachers may offer a solution or change group membership if the problem proves intractable.

Effective Group Work Skills

To work effectively in a group, students must practice a number of group work skills. These include social skills, such as active listening, sharing, and supporting; explaining skills, which convey understanding and meaning in academic tasks; and leadership skills, such as planning and demonstrating initiative and enthusiasm. Time spent discussing and role-playing these skills is time well spent. Teachers also often find games such as those in Cohen's (1994a) *Designing Groupwork* to be useful tools.

Social Skills

Active listening includes listening to others without interrupting, being able to summarize others' ideas, incorporating them into the ongoing discussion, and using them constructively in completing the group's assignment. Sharing materials and taking turns are also necessary for effective cooperation. Another social skill is giving support, which includes accepting differences, being friendly, and encouraging others. Students who lack social skills may insist on doing things their way, argue frequently, ignore or put down another student's contributions, or not participate in the group's work.

The ability to work in a group depends on social skills, so teachers usually emphasize their development. One way to do so is to teach students the skills needed for group work as group activities are introduced at the beginning of the year. They may even teach certain phrases for students to use in summarizing, questioning, or expressing disagreement. Teachers should also reinforce appropriate use of social skills throughout the year.

Explaining Skills

Explaining skills are an important aspect of group work, and they are critical to the development of academic outcomes. Indicators of explaining skills are comments that describe a problem, assignment, or goal. Student comments might also identify steps to be accomplished or followed to complete a task as well as reasons for the steps. Students might summarize the work they have done or plan to do. If a group assignment includes answering questions, students can give their answers and explain how they arrived at them.

Another important component of the explaining process is seeking explanations from others. This may involve students' describing what they do and do not understand and asking for help from other group members. Such requests are unlikely to occur unless other students in the group practice good social skills. To encourage students to seek help, the teacher might say, "No one knows everything. If there's something you don't understand, it's smart to ask for help from the group. And if someone asks for help, the friendly thing to do is to give a good explanation."

Interactions about content are essential to the process of constructing meaning. They enhance comprehension and are critical to learning. Most students need encouragement to engage in these behaviors because conversations about content are not a natural part of their interactions. Some ways to encourage them include the following:

- Assign the role of summarizer to a student and rotate the role.
- Have students turn to a partner and explain something; then have the partner "explain back."
- Have each student in the group write one question; then the members of the group answer it.
- Conduct role plays of asking for help and explaining; demonstrate and discuss.
- Lead a discussion about how to give a good explanation and how to ask for help.
- Have students write their group's ideas on a chart and present them to the class.

Leadership Skills

When a group has someone who steps up and says, "Let's figure out what we need to get this job done," it has someone who is practicing a leadership skill. Desired attributes include demonstrating initiative, planning, and enthusiasm. Good social skills also complement this repertoire, as does basic competence in the content relevant to the group's task. Teachers can help students develop leadership skills by assigning roles such as presenter or discussion leader, which give students the opportunity to demonstrate initiative and gain confidence. Such roles should be defined clearly and the tasks delineated. Roles should be rotated so that every student gets an opportunity for practice. Most teachers value these skills highly and try to form groups with at least one student who exhibits them "naturally."

Although leadership skills are developed over time and students possess them in varying degrees, all students can make some progress toward learning and achieving them.

⊚ FOR REFLECTION

Supporters of the use of cooperative learning emphasize the interdependent nature of social life, including work and family settings. They also emphasize the social nature of learning and the importance of interaction in constructing meaning. Some educators and commentators, however, have expressed concerns about over-reliance on groups, arguing that group learning wastes time, especially of gifted students who must help their less able peers. These critics also dislike the focus on group rather than individual performance. What is your position on these issues? Should groups be used more or less frequently in your teaching field? To accomplish which goals?

⊙⊙ Beginning the Use of Cooperative Learning Groups

Whether you begin to use groups at the start of the year or wait until later, you should address several matters. It is important that the physical arrangement of the classroom support the use of groups, especially if you intend to use them extensively. You should also choose carefully the initial tasks for the groups because you want a successful experience to set the stage for subsequent group activities. Group composition is important; students must be able to work constructively with each other and aid each other's learning. Finally, you must plan how to teach the group skills needed for effective group functioning.

Room Arrangement

Try to arrange places for students to meet in groups so that you can monitor them easily. Establish a central materials storage area with easy access so that your "materials managers" can obtain needed supplies quickly. Other important aspects of room arrangement were discussed earlier in this chapter, as well as in Chapter 1.

Procedures and Routines

Don't assume that because students follow the rules during whole-class and seatwork activities, they will automatically do so during group work. Instead, be prepared to teach students your specific expectations for talk and movement during group work. (For example, talk only to your own group members.) Also teach a group attention signal so that you can refocus class attention as needed. These procedures should be explained to students and rehearsed when feasible, with students receiving feedback on their ability to follow them.

Forming Groups

Your initial use of groups may involve pairs only, having the students simply check each other's work or discuss a question or problem. You also might use pairs to work on a classwork exercise or to practice spelling words or number facts. When pairs are used in such straightforward ways, most students do not have to move to new locations, and the activity is brief, placing fewer demands on the students and on you.

When groups are used more extensively and frequently, group membership becomes more critical. Teachers usually form groups ahead of time and seat students accordingly rather than have students move to new locations for group work, although that is not always the case. Different groups might be formed for math, for example, than for reading and social studies.

When assigning students to groups, a main consideration of most teachers is to represent in each group a range of achievement in the subject. A second concern is often to place a leader (see the section on leadership skills) in each group. Teachers also try to avoid personality conflicts. Students who are argumentative often work best in groups that have a student with good leadership abilities, including social skills.

Some teachers avoid placing in the same group students who are at extremes in achievement levels in the content area; for example, they would not place a very high achiever and a very low achiever in the same group. Instead they seek less variation, although their groups are still more heterogeneous than are separate groups of high- and low-achieving students. These teachers' concern is that the pace of work and the discourse patterns in the groups with very high-achieving students may be inappropriate for and intimidating to the lower-performing students, resulting in their withdrawal and task avoidance. In groups having midrange achievers, the pace and vocabulary are more likely to encourage the lower achievers' participation. This principle obviously depends on the degree of social and explaining skills possessed by the various students.

No hard-and-fast rules can be stated about how long groups should stay together. Some teachers change group membership frequently, as often as every few weeks. Most leave students in the same groups for longer times but reshuffle the deck at least a few times each year. Some teachers allow students to form their own groups for special activities or projects or as a change of pace, but rarely do they allow self-selected groups for an extended time, except in a special project.

At the beginning of the year, before you know your students very well, it may be instructive to allow students to choose partners for a few initial activities. Limit the length and scope of these activities and monitor closely to make sure that no child feels left out. An alternative grouping technique is to group the students by interest. Place several topics or types of activities on the board. Have the children write down their first, second, and third choices. Collect the choices and assign students to groups based on their first or second choice. Doing so provides valuable information about who works well with whom, which you can use when forming more permanent groups. After groups are formed, they should be monitored for signs of conflict. Don't be too quick to step in with a solution, but do ask groups to address such problems. Giving students responsibility for dealing with group problems can create an opportunity for learning. As students acquire group skills and experience success in working together, conflict usually diminishes. When conflicts cannot be resolved in a reasonable time within a group, however, most teachers choose to move antagonistic students to new groups. Later in the year, when such students have become more adroit at cooperating, they might be given an opportunity to work together again.

Initial Group Tasks

Students who don't have much experience with working in groups will have to develop their skills in uncomplicated tasks rather than in complex projects. Holubec (1992), a pioneer in the development of cooperative learning groups, describes a number of simple, easy-to-implement activities for beginning group work. Her suggestions include the following: Turn to your partner. Explain something or compare answers to a problem or exercise. Students might also choose the next step or add to an answer. As the students gain experience, this format can be used for problem solving.

DRILL PARTNERS

Partners practice material that must be memorized.

READING BUDDIES

Students read to each other. The teacher can build on this after a while by asking students to summarize or make up questions for their partners.

CHECKING

Students compare answers and resolve discrepancies. Each student must be able to explain the answer.

REVIEWERS

Students review for a quiz or test or prepare for an oral report by working together to develop questions. They ask and answer each other's questions.

It's important not to rush into group work until you build a foundation of practice and skills. Teaching group skills is easier in simpler formats with uncomplicated procedures. After your students have had success in some of these initial group tasks, they will be ready for more complex group formats and assignments.

Teaching Group Skills

Decide on a set of basic skills that your students should acquire. One set might include listening, explaining, asking for help, encouraging, and sharing. A good way to begin the teaching process is to have a whole-class discussion about what is needed to work cooperatively. To build a rationale for working together, some teachers like to broaden the discussion to include home, playground, and neighborhood as well as classroom groups, and to discuss the character and life skills needed. Eventually, of course, the discussion has to address concrete behaviors that constitute good listening, explaining, and so forth. Signs can be posted listing desired group behaviors (a school-supply store may have some that pertain specifically to group activities).

Providing students with examples and models of desired group behaviors is important and should be accompanied by practice and feedback. Remember that it takes many weeks for some students to become comfortable with the new demands of group participation. Be patient. Rather than reviewing all desirable group skills, pick one and spend time discussing it. Let students practice it, and give them feedback as they work in groups. Introduce other skills in subsequent days or weeks.

> Mrs. Walker focused on one group skill per week until her fifth graders developed an effective repertoire by the end of the first six weeks of the school year. During the first week, she emphasized participating during group work; the second week, she focused on remaining on-task. Subsequent weeks were devoted to cooperating, encouraging, explaining, and active listening. Mrs. Walker introduced each skill in a whole-class discussion, soliciting examples, suggestions, and a rationale from her students. During the first week, she displayed a five-point rating scale for "participating" and indicated what she would be looking for as students worked in groups. At the end of several group activities that week, she engaged students in a discussion about the skill, asked them to review their performance, and shared her assessments with the groups. In each subsequent week, Mrs. Walker added a new scale, so that groups received feedback about their progress in acquiring the skills.

Students need feedback about how they are performing group skills. Mrs. Walker's use of scales is one way to focus students on specific components of group work. Another way is to conduct whole-class discussions about group work activities. Begin with a request that students evaluate an aspect of their group work, indicating what went well and what could be improved, or they might be asked to describe how someone in their group performed one of the group skills effectively. Students might also describe what makes it difficult to perform a particular skill, and how that problem might be overcome. Getting students to talk about their group experience is one of the best ways to help them develop good monitoring and self-regulation skills.

Teachers can provide feedback to a particular group or to an individual, as needed. Usually such feedback occurs as the teacher moves around the room, monitoring the activity. During the initial stages of group work, when students are acquiring group skills, it is especially important that appropriate behaviors be identified and supported. Interventions with students who aren't practicing good group behaviors can sometimes be addressed as a group problem. "Roberto isn't participating yet. What can the group do to let him know that it supports his participation?" At other times, discussing the situation with the individual student may be the best way to encourage attempts to practice group behaviors.

Some group skills can be taught by the assigning of roles to individual students in a group. Roles such as materials manager, recorder, discussion leader, encourager, discussant, or reporter entail the use of specific skills. By assigning some of these roles to students, teachers encourage them to practice new behaviors. Rotating the roles among group members permits all students to gain experience in the skills. Using roles also helps promote interdependence among the group members because each student has a unique job to perform for the group. Roles that are frequently used can be written on cards, along with key behaviors, and laminated. Posters with role descriptions can also be displayed at easy-to-see locations until students have mastered the basics.

Student Goals and Participation

Students should be told the purpose of their group work and given direction about how they are to proceed, consistent with the task they are to accomplish. Cohen (1994b) makes an important distinction about the nature of group tasks. She summarizes research indicating that the nature of a teacher's directions depends on the degree to which the group's task is structured. For outcomes that are well defined and for which there are a limited range of suitable strategies (e.g., completing a worksheet, performing a specific laboratory procedure, answering comprehension questions, reviewing material presented in a text or by the teacher), teachers can give explicit instructions about steps to follow and can monitor the groups for satisfactory progress. On such tasks, the teacher might prepare a list of steps that should be followed and then display it on a chalkboard, on an overhead projector, or on a handout. A student can be assigned to monitor, noting when a step has been completed, or the whole group can be asked to keep track of progress.

However, when the task is less structured, the nature of the product and steps to achieve it are not as evident, nor is there an easily identifiable strategy. Teachers then must be less directive about how the group proceeds. The teacher might delegate some responsibility to the group to decide on its procedures and to select appropriate resources. Typically, the goal of such group tasks includes higher-order thinking and problem solving. Too explicit a set of directions about how to proceed may stifle the types of thinking such a task is intended to promote.

For example, suppose a teacher's goal in assigning the development of a group report is to promote critical thinking and problem solving about the topic. If the teacher is highly directive about how the group is to function and what resources it can use, the students may simply try to develop a report that satisfies *pro forma* the assignment requirements. If, however, the teacher's directions offer the students latitude, and if responsibility is delegated, there is a better chance that students will draw on their own creativity and be more engaged in the group process.

Using Group and Individual Rewards

Most students consider working in groups to be a desirable activity, so it is not usually necessary to establish an extrinsic group or individual reward structure to accompany the use of cooperative learning groups. However, teachers sometimes find using rewards helpful as an extra motivational tool to encourage students to practice appropriate group skills or to improve the participation of undermotivated students.

> Mr. Galvan used a weekly raffle system, rewarding students with "tickets" for desirable group behavior. A group also could receive bonus tickets when all of its members did well on an assignment. Students initialed their tickets, and at the end of the week, Mr. Galvan drew four or five from a box; winners received small toys or privileges as prizes.

> Ms. Frank gave points to groups for desirable behaviors, such as getting ready or cleaning up promptly, helping and sharing, or listening and explaining. She awarded points during group work, for example, by telling a group, "I really like the way you have been explaining the ideas to each other. Your group has earned a bonus point." She also awarded points during wrap-up discussions with the whole class, noting that she observed good examples of desirable behavior during group work. She kept a tally of points for each group on the chalkboard; when a group reached a set number of points, its reward was to eat lunch with Ms. Frank in the classroom.

Judicious use of rewards can direct student attention to important behaviors and make it more likely that students will employ them. Group rewards, moreover, can strengthen cohesiveness through a common goal and the shared positive feelings that result when the group succeeds. As noted in Chapter 7 in the discussion on intrinsic motivation, extrinsic rewards should be a supplement to more natural consequences of student accomplishment, such as recognition, positive feedback, other forms of praise, and the satisfaction that accompanies learning and goal attainment. As long as these consequences are abundant, the use of additional group and individual reinforcers should not interfere with intrinsic motivation.

Further Reading

Baloche, L. (1998). *The cooperative classroom: Empowering learning.* Upper Saddle River, N.J.: Prentice-Hall.

This text helps teachers to understand the power of students working together and to develop the knowledge and skills for creating empowering classrooms. It addresses issues such as why use cooperation as well as when, how, and how much to use it.

Cohen, E. G. (1998). Making cooperative learning equitable. *Educational Leadership, 56,* 18–21.

Status differences among students reduce the participation and learning of lower-status students. Cohen provides some practical strategies teachers can use to improve lower-status students' opportunities, including teacher emphasis on the multiple abilities needed to accomplish many group tasks and altering student expectations about the competence of the lower-status students.

Johnson, D. W., & Johnson, R. T. (1999). Making cooperative learning work. *Theory Into Practice, 38*(2), 67–73.

Cooperative learning is defined in comparison to other learning activities (individualistic, competitive, pseudolearning group, and traditional). Three types of cooperative learning (formal, infor-

mal, and base group) are described, and benefits for students involved in cooperative leaning are detailed in the areas of achievement, interpersonal, and personal growth.

Slavin, R. E. (1995). *Cooperative learning: Research, theory, and practice* (2d ed.). Boston: Allyn & Bacon.

This authoritative book provides a good overview of cooperative learning approaches along with a careful description of research. The author has done extensive research and development in this field, and this book provides a thorough review of his and his colleagues' work.

www.co-operation.org

The website for the Cooperative Learning Center at the University of Minnesota gives detailed information about cooperative learning and how it is accomplished.

www.psychologymatters.org/jigsaw.html

This website, sponsored by the American Psychological Association, provides references and updated research on using Jigsaw grouping in classrooms.

www.findarticles.com/p/articles/mi_m0341/is_4_55/ai_62521561

The Looksmart findarticles website lists hundreds of articles on educational topics. This link takes you to one by Robert Slavin and Robert Cooper (1999): Improving Intergroup Relations: Lessons Learned from Cooperative Learning Programs, *Journal of Social Issues, Winter Issue.*

http://home.att.net/~clnetwork/thinkps.htm

Think-Pair-Share is one of the most common cooperative learning structures and one of the easiest to implement. It can be used for higher-level thinking as well as for basic review and recall. The steps and pitfalls are spelled out in this article.

 ## Suggested Activities

1. Observe in a classroom using cooperative learning. As you do so, note room arrangement features and routines that support group learning. Use Checklist 6 as an observation guide.

2. Choose a lesson or unit that you have observed being taught in an individual or whole-class instructional format, or find one in a teacher's edition or curriculum guide. Identify ways to use cooperative learning groups to teach a component of the lesson or unit. Discuss the modifications you would make to incorporate concepts presented in this chapter.

3. In a group, discuss problems associated with fostering individual responsibility in a group-based task, and how to give feedback to individuals about academic performance and individual behaviors in the group setting. What are some workable, efficient strategies for enhancing responsibility and providing feedback?

4. Reread Case Study 4.2, which illustrates one teacher's approach to introducing cooperative groups at the beginning of the year.

   a. Note concepts described in this chapter that are evident in Ms. James's procedures and strategies. What functions do the associated procedures and strategies serve?

      b. Are any areas discussed in this chapter not present in Ms. James's classroom during the first three days? Would you suggest introducing them? Why or why not?

      c. Ms. James teaches in a departmentalized sixth-grade math class. What changes might be appropriate for earlier grades? For different content areas? For project-based, integrated-subject units?

5. Review some plans for cooperative group lessons by going to the website www.eduref.org and clicking on "Lesson Plan." You can search this site's large lesson plan collection by grade level and subject. To find examples of Cooperative Group lessons, type "cooperative groups" in the search descriptor. Share a favorite lesson plan with colleagues. What management issues could arise if you were to teach this lesson? Get feedback from others in your group.

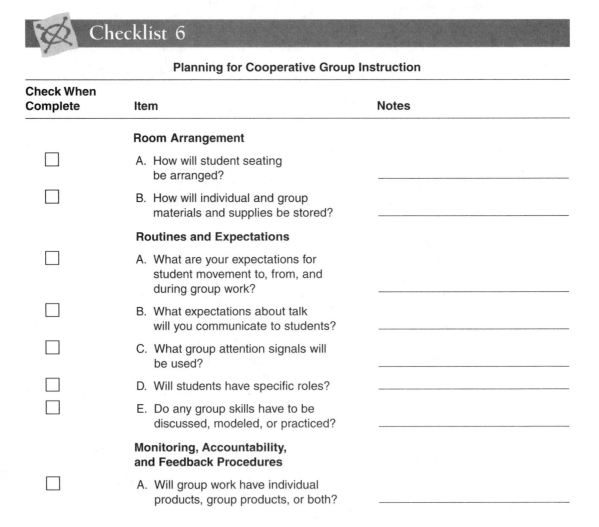

Checklist 6

Planning for Cooperative Group Instruction

Check When Complete	Item	Notes
	Room Arrangement	
☐	A. How will student seating be arranged?	_____
☐	B. How will individual and group materials and supplies be stored?	_____
	Routines and Expectations	
☐	A. What are your expectations for student movement to, from, and during group work?	_____
☐	B. What expectations about talk will you communicate to students?	_____
☐	C. What group attention signals will be used?	_____
☐	D. Will students have specific roles?	_____
☐	E. Do any group skills have to be discussed, modeled, or practiced?	_____
	Monitoring, Accountability, and Feedback Procedures	
☐	A. Will group work have individual products, group products, or both?	_____

Check When Complete	Item	Notes
☐	B. How will individual or group work be assessed?	_____
☐	C. How will you monitor student behavior and work during group activities?	_____
☐	D. How will students receive feedback about individual and group performance?	_____
☐	E. How will students receive feedback about their behavior in groups?	_____

Group Skills That Must Be Discussed, Modeled, or Practiced

☐	A. Social skills?	_____
☐	B. Explaining skills?	_____
☐	C. Leadership skills?	_____

7
Maintaining Appropriate Student Behavior

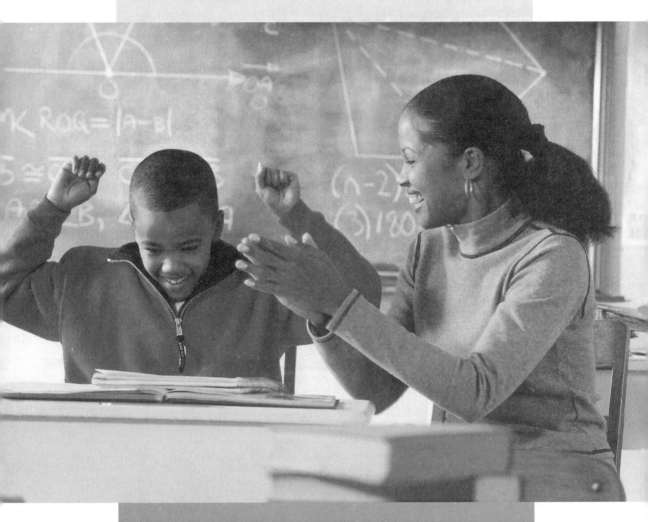

As you have seen in the first six chapters, good classroom management depends on careful planning of the classroom's organization, rules, procedures, initial activities, and instruction. This planning and preparation will pay large dividends when the students arrive. However, being ready is not enough. To sustain good behavior throughout the year, you will have to be actively involved in maintaining student cooperation and compliance with necessary classroom norms, rules, and procedures. You cannot assume that students will behave appropriately just because you carefully taught them what was expected of them. In primary grades, children are in the early stages of learning "going to school" skills, so you will need to pay constant attention to prompting good behavior. Even in the intermediate grades, children need teachers who encourage good behavior by establishing their rules, procedures, and consequences consistently.

In particular, don't be lulled into complacency by the good behavior of your students at the beginning of the year. Most elementary classes are quiet and subdued on the first day or two of school. Without your careful attention to maintaining good behavior, even a class that begins very well may ultimately become disruptive and difficult to control. The following brief example illustrates such a class and also suggests some of the reasons management problems developed.

> Ms. White carefully discussed her classroom rules and procedures with her fifth-grade class at various times on the first several class days, and students were generally well behaved. However, at the start of the third week, problems are beginning to occur. While leading whole-class discussions, Ms. White stands at the front board to jot down important points. When she turns away to write on the board, students at the back of the room begin talking quietly among themselves. Some pass notes, throw paper wads, and wander around the room during quiet work time. If Ms. White reprimands students for talking, they say they do not understand what to do and that they are asking for help from others. If she allows students to help each other, before long everyone is talking, few are working, and the noise level increases.
>
> At first, students raised their hands for permission to speak. Later, some students called out comments, and rather than ignore the contributions, Ms. White began to accept them when they were substantive. Now, more and more students have become loud and distracting. Because discussion activities do not seem to work well, Ms. White has begun to reduce the amount of time spent on these activities and to assign more individual work.
>
> During reading instruction, Ms. White meets with students in small groups while the rest of the class works on individual assignments. While working with the small group, Ms. White is interrupted more and more frequently by students who are having problems with the individual assignments. At other times, she has to interrupt small-group instruction to deal with misbehavior outside the group. At the end of the small-group instruction period for reading, Ms. White frequently is dismayed to see what little progress students have made on their independent work.

Problems such as those occurring in Ms. White's class often have a gradual onset, developing over several weeks or even months. It is usually possible to avoid these problems, but to do so you must first understand why they occur and what you can vent them. Because they develop gradually, the causes are not always ap- the teacher or even to an observer unfamiliar with the history of the class- wever, the short account of events in Ms. White's class suggests why things ...ginning to go awry. One problem is that Ms. White is not monitoring behavior carefully enough. Talking, inattention, and misbehavior are going undetected until the noise or commotion level is high. In addition, Ms. White is not checking student progress on assignments frequently enough. This reduces her students' accountability and prevents her from helping students achieve the learning objectives.

A second problem is that Ms. White is being inconsistent in her use of procedures and in her reaction to students when they do not follow the procedures. By accepting some call-outs and by allowing noisy talk during independent work, she invites students to continue to test the limits until the procedures finally break down.

A third problem, related to the first two, is that too many inappropriate behaviors are being ignored. As a result, students are unsure of behavior standards, and minor events escalate into major disruptions involving substantial numbers of students. A fourth problem is that the teacher's attention is becoming more and more directed at inappropriate behavior; no attention or incentives for appropriate behavior are evident.

These problems can be prevented or handled by following these four important guidelines:

- Monitor student behavior and academic progress carefully.
- Be consistent in the use of procedures, rules, and consequences.
- Deal with inappropriate behavior promptly.
- Build a positive climate with an emphasis on reinforcing appropriate behavior.

The remainder of the chapter considers how these guidelines can be implemented.

FOR REFLECTION

Before we examine ways to maintain appropriate behavior, identify exactly what "appropriate" behavior means to you. Imagine your own classroom. When students are behaving appropriately, what will it look and sound like? How much movement and talk do you find acceptable? Picture different instructional settings—a whole-class discussion, individual work time, cooperative groups. When you have thought through your expectations, look for suggestions in this chapter that will help you help students meet them.

Monitoring Student Behavior

To monitor classroom behavior effectively, you must know what to look for. Two categories of behavior are especially important to monitor:

1. Student involvement in learning activities.
2. Student compliance with classroom rules and procedures.

Student involvement is indicated by many behaviors, including attention during presentations and discussions and satisfactory progress in individual work and other assignments. Student compliance with classroom rules and procedures is easy to monitor if you have clear expectations for behavior and have communicated these to the class.

Monitoring behavior during whole-class presentations requires that you stand or sit where you can see the faces of all students and that you scan the room frequently. Some teachers are not effective monitors of behavior during whole-class activities because they focus their attention on a limited number of students (usually those seated in the middle rows or tables and at the front desks); other teachers "talk to the chalkboard." In either case, the teacher does not have a very clear perception of overall response to the presentation, nor is the teacher fully aware of what may be occurring at the periphery of the classroom. During your presentations, try to move around and develop "active eyes." If you notice a commotion involving several students and you have no idea what is going on, this is a sign that you have not been monitoring closely enough.

When instructing a small group of students while the remainder of the class is engaged in individual work, sit where you have an unobstructed view of all students. Don't become so absorbed in working with the small group that you lose track of the other students. Look up frequently and be alert for problems. After finishing with one group, circulate around the room and provide needed assistance before calling the next small group.

When students are working on individual assignments and you are not instructing a group, monitor the class by moving around the classroom and checking each student's progress periodically. You will, of course, help students who request assistance; however, you should not just "chase hands," or you will not be aware of the progress of other students. One way to prevent having to chase hands is to establish a procedure by which students can ask questions of members of their group or their neighbors. This can free you to work with other students.

It is difficult to monitor progress on assignments from your desk or from any other fixed location, so don't spend too much time in one place. If you must work at your desk for an extended time, get up periodically and circulate around the room, looking at each student's work. If you must spend a long time (more than a minute or two) helping an individual student, avoid doing it at the student's desk unless you can monitor the rest of the class from that position. If the student's seat is in the middle of the room, for instance, half of the class will be behind you. In such a case, call the student to a small-group worktable, to your desk, or to some other location from which you can easily see the students. Finally, when you work at your desk or at any other location, don't let students congregate around the area. They will obstruct your view of the class, and they will probably distract students seated nearby. Instead, call students to you one at a time.

Monitoring cooperative groups can present special challenges. To be sure each group understands your expectations, move quickly from group to group as students begin to work. Then stop and spend more time with each group, listening and occasionally contributing as a group member. In this way, you can gather information about the group's progress, provide a model for participation in a group, and help guide discussions to higher levels.

A critical monitoring task is checking assignments. Collect them regularly and look them over, even when students check their own work in class. Keep your grade book current so you will be able to detect students who skip assignments. If you give a long-term assignment, check progress regularly. You may even give a grade or assign points toward a grade at these times. In upper elementary grades, students can keep a checklist of assignments and due dates.

Because an important part of monitoring is checking student progress and understanding, build into your assignments ways to monitor these areas. For example, ask small groups to report on their progress; have individuals make and update daily or weekly work plans; follow up individual work time with brief discussions of concepts with oral checks for understanding. (See Chapter 5 for different ways of checking for understanding.)

Consistency

In the classroom, consistency means retaining the same expectations for appropriate behavior in a particular activity at all times and for all students. For example, if students are expected to work silently during independent work on Monday, the same procedure must be in effect on Tuesday, Wednesday, and the rest of the week. Penalties should also be applied consistently. For example, if the penalty for missing assignments is losing one's place on an honor list, the teacher must make sure that all students who skip assignments receive the penalty. This procedure should be followed even when it is inconvenient to administer and in spite of the pleading of individual students for exceptions. Obvious inconsistency in the use of procedures or in the application of penalties can cause confusion about what is acceptable behavior. Students then frequently "test the limits" by not following the procedure or by repeating whatever behavior evoked the penalty. These events can rapidly escalate and force the teacher either to abandon the procedure or to tolerate high levels of inappropriate behavior. Because neither outcome is desirable, avoid the problem by learning to be consistent from the start. Of course, it is not possible to be totally consistent; there are occasions when the most reasonable course of action is to make an exception to a rule or procedure. Thus, a deadline for an assignment may be extended when a student has a valid reason, or some procedures might be ignored during an emergency. Note that using certain procedures routinely for some activities but not for others is not inconsistent. For example, you may require that no students leave their seats without permission during discussions or presentations, but you may allow them to get materials, sharpen pencils, or turn in papers as needed without permission during individual work time. Differentiate between these activities when you explain the procedures to the students.

Undesirable inconsistency usually arises from three sources: First, the procedures or rules as presented are not reasonable, workable, or appropriate. Second, the teacher fails to monitor students closely and detects only a fraction of the inappropriate behavior. This creates the appearance of inconsistency. Third, the teacher may not feel strongly enough about the procedure or rule to enforce it or to use the associated penalty. If you find yourself being inconsistent in ways that cause problems, consider these alternatives:

1. Reteach the procedure. Take a few minutes to discuss the problem with the class and to reiterate your desire that they follow the procedure. Then enforce it.
2. Modify the procedure or consequence and then reintroduce and use it.
3. Abandon the procedure or consequence and possibly substitute another in its place.

Your choice of alternatives depends on circumstances and the importance of the issue to your classroom management system.

Management of Inappropriate Behavior

Inappropriate behavior must be handled promptly to keep it from continuing and spreading. Behaviors that you should be concerned about include lack of involvement in learning activities, prolonged inattention or work avoidance, and obvious violations of classroom rules and procedures. It is not a good idea to ignore such behavior. Prolonged inattention makes it difficult for the students to learn and to complete assignments, and violations of rules and failure to follow procedures create many problems we have already discussed. These behaviors should be dealt with directly but without overreaction. A calm, reasoned tone or approach is more productive and less likely to lead to confrontation. The following alternatives are recommended.

1. Make eye contact with or move closer to the student. Use a signal, such as a finger to the lips or a head shake, to prompt the appropriate behavior. Monitor until the student complies.

2. If the student is not following a procedure correctly, a simple reminder of the correct procedure may be effective. You can either state the correct procedure or ask the student whether he or she remembers it.

3. When the student is off-task—that is, not working on an assignment—redirect his or her attention to the task: "Sammy, you should be writing now," or "Cynthia,

the assignment is to complete all of the problems on the page." Check the student's progress shortly thereafter to make sure he or she is continuing to work.

4. Ask or tell the student to stop the inappropriate behavior. Then monitor until it stops and the student begins constructive activity.

Sometimes it is inconvenient or would interrupt the lesson flow to use these procedures immediately. If the behavior is not disruptive, or is not likely to spread to other students, make a mental note of the problem and continue the activity until a more appropriate time occurs. Then tell the student that you saw what was happening and discuss what the appropriate behavior should have been.

The four procedures outlined here are easy to use, cause little interruption of class activities, and enable students to correct their behavior. However, if a student persists in an unacceptable behavior, other alternatives should be used. If the rest of the class is working appropriately and does not need your immediate attention, a brief talk with the student may be sufficient. If that doesn't settle the matter, or if an immediate conference is not desirable or feasible, stop the child's behavior and assess whatever penalty is appropriate. Some teachers use a "time-out" desk or chair as a holding area for erring students. Note that the four procedures apply to relatively minor forms of misbehavior. Many additional measures for dealing with problem behaviors are described in Chapters 8 and 9.

Building a Positive Climate

This chapter emphasizes maintaining appropriate behavior by applying procedures and rules consistently, handling problems promptly, and using nonintrusive interventions when possible to maintain activity flow and student involvement in lessons. We now want to emphasize the importance of keeping a positive perspective and avoiding overdwelling on misbehavior or inadequacies. Sometimes teachers get caught in the trap of seeing only faults and problems and overlooking the better features of students' behavior. Instead of rejoicing when twenty-nine students are involved in learning, we complain about the one student who is off-task.

> Mr. Acerbic's sixth-grade physical education class could do nothing right. Although most of the students initially participated willingly in the class activities, students never seemed to perform quickly or well enough for their teacher. "Come on, you horseflies, quit buzzing and listen up," he would yell when he heard talking. "Laps" around the gym were given for even slight infractions such as brief inattention; there always seemed to be three or four students making the rounds at any given time. Instead of feedback about good performance, criticism was usually given for inadequacies. Although students took the constant carping in stride, they displayed little zest for the class.

Although poor performance should not be ignored—students need specific, corrective feedback to know what they need to improve—it is important that the climate for learning be positive. This means that students should look forward to the class. They should expect to learn, to receive assistance when they encounter difficulty, and to feel supported in their efforts. Teachers can foster such a climate by communicating positive expectations to students, by praising good performance, and, at times, by using additional rewards.

The teacher's expectations can be communicated in a variety of ways, some obvious and others subtle. (For a thorough description of this, see Good and Brophy 2003.) Teachers can do the following:

- Identify appropriate instructional goals and discuss them with students so that they are clear about what is expected.
- Insist that students complete work satisfactorily.
- Refuse to accept excuses for poor work.
- Communicate acceptance of imperfect initial performance when students struggle to achieve new learning.
- Convey confidence in the student's ability to do well.
- Display an encouraging "can do" attitude that generates excitement and self-confidence.
- Avoid comparative evaluations, especially of lower-ability students, that might cause them to conclude that they cannot accomplish the objectives.

By communicating positive expectations, you lay the foundation for students to attempt new tasks and reach new goals. When students know that their teacher believes them to be capable, they are more likely to try harder.

A positive climate for learning is also created by appropriate praise. When used well, the teacher's praise can be uplifting and provide great encouragement to a student. The most powerful type of praise provides the student with information about which aspect of performance is praiseworthy and also demonstrates that the teacher is impressed with the quality of the student's work. In other words, effective praise provides both informative feedback and genuine approval. It can also accompany suggestions for improvement (constructive criticism) without loss of effect.

For students from about the third grade and up, public praise that focuses on accomplishment works better than praise for effort. When teachers praise students for "working hard," many older elementary students are likely to assume that the teacher thinks they aren't very able. When you know that a student put forth considerable effort and you want to acknowledge it, be sure the praise also includes an emphasis on the student's achievement. "Gloria, all of your hard work paid off—your project was beautifully done. The organization of ideas and the extra details in the descriptions were outstanding!" Likewise, praise should be deserved and it should not be too easily obtained. Public praise of a student for success on an easy task can communicate to the rest of the class (and the student who was praised) that the teacher believes he or she has little ability.

It is a good idea to look for private ways to provide praise. Written comments on papers, tests, and other assignments and personal notes offer excellent opportunities for quality praise. Private conversations, conferences with parents, notes home, and informal contacts also offer opportunities for praising students. Private praise avoids some of the complications of public praise and permits the teacher to include a greater variety of performances and behaviors as the focus of praise. Further discussion of the uses of praise can be found in Emmer (1988) and Brophy (1981).

Improving Class Climate through Incentives and Rewards

Extra incentives and rewards can help build a positive climate. The improvement in class climate occurs because the incentives add interest or excitement to the class routine while also directing attention toward appropriate behavior and away from inappropriate behavior. Moreover, students are more likely to respond positively to the teacher, contributing to a mutually supportive pattern of interaction.

Rewards can have beneficial effects at some times, but they can have negative effects under certain circumstances. The following sections cover different types of rewards and incentives as well as cautionary guidelines regarding possible negative effects on student motivation.

Before using an added incentive, consider several factors that might affect its appropriateness and effects. Check your school or district policies, because sometimes certain incentives are prohibited, and you would not want to promise a field trip or party only to find out that it was not allowed. Your rewards should target the behaviors you would like to encourage. Rewards too easily earned or too difficult to achieve lose their motivational effect. Also, be concerned about whether the use of a reward takes too much class time for record keeping or other administrative tasks. Avoid using complex systems that distract you and your students from a focus on learning. Start with simple procedures, and add to them if that seems reasonable.

Be careful not to create incentives that only the most able students can achieve. Systems that encourage excessive competition for scarce rewards discourage students who don't believe they have much chance. The examples in this section and in the activities at the end of the chapter include a variety of types. Combine these ideas with those of other teachers and your own experience to create rewards for use at various times of the year.

Many types of rewards, including recognition, activities, symbols, and materials, can be used with elementary students. Let's look at each of these rewards and consider some examples.

Recognition

Recognition rewards involve a means of giving attention to the students. Examples are displaying student work; awarding a certificate for achievement, for improvement, or for good behavior; and orally citing accomplishments. Recognition rewards may be given on a weekly or monthly basis using a system such as "Super Stars of the Week," a class honor roll, or "Good Worker's Award." Be sure to explain the basis for awards—for example, good attendance, achievement, improvement, hard work, good conduct, or citizenship. The more specific you can be when describing the desired behavior, the more likely it is that you will obtain it.

Some teachers encourage competition among work teams or other groups. These competitions may be simple and short (for example, in a first-grade class, the teacher might say, "Let's see which table is ready first!"); at higher grade levels, competitions may run for a week, a month, or a grading term and may be based on behavior or a specific academic task. If competition among groups is encouraged, this fact should be kept in mind when the teacher forms the groups. Group composition should be balanced so that all groups have an equal chance to succeed. Competing for awards and prizes can be fun and spurs interest and effort.

Activities

Permitting or arranging for students to do something special or enjoyable constitutes giving an activity reward. Sometimes you can let students choose what this might be. If they have a voice in what the activities are, they are more likely to "buy in." Examples are privileges such as free-reading time, game time, visits to the school library, extra time on the computer, or appointment as a room monitor, game leader, or special helper.

When activity rewards are used as incentives for the whole class, students can participate in their identification and selection. Ideas for activity incentives can be solicited from students during a discussion, or the teacher might start with a short list and ask students to suggest additions to it; either way, the class can vote for a favorite. Some whole-class activities that might be used as incentives include watching a videotape, fifteen minutes of free time, playing a game, listening to music, having a popcorn party, or no homework. A group activity reward should be made contingent on specific desirable behaviors; if the group cooperates, they receive the incentive. If not, they lose some or all of the time in the activity. Because the purpose of using an activity reward is, in part, to promote positive climate building, don't let one or two students spoil the fun for the rest of the class. A chronically uncooperative student can be invited to participate but can be excluded from the reward if he or she persists in noncompliance. In most cases, positive peer pressure encourages such a student to cooperate without the teacher's having to resort to exclusion.

Symbols

Elementary teachers use a variety of symbols to communicate a positive evaluation of student work. Examples include letter grades and numerical scores, happy faces, checks and check pluses, and stars and stickers with an appealing design. At all elementary grade levels, the teacher's positive evaluation and written comments are a source of satisfaction for students. For younger children, especially, this reward should be provided as soon as possible after they complete a task and on a daily basis. Assignments in the early grades can usually be checked quickly, so there is no reason to delay feedback. One effective procedure for checking assignments such as worksheets, writing, or math is to have the children place them on a corner of their desks when finished. As you circulate through the room, you can check completed assignments, write an E, put a star, check, or other symbol on the paper, and praise good effort, correctly done work, or neatness.

In the upper grades, where assignments are sometimes more complex or some-what lengthy, you are more likely to collect assigned work to check it and record the grades in your grade book. Acquire a box of stars or other stickers, or buy hand stamps with a happy face or other symbols to supplement your numerical or letter grades. Be liberal in your use of these. Reward improvement and good effort so that all students have access to these incentives. Obviously, you should not reward poor performance, but do give feedback and encouragement so the student can improve.

In addition to their use for daily feedback, symbols are also used on report cards. Elementary-grade children, even first graders, place a positive value on high grades (or "lots of E's"), and it is not uncommon to hear young children compar-ing report card grades. However, most first or second graders are not likely to have a clear conception of a specific relationship between daily work and long-term grades. Consequently, report card grades are not particularly useful incentives for encouraging young children to complete daily work. In the upper elementary grades, however, students are better able to understand a connection between their effort on daily assignments and the grades they receive in particular subjects. There-fore, it is a good idea to explain your grading policies to these children so they will understand that the value you place on good effort and performance on daily work will translate into a report card grade. However, do not expect report card grades to be the major source of motivation for most students; plan to rely more on the daily use of symbols, positive feedback to students, and other rewards.

Material Incentives

Material incentives are objects of value to students. Examples include food, a pen-cil or eraser, discarded classroom materials, games, toys, and books. You must con-sider your own financial circumstances as well as school policy before deciding to use such rewards.

A procedure combining several types of rewards is the use of an honor roll sys-tem (an all-star list, super stars, gold record club) or competition among groups or teams in conjunction with other incentives. Badges, stickers with appealing designs, food treats, activity privileges, or a party can be used as rewards along with the recog-nition of being an award winner. It is best to spread the honors around and include a good portion of the class. Do not give awards only for outstanding achievement; have awards for improvement, excellent effort, good conduct, and so on.

A major consideration in the use of rewards is their feasibility. Some rewards require a great deal of planning, record keeping, or other preparation. Other rewards require little preparation or effort. Examples are giving positive verbal feedback, placing a symbol or other positive comment on an assignment sheet, and awarding simple privileges such as leading the line to lunch, passing out materials, taking up papers, and being a room monitor.

Between the two extremes of much effort and little effort are a large number of rewards that require a modest amount of the teacher's time or effort. These include things such as awarding free time for reading, play, computer time, or games; sending home a positive note to parents; awarding prizes such as a pencil with the school name on it; allowing extra time in the library or for some other activity; and establishing an honor roll or "Super Star" list, but don't try too much too soon. Start with simple procedures and add to them if you can. The examples at the end of the chapter illustrate a number of possibilities.

Caution in the Use of Rewards

Some researchers (e.g., Deci, Koestner, & Ryan 1999) have urged caution in the use of extrinsic rewards by pointing out that in many cases their use erodes students' intrinsic motivation to engage in the activity that is rewarded. Rewards that are expected, tangible, and related to task performance generally interfere with both the *process* and the *quality* of learning.

These researchers point to the difference between rewards that are expected or unexpected, tangible or verbal/symbolic, and task contingent or performance contingent. In general, they found that expected, tangible, and task-contingent rewards had a negative effect on a student's inner motivation and caused a shift of attention away from the content to be learned, the challenge to a student's natural curiosity, and a desire to be competent. Further, frequent use of these types of rewards may result in passive learning and undermine creativity instead of supporting the teacher's goal of developing self-regulation, deep understanding, and appreciation of knowledge and skill. In other words, students expecting a reward, consciously or unconsciously, may be working primarily for the reward.

Teachers need to differentiate between rewards given to control or shape behavior and those designed as feedback to student competence or that support a sense of mastery (Reeve in press). If the teacher's objective is to control student behavior through prizes or other extrinsic rewards, students may comply with specific standards. However, they may not develop a sense of self-regulation or an appreciation of the need for competence.

Not all rewards are perceived to have this dampening effect. Those tied to progress, competence, or a sense of mastery may actually increase inner motivation and validate a student's sense of personal ability. Praise, symbols, or prizes should be tied as specifically as possible to positive behavior. The informational aspect of the reward also is important and nurtures students' inner motivation.

The most reasonable application of the research results for classroom use of rewards is to be thoughtful about their use. No purpose is served by rewarding activities that are already highly interesting to students. In fact, the evidence suggests that to do so reduces motivation. However, many classroom tasks are not highly interesting, especially those in which extensive repetition is needed to produce skilled performance and learning. When student motivation flags, external incentives may be necessary to maintain engagement.

Finally, when rewards are used, the teacher can counteract the potentially negative effects on intrinsic motivation by pointing out to students the usefulness of the skill to be learned, by choosing materials and activities that have high potential for sustaining interest, and by modeling and demonstrating personal interest and enthusiasm for the task.

Further Reading

Brophy, J. E. (2004). *Motivating students to learn.* (2nd ed.). Hillsdale, N.J.: Erlbaum.

This very readable book addresses teachers directly and offers strategies and principles to use in motivating students to learn. Based on the author's research on motivation and effective teaching practices, the book identifies parts of the literature that are most relevant to teachers, summarizes research in everyday language, and provides helpful examples with an eye toward the complexities of the classroom setting.

Burden, P. R. (2000). *Powerful classroom management strategies: Motivating students to learn.* Thousand Oaks, Calif.: Corwin Press/Sage.

This teacher-friendly publication describes the varieties of motivation accessible to educators for use in the classroom. Throughout the reading, the author has provided first-hand accounts from practicing teachers that highlight the text discussion. Planning, assessment, and working with the hard-to-reach student are also covered in this book.

Freiberg, H. Jerome (1996). From tourists to citizens in the classroom. *Educational Leadership, 54,* 32–36.

An emphasis on creating a positive classroom climate characterizes this article. Based on research he has conducted, Freiberg recommends increasing student participation in rule setting, allowing students to volunteer for classroom jobs, and making the school a more caring and personal place.

Mueller, C. M., & Dweck, C. S. (1998). Praise for intelligence can undermine children's motivation for performance. *Journal of Personality and Social Psychology, 75*(1), 33–52.

Through a series of six studies, the authors demonstrate that students who receive positive feedback based on their effort continue to exert effort in learning. These students associate struggles with a lack of effort, therefore exerting more. Students who receive positive feedback based on their intelligence seek to continue looking smart and may choose activities with less challenge. These students associate struggles with lack of ability and, therefore, may not make further attempts.

Raffini, J. P. (1996). *150 ways to increase intrinsic motivation in the classroom.* Boston: Allyn & Bacon.

Many useful strategies are presented in this compendium of classroom activities designed to enhance motivation. Teachers looking for alternative ways to build classroom climate will find Chapters 4 and 6 especially relevant.

Reeve, J., Bolt, E., & Cai, Y. (1999). Autonomy-supportive teachers: How they teach and motivate students. *Journal of Educational Psychology, 91*(3), 537–548.

The authors examine motivating style in terms of a teacher's disposition to control students or support their autonomy. Autonomy-supportive teachers show a distinctive motivating style measured by their conversational behaviors, interpersonal style, and attempts to support students' intrinsic motivational and internalization processes.

Strengthening student engagement [Special issue] (1995). *Educational Leadership, 53*(1) 1–69.

This issue of the journal Educational Leadership *contains several articles that focus on maintaining involvement in the classroom. Topics in the issue include the use of rewards, student views of schoolwork, strategies for engaging students in specific content areas, and cultural factors in improving classroom climate.*

Suggested Activities

1. In Problem 7.1 Ms. Greene is encountering problems maintaining her management system. Use the information in this and previous chapters to diagnose her problems and to suggest what she can do to improve student behavior. Refer to the key in the Appendix for other suggestions.

2. Read Examples 7.1 through 7.4 and consider how you might adapt these descriptions of reward systems to your own classroom. Analyze each example using the following questions as the starting point:

   a. What teacher and student roles are encouraged?

   b. Is the system primarily intrinsic or extrinsic?

   c. Is the system cooperative or competitive?

   d. What kind of classroom environment is the system likely to foster?

3. Find out about school policies that will affect your use of rewards. Also, note any schoolwide system that you will have to incorporate in your own classroom procedures.

4. Review Checklists 2 and 3 in Chapters 2 and 3 and identify the rewards you intend to use with your major conduct and accountability procedures. By planning ahead, you will be better able to explain these incentives and be consistent in their use.

5. How can you help students see the intrinsic rewards in activities in your classroom?

   ■ *Example 7.1: Shoot for the Moon* Mrs. Li used a reward system called "Shoot for the Moon" to give feedback to second-grade students for behavioral and academic performance. She decorated a large bulletin board with blue paper, a large round moon, a few clouds, and a title, "Shoot for the Moon." Each child's name was written on a small construction paper spaceship. The spaceships were lined up at the bottom of the bulletin board at the start. At the beginning of the year, Mrs. Li discussed with her class the kinds of behaviors that would result in the movement of each spaceship closer to the moon. Daily completion of assignments and good behavior in the classroom, at lunch, and on the playground would result in the spaceship's moving two inches closer to the moon. For bad behavior (such as misbehavior in the lunchroom or during instruction, not working in class, or not turning in an assignment), a student's spaceship would be moved one inch away from the moon. When students reached the moon, they were rewarded by being able to keep their spaceships decorated with a star. The teacher then started another spaceship for them at the bottom of the board. Sometimes students were required to reach the moon by a certain deadline to get a special reward such as a privilege or a popcorn party. Mrs. Li was consistent in rewarding appropriate behavior each day and in penalizing inappropriate behaviors, and she also occasionally rewarded individual students for being especially quiet or helpful or for improving their work or grades. This worked well with students who had particular behavior or academic problems.

   ■ *Example 7.2: Regular Feedback* Ms. Harmony's first-grade class functioned smoothly and productively without many obvious rewards and penalties. Although she only occasionally rewarded individuals or groups with public compliments, Ms. Harmony maintained a high level of student involvement through interesting, well-paced lessons and assignments with a high level of student success and by promptly returning assignments and giving students feedback regarding their work. She dealt with inappropriate behavior by brief verbal correction of students or short private conferences with individuals inside the classroom. Often she simply mentioned what the student should be doing if all the rest of his or her work was finished. Ms. Harmony made extensive use of telephone contacts with parents to inform them of their children's progress and particularly to identify when a student was not completing assignments satisfactorily. She did this frequently during the first few months of the school year, with long-lasting results.

■ *Example 7.3: A Token Exchange System* Mr. Young used a variety of strategies, some simple and some elaborate, for encouraging appropriate behavior in his third-grade class. Throughout the year, he used a system in which the class as a whole earned blue chips for good behavior and red chips for poor behavior. When a monthly goal for the number of blue chips was reached, the class was rewarded with a treat or special privilege. Goals and rewards escalated during the course of the year, beginning with a class party at the end of the first month. During each day, blue chips were dropped into a container for various appropriate behaviors— two for good behavior during the time a visitor was in the room, ten for each satisfactory cleanup, one for each student who had completed his or her individual contract work by the end of the day, and so on. Red chips were dropped into the container for excessive noise, throwing trash on the floor, bad behavior on the way to lunch, or other transgressions. Shaking the can that contained the chips was often used to signal that there was too much talking or misbehaving and that failure to become quiet would result in another red chip. At the end of the day, red chips were counted, and an equal number of blue chips were deducted from the blue chip collection.

In addition to the chip system, Mr. Young complimented good workers aloud, sometimes let best-behaved or best-prepared students line up first, put names of cooperative students on the board under a "Super People" title, and awarded happy faces to students who did all of their work that day.

6. Read Example 7.4 and review what research has to say about expected, tangible and task-contingent rewards. What message is Ms. Woodmore sending regarding her expectations of her students' academic and personal behavior?

■ *Example 7.4: Token Reward System for Grades 4–6* In Ms. Woodmore's class, students were issued a "credit card" on the first day of school. Each day they were able to earn three dollars of credit: one dollar for being at school on time, one for turning in all work for the day, and one for receiving no more than one warning about misbehavior. At the end of the day, Ms. Woodmore recorded the number of dollars each student had earned. On the last day of the marking period, Ms. Woodmore held an auction. Students bid based on the accumulated dollars in their accounts. Items for sale at the auction included prizes donated by parents, books, pens, free homework passes, computer passes, and a pizza lunch to be shared with a friend. There were enough prizes in the auction for every student to get a prize. Dollars not spent could be "rolled over" to the next six weeks.

PROBLEM 7.1

MISBEHAVIOR IN A THIRD-GRADE CLASS

Ms. Greene's third-grade students never seem to settle down. Regardless of whether the children have been assigned independent work or are supposed to be paying attention to a presentation, some degree of commotion or noise is always present. During the first few days of school, the class seemed well-behaved and was seldom out of order, and almost all of the children were cooperative and did their work. Gradually, however, more and more inappropriate socializing, loud talk, call-outs, and other interruptions occurred, even from previously quiet students.

During Ms. Greene's presentations to the class, students are frequently inattentive, and she is able to complete lessons only with difficulty. Sometimes she even stops lessons short because the children are so difficult to control. At times, the only way she can restore a semblance of quiet is to start writing names on the board and assigning detention. However, even that tactic doesn't work for long because so many students are inattentive that the list of names gets very long and not being on the list becomes something of a social stigma.

During a recent reading-group period, three students talked continuously while Ms. Greene was working with one of the small groups. Two other children wandered around the room and a half-dozen others made frequent trips to the drinking fountain, restrooms, and hamster cages.

What has gone wrong in this class? How might Ms. Greene attempt to gain better cooperation from her students?

8

Communication Skills for Teaching

Throughout this book, we have emphasized classroom management's preventive and instructional aspects. Not all problems can be prevented, however, and sometimes unobtrusive handling of inappropriate behavior during instruction is not sufficient. The approaches described in this chapter provide additional means for dealing with persistent problems. This example illustrates such a situation:

> During the past several days, Debra and Diane have been increasingly inattentive in Ms. Harris's fifth-grade class. Their off-task behavior has included whispering with other students and each other, teasing boys seated nearby, and displaying exaggerated boredom with class discussions. Ms. Harris first asked the girls to stop bothering the class, and when that had no effect, she moved the girls to different seats. However, Debra and Diane continued to disrupt by passing notes and calling out loudly to one another.

We will not second-guess Ms. Harris by wondering whether she had communicated expectations clearly or had taken action promptly enough: Let us suppose that she had, in fact, practiced good preventive management skills, but the students misbehaved anyway. No strategy works all the time! What options are now available to Ms. Harris to deal with the situation? Possible approaches include the following:

- Ignore the problem and hope it goes away.
- Refer the students to the principal.
- Call the students' parents and ask for their help.
- Apply a consequence, such as detention or some other punishment.

Each of these approaches has advantages and limitations. For example, ignoring the problem requires little effort and might work if the students are mainly seeking the teacher's attention. The description does not, however, suggest that this is a likely reason for the behavior, and ignoring may only allow it to intensify and spread to other students. Referral has the advantage of taking little of the teacher's time, at least in the short run; it also temporarily removes the disruptive students, and it can have deterrent value. However, it may do nothing in the long run to deal with the problem the students are causing in the class, and although referral may sometimes be a reasonable approach to serious misbehavior, it can easily be overused.

A telephone call to parents sometimes works wonders and is usually worth a try. However, parents cannot always stop misbehavior. They do not, after all, accompany their child to your class, nor do they control the cues that are eliciting the misbehavior. Punishing the students by assigning detention or withholding some desirable activity or privilege is another possible reaction. Punishment, as discussed in Chapter 9, can stop misbehavior temporarily, and it can deter other students. But punishment can have the disadvantages of creating hostility or resentment and of trapping the teacher and students in a cycle of misbehavior–reaction that leads to power struggles. By itself, punishment does little to teach the student self-control and responsibility.

Because each of these approaches has limitations, you need additional means of coping with problems. This does not mean that other approaches such as ignoring, referral, applying consequences, or involving parents will be supplanted. It does mean that communication strategies should be added to your repertoire to deal with problems that cannot be corrected with minor interventions and to help students learn to take responsibility for their own behavior.

In addition to being helpful in dealing with students whose behavior is creating a problem for the teacher or for other students, using communication skills can assist students who are themselves experiencing problems. Teachers frequently become aware of student problems caused by factors both inside and outside the classroom. Sometimes, teachers can help students by being good listeners and by encouraging them to consider alternative ways to solve problems or to adapt to difficult situations.

We use the label *communication skills* for the set of strategies described in this chapter to emphasize that the approach focuses on communicating clearly and effectively with others to help bring about a change in their behavior, in their thinking, or in the situation that has caused the problem. But communication also means being open to information, so teachers also have to be good listeners and try to understand the student's (or parents') concerns and feelings. To become an effective communicator, three related skills are needed:

1. **Constructive assertiveness:** Describe your concerns clearly, insist that misbehavior be corrected, and resist being coerced or manipulated.
2. **Empathic responding:** Listen to the student's perspective and react in ways that maintain a positive relationship and encourage further discussion.
3. **Problem solving:** This component includes several steps for reaching mutually satisfactory resolutions to problems; it requires working with the student to develop a plan for change.

The three elements are derived from a variety of sources, including Kottler's *Students Who Drive You Crazy* (2002), Glasser's *Reality Therapy* (1975), Alberti's *Assertiveness* (1977), Zuker's *Mastering Assertiveness Skills* (1983), and others. The treatment of communication skills in this chapter is an introduction; if you are interested in further reading, one or more of the cited books would be helpful.

Although this chapter's treatment of assertiveness, empathic responding, and problem solving focuses on their use with students, the skills are helpful when dealing with parents—especially during parent conferences—and with other adults. Thus, the skills described here have a variety of applications and can improve your effectiveness in handling many classroom and school-related situations.

◎ FOR REFLECTION

Most teachers are sensitive to, or self-conscious about, some aspect of their image or background. Height, weight, appearance, content knowledge, inexperience, marital status, and acceptance or respect are among the areas that may be a source of insecurity or concern. Because teaching is such a public event, and because students are astute observers of teachers' reactions, teachers often

(continued)

reveal much of themselves in their reactions when their students find the right "button" to "push." Think about an area that represents a source of insecurity to you. Consider how your communication with students may be affected if a student pushes that button.

Constructive Assertiveness

Assertiveness is the ability to stand up for one's legitimate rights in ways that help ensure that others cannot ignore or circumvent them. The adjective *constructive* means that the assertive teacher does not deride or attack the student. Assertiveness is a general characteristic or attribute that we use in a wide variety of settings or as a set of skills that are more situation specific. Some individuals are assertive in a variety of settings (e.g., interacting with strangers, on the job, at parties, in school), whereas others lack assertiveness in many social situations.

Even if you are not generally assertive, you can learn to use assertive behaviors while you are teaching. In fact, doing so may generalize to other situations as you become more confident of your skills. People who are very unassertive (e.g., feel extremely nervous whenever they are expected to lead a group; are unable to begin conversations or to make eye contact with others; accede to inappropriate demands readily; are unable to ask others to respect their rights) find teaching uncomfortable and have particular difficulty with discipline. Such people can help themselves in several ways, especially by reading about assertiveness and practicing some of the skills, preferably in situations that are not too uncomfortable, until they begin to develop more confidence. It is also possible to obtain professional help, such as from a counseling center, or to enroll in a course or workshop on assertiveness training. A good training program usually includes cognitive restructuring to reshape negative thought patterns that interfere with appropriate social interaction, anxiety-reduction exercises, and skills training and practice to develop more effective behaviors.

The elements of assertiveness include:

- A clear statement of the problem or issue
- Unambiguous body language
- Insistence on appropriate behavior and resolution of the problem

Assertiveness is not

- Hostile or aggressive
- Argumentative
- Inflexible

Assertiveness lies on a continuum of social response between aggressive, overbearing pushiness and timid, ineffectual, or submissive responses that allow some students to trample on the teacher's and other students' rights. Assertiveness skills allow you to communicate to students that you are serious about teaching and about maintaining a classroom in which everyone's rights are respected. Assertiveness does not limit or hamper teachers' and students' caring for one another.

Following are aspects of constructive assertiveness that have special importance for teachers.

Stating the Problem or Concern

Student misbehavior usually causes problems for teachers by making it difficult to conduct lessons, by slowing down activities, by subverting routines that help a class run smoothly, and by distracting other students from their work. When misbehavior persists, the teacher must let the student know what the problem is, from the teacher's point of view. Sometimes just a simple description of the problem results in students' changing their behavior because they become more aware and begin to monitor themselves better. Stating the problem has two parts, (1) identifying the behavior and (2) describing its effects, as in the following examples:

> "Loud conversations in the library corner distract other students."
> "Please raise your hand so that I can call on you."
> "Wandering around the room disturbs the class."
> "Calling other students names causes hard feelings."

By focusing on the behavior and its effects, you can reduce the potential for student defensiveness and keep open the chance for a satisfactory resolution to the situation. Conducting the conference privately (e.g., after class or during a conference period) when possible lessens the potential for embarrassing the student in front of peers and reduces the likelihood of a confrontation or power struggle that challenges the teacher's authority. However, sometimes you will be forced to act immediately.

Notice that the problem descriptions do not label students or their behavior; that is, students are not accused of being bad, rude, and annoying or behaving in an inconsiderate and stupid manner. Such labeling, whether for a student or the student's behavior, impedes behavior change by suggesting that a student's behavior is a permanent characteristic that the student might accept as valid. Notice also that statements rather than questions are used. Quizzing students (e.g., "Why are you talking?" "Do you think that you should be calling someone that name?") invites defensive, sarcastic, or oppositional responses that lead to arguments.

Body Language

Constructive assertiveness with students needs the visual reinforcement of appropriate body language in three areas. The first is making eye contact when addressing the student, especially when describing the problem and when calling for behavior change. Note that there is a difference between eye contact that communicates seriousness and resolve and an angry, hostile glare. Breaking eye contact from time to time relieves tension. A second area of assertive body language is maintaining an alert posture and body orientation toward the student (but not so close as to be threatening). Maintaining an erect posture and facing the student communicates your attention and involvement in the conversation. A third area is matching your facial expressions with the content and tone of your statements (e.g., not smiling when making serious statements).

Obtaining Appropriate Behavior

Assertiveness requires that the teacher not be diverted from insisting on appropriate behavior. Students may engage in diversionary tactics in several ways: by denying involvement, by arguing, and by blaming others (including the teacher). When dealing with such tactics, remember: There are many reasons, but no excuses, for misbehavior. Although it is possible that others contributed to the problem, the student must accept responsibility for his or her own behavior. Listen carefully to understand the student's point of view, but in the end, if the student's behavior is interfering with your ability to teach, the behavior must change. Thus, if a student begins to argue or to deny responsibility for the behavior, avoid being sidetracked; the bottom line is that the student's behavior is not acceptable, whatever the reason for it.

Being an assertive teacher means that you let students know your concerns and wants in a manner that gets their attention and communicates your intent to carry through with consequences and to deal with the situation until it is resolved. You don't have to lose your sense of humor or treat students impolitely. A little humor can reduce tension, and treating students with courtesy models the kind of behavior you expect of them. Developing a level of assertiveness that is comfortable for you and understanding how your behavior is perceived by others are important; working through the activities at the end of this chapter will help.

Empathic Responding

Another important communication skill is responding empathically to students. This skill shows that you are aware and accepting of the student's perspective, as well as willing to seek clarification of it when necessary. Empathic responding helps keep the lines of communication open between you and your students so that problems can be understood and resolved in mutually acceptable ways. Such skills are especially appropriate when a student seems excessively concerned, under stress, or otherwise upset. As a teacher, you have to be able to respond in a manner that helps students deal constructively with those emotions or at least avoids further discomfort or distress. Empathic responding can also be used as a part of the problem-solving process when dealing with students who must change their behavior. In such situations, students may be resistant and express negative feelings; the teacher's empathic response can then help defuse these reactions and increase the acceptance of a plan for change.

Empathic responding complements constructive assertiveness. Whereas assertiveness allows teachers to express their wants, empathic responding solicits and affirms the student's viewpoint. The use of empathic responding skills does not imply that misbehaving students are entitled to "do their thing" without regard for others; rather, the purpose is to understand and take into account the student's views to reach a satisfactory solution. If the teacher shows some openness toward the student's perspective, there is a better chance that the student will make a commitment to change. Conversely, a teacher who shows no interest in the student's feelings is more likely to encounter defiant behavior and an unwillingness to cooperate or to accept responsibility.

Compare the following two episodes.

Episode A

STUDENT: I'm not staying. You can't make me.
TEACHER: You'll have to stay after school. You haven't completed your work.
STUDENT: No, I can't stay.
TEACHER: That's life. If you don't serve your time now, it's doubled. That's the rule.
STUDENT: (Angry) I'm leaving.
TEACHER: You'd better not.
STUDENT: I'm going! (Student leaves.)

In Episode A the teacher's response does nothing to resolve the situation. It's likely that the student is aware of the consequences of skipping detention, so the argument only provokes a confrontation, which the student wins, at least temporarily, by leaving.

Here is another way to handle the same situation:

Episode B

STUDENT: I'm not staying. You can't make me.
TEACHER: It's true, I can't. It's up to you.
STUDENT: I can't stay.
TEACHER: Staying after school is a problem for you?
STUDENT: I have to be at home right away.
TEACHER: So it would be a problem for you to get home late.
STUDENT: Right, we're going somewhere after school today.
TEACHER: That's a difficult situation. Would you like to talk about what you could do?
STUDENT: Okay.

In Episode B the teacher avoids arguing with the student and instead acknowledges the student's concern and invites further discussion. The student responds to the teacher's approach by stating his or her concern more explicitly. Notice that the teacher's role in this conference is that of listener or helper rather than opponent. Notice, too, that the teacher does not offer to solve the student's problem by dropping the detention penalty. Instead, the student is led to consider what options are available. Of course, there is no guarantee that the situation will be resolved to everyone's satisfaction. But the approach at least offers the possibility of resolution, and it avoids the confrontation that occurred in Episode A. Further, it maintains the student's responsibility for dealing with the situation rather than giving the student yet another excuse for avoiding responsibility.

Empathic responding has several advantages. It provides the teacher with a way to deal with a student's strong emotions without taking responsibility for solving the student's problems. At the same time, the strategy helps defuse an emotionally charged situation. Intense feelings are often transient and persist only when fed by an intense response. By not reciprocating with similar emotional intensity, the teacher avoids fueling the fire. Also, the calm, empathic teacher serves as a good model for constructive problem solving.

Empathic responding has two components: listening skills and processing skills.

Listening Skills

Listening skills acknowledge or accept the student's feelings or ideas. At a minimal level, the listener merely indicates attention. Sometimes an interested look encourages the student to continue speaking. Other examples of nonverbal listening behaviors are nodding, making eye contact with the speaker, and other body language that communicates openness to discussion. Verbal encouragement is indicated by utterances such as "Um hm," "I see," "Go on," "That's interesting," and the like. At other times, a little more encouragement may be needed. A child who expresses feelings of rejection or discouragement and who needs reassurance may respond to a friendly touch, a pat on the shoulder, or a hug. Beyond this level of response, the teacher can invite more discussion with statements such as, "Tell me more," "I'm interested in hearing your ideas about this," "Would you care to comment?" "What do you think?," and "You've listened to my opinion. I'd like to listen to yours."

Processing Skills

Processing skills allow you to confirm or clarify your perception of the student's message. Consider the following interchanges and identify the one that would be most likely to lead to further discussion:

STUDENT: I can't do this assignment.
TEACHER (A): You're having difficulty?
TEACHER (B): Come on, try harder—you'll get it done.

STUDENT: (Tearful) I hate Angela. She's not my friend anymore.
TEACHER (A): It's upsetting to lose a friend.
TEACHER (B): Don't be silly. She's your best friend. Just tell her you're sorry.

In these interchanges, the A responses are more accepting of the student's feelings, whereas the B responses ignore the student's emotional tone and tend to block further communication. The B comments are judgmental and suggest a solution without obtaining enough information about the situation and without giving the students the opportunity to deal with their own problems.

To process a student's comments, you can repeat or summarize what the student says. If the student has given multiple messages or a confusing array of statements, select what seems to be most important and paraphrase it. This paraphrase can simply be stated back, or you can "reflect" or "bounce back" the paraphrase as a question. Whichever you do, the student usually either acknowledges the correctness of your perception or offers clarification or elaboration. Consider the following interchange from a short afterschool conference:

STUDENT: I hate this place. School is stupid!

TEACHER: Would you like to talk about it?

STUDENT: I just don't like it here.

TEACHER: There's something about school that bothers you.

STUDENT: (*Crying*) Yes. Sean and Billy laugh at me.

TEACHER: (*Puts arm around student*) You feel sad because they're making fun of you?

STUDENT: Yes.

TEACHER: Can you tell me about that?

STUDENT: They call me stupid and dummy.

TEACHER: It hurts a lot to be called those names. Are you worried that they really think that about you?

STUDENT: No. I'm not dumb.

TEACHER: You're not, and I'm glad you don't think so. I don't think so either. Would you like to talk about what to do when someone calls you a name or makes fun of you?

In this example, the teacher uses a variety of responses with an unhappy student and progresses to the point at which the student can express, at least partially, the basis for the feelings. The teacher then offers to help the student learn how to deal with the problem. Although it is not realistic to expect that major problems will be resolved by a single empathic interchange, it is not unusual for the sharp edge of negative emotions to be blunted and for the conversation to end on a positive note. At the least, the student knows that an adult cares enough to listen, and the teacher is in a better position to guide the student in the future.

The skills of empathic responding—both listening and processing—have been presented in the context of interactions with an individual student, but they are also helpful when problems arise in group settings. Using these tactics helps prevent teachers from responding defensively when students react emotionally or express a problem during class. They also "buy time" for the teacher to consider alternatives for dealing with a problem. In addition, listening and processing skills are useful for leading group discussions and for interacting with parents.

Although empathic responding skills are very helpful in some situations, they are not the primary means of dealing with students who are acting out, breaking class rules, or interfering with other students. Such misbehavior has to be dealt with using approaches discussed in Chapters 7 and 9 and in the other sections of this chapter. However, listening and processing will support these other measures.

Another limitation of empathic listening skills is choosing the right time and place to use them. It would be awkward, to say the least, to respond empathically to every expression of emotion or opinion during class activities. Such reactivity would cause slowdowns and undermine your students' attention. How frequently and in which circumstances you use these skills depends on a variety of factors, including opportunities, your goals and values, and how competent you feel. At the least, develop your skills so you are able to respond empathically in situations in which the use of the skills is helpful. Doing so effectively requires practice and observation, and working through the activities at the end of the chapter can help.

Problem Solving

Problem solving is a process that is used to deal with and to resolve conflicts. Conflicts arise between teachers and students because different roles give rise to different needs and because individuals have different goals and interests. In a crowded classroom, diverse paths can cross, and individuals can find themselves at odds with one another. If conflict arises, teachers need a way to manage it constructively so that teaching and learning can continue in a supportive classroom climate. An effective means of accomplishing this is the problem-solving process in which the teacher works with the student to develop a plan to reduce or eliminate the problem. Steps in the problem-solving process include (1) identifying the problem, (2) discussing alternative solutions, and (3) obtaining a commitment to try one of them. Depending on circumstances, problem solving may also include attempts to identify the causes of the problem and may specify the consequences of following or not following the plan. Because it generally requires more than a brief intervention, problem solving is usually conducted during a conference with the students it concerns. Often, the skills of constructive assertiveness and empathic responding are helpful in reaching an agreement for solving the problem.

Problem-solving conferences are usually reserved for chronic situations that have not yielded to simpler remedies. Action must be taken to stop the behavior because allowing it to continue would interfere with your ability to teach, with other students' opportunities to learn, or with the student's long-term functioning in your class or school. Consider the following examples:

1. Brad likes to be the center of attention. Whenever you ask a question, he calls out the answer without raising his hand and with no regard for the fact that you have already called on another student. Although you have reminded him of correct behavior and have tried to ignore his call-outs, the behavior continues to interfere with your class discussions.

2. Alice and Alicia never seem to clean up materials, supplies, or their work areas when they have finished a project or assignment. They resent your reminders and insistence that they observe class procedures, but unless you monitor them closely, they avoid all responsibilities. Lately, they have been arguing and complaining whenever they are asked to complete a task. Their foot-dragging seemed trivial at first, but it has become a constant source of irritation.

3. Terrence has skipped his last three arithmetic assignments, even though you allowed ample time in class to work on them. He seems to have a lackadaisical attitude about academic work, and he uses his time in class for goofing off whenever he can get away with it. Twice last week, he was kept in from recess to work on his

missing assignments, but he did not finish them, and he resented the loss of his midmorning break. During the previous grading period, he had several unsatisfactory grades on his report card, and skipping assignments is sure to prevent his making satisfactory progress in learning arithmetic skills.

Each of these examples illustrates a situation that has reached a stage at which a problem-solving conference might be useful. In each case, routine interventions have not changed the student's behavior; in each case, more of the same teacher response is likely to result in a continuing power struggle or in a deterioration in the student's ability to behave constructively.

What is evident in the three examples is that the students are not accepting responsibility for their behavior. It may be that what is needed is a stronger consequence (i.e., a penalty) that is clearly tied to the misbehavior. In fact, this strategy can be an alternative discussed with the student during a problem-solving conference. But until the student makes a commitment to change the offending behavior, the use of punishment will probably be perceived as coercive and controlling rather than as a natural consequence of the behavior and thus may do little or no good. It also appears that the basis of the problem in each of the three examples is not totally clear. Why won't Brad wait his turn? Why can't Alicia and Alice follow simple clean-up procedures? Is Terrence having difficulty understanding the content, or is some external problem the source of his reluctance to do his work? Giving the students a chance to discuss their situations might provide insights that would lead to better solutions. It would also permit the teacher and students to become more aware of each other's perceptions and possibly prevent the development of additional problems.

Steps in a problem-solving conference are described next.

STEP 1: Identify the problem. You can begin the discussion by stating the purpose of the meeting and asking the student to express his or her viewpoint. Obtaining the student's views gives you useful information for later steps, and it also enables you to gauge the student's degree of cooperation and understanding of the situation. An alternative opening is to describe the problem yourself and ask the student for a reaction; this alternative is especially needed when dealing with young children, with students having limited verbal skills, and with evasive and dissembling students. Unless the student's attitude is cooperative, you must be assertive in expressing your concerns. As explained earlier, this can be done by describing, without labeling, the behavior of concern and the problem it is causing. You may also have to stress that the problem will not be allowed to continue and that something must be done to solve it.

Glasser (1975) recommends asking students to evaluate whether their behavior is helping or hurting them or has good or bad effects. The logic is that a student who understands and admits that a behavior has negative consequences is more likely to participate in the search for and commitment to a solution. A student who denies responsibility or who sees no harmful effects seldom makes a meaningful commitment to change. It may be helpful to ask such a student what might happen if the behavior continues.

During this initial phase of the conference, students may react defensively or emotionally, and they may try to avoid responsibility by blaming others, arguing, citing extenuating circumstances, and so forth. When such behavior occurs, you must decide whether the student's reactions are primarily for the purpose of evading responsibility or whether they have some validity. If the latter is the case, you can use listening and processing skills to respond. This communicates your willingness to hear the student's point of view and may increase subsequent cooperation. By modeling such desirable behavior, you encourage its use by the student. A disadvantage of using empathic responding during this phase of problem solving is that the student's excuses, arguments, and extenuating circumstances may simply be a means of avoiding responsibility. Because you do not want to get sidetracked from the issue that brought the student to the conference in the first place, be sure to return the focus to the main problem after the student's concerns have been expressed. When the problem has been identified and agreed on, the conference can move to the next step.

> **STEP 2: Select a solution.** One way to begin this phase is to invite the student to suggest a solution to the problem. If the student is unable to do so, you can offer one. Whenever possible, it is best to have two or more alternatives so that options can be compared and the most desirable one chosen. Frequently the student's solution is stated negatively, focusing on simply ending an undesirable behavior. Although this is a step in the right direction, it is best to include a positive focus as well by suggesting a plan for increasing desirable behavior. Thus, you should be ready to work with the student's ideas and also to suggest modifications.

If you are the one who suggests a solution, seek the student's reaction to check whether the plan is understood and accepted. Also, evaluate the plan's appropriateness: Is it realistic? Will it significantly reduce the problem? Does it call for changes in other students or in the classroom environment, and are such changes feasible? Can it be evaluated readily? Occasionally a student may try to avoid responsibility by proposing a solution that places the burden for change on the teacher or on other students; for example, to design more interesting lessons or to get other students to "leave me alone." Consider such changes to the extent they are appropriate and reasonable but don't allow a student to shift responsibility to others—unless, of course, that is where responsibility for the problem lies. A reasonable response is, "Yes, such changes would help, but what will you contribute?" Once a mutually agreeable solution is reached, you are ready for the third step.

> **STEP 3: Obtain a commitment.** In this step, the teacher asks the student to accept the solution and try it for a specified period, usually with the understanding that it will be evaluated afterward. The student's commitment can be given orally or in written form, as in a "contract." Sometimes contracts are printed with an official-looking border, seal, and script, with space for the student's and the teacher's signatures and for listing contract terms and consequences for following or not following the plan.

Whether consequences are specified in case the plan is not followed will depend on the severity of the problem and whether it is a first conference or a follow-up for a broken contract. Some teachers like to give students a chance to correct their behavior without resorting to penalties, the rationale being that long-range cooperation is better when the teacher uses the least controlling or coercive approach. However, if the student is not making a reasonable effort to comply with the plan, or if the misbehavior is dangerous or too disruptive to be allowed to continue, spelling out the consequences may be needed to get the student's attention and to communicate the seriousness of the situation: "You will have to choose between following our agreement and discussing your behavior with our principal and your parents."

If the plan fails to solve the problem, you'll have to either follow through with whatever consequence was stipulated or work with the student to alter the plan and produce a more workable solution. A major consideration is the amount of time and energy you can or should devote to pursuing the plan versus using a referral, a detention, or some other consequence available in your school. You might also consult with a counselor, an assistant principal, or another teacher before taking further action to get another perspective on the problem.

When problem-solving conferences fail to make progress (e.g., the student does not make a sincere commitment to a plan or simply does not cooperate), the teacher should evaluate his or her assertiveness and empathic responding skills before concluding that the problem-solving approach does not work with that student. Poor assertiveness skills—hostile, critical, or attacking behaviors—and their opposites—timid, tentative responding—interfere with the problem-solving process. An excessively assertive, hostile style reflects a reliance on power and cuts off communication. An unassertive, timid style abdicates authority and is easily ignored; the teacher is not seen as credible, and students simply do not believe that he or she will insist on correct behavior or will follow through with consequences. A constructively assertive teacher, however, captures the students' attention and communicates seriousness of intent in changing the situation. Empathic responding communicates a willingness to listen to the student's point of view and permits the teacher to clarify and react to a student's statements without closing off further discussion. Such skills are especially needed during problem-solving discussions because they allow the teacher to deal constructively with defensive behavior. They also help to clarify solutions as they are discussed and improve the chances of obtaining a sincere commitment to change.

When you use these skills, be patient and give them a chance to work. Teachers often use a problem-solving approach after a situation has become chronic or for behavior that has been established over a long time. In such cases, you cannot expect miracles; change may occur only gradually and imperfectly. However, problem-solving conferences can be helpful in many cases and should be a component of your set of management and discipline skills.

Examples of problem-solving conferences are presented in Dialogues 8.1, 8.2, and 8.3. In addition, exercises on problem solving are presented in activities at the end of the chapter.

◎⊚ Talking with Parents

As we have already mentioned, constructive assertiveness, empathic responding, and problem solving can be useful strategies in your interactions with students. They can also be effective in working with parents. Think about the following suggestions in your interactions with parents or when holding parent conferences.

- Approach parents as team members. Both you and the parents want what's best for the child; the point of a conference is to find ways to work together.
- Parents who had difficulty in school themselves may be intimidated by schools and teachers. This may come across as avoidance, anger, or defensiveness. Be respectful, open, and nonthreatening.
- Respect parents' knowledge of their children.
- Show your appreciation for parents' efforts to rearrange work schedules to meet with you. Use the time wisely by being prepared and organized.
- Stick to descriptions of behavior rather than characterizations of students (e.g., "Abigail calls other children names," rather than "Abigail is mean").
- Whenever possible, document your concerns. For example, if you feel a student's work is sloppy, have samples available to show parents. If the student isn't turning in assignments, give them the assignment sheet with due dates.

For more information on working with parents, see Chapter 9 and the Further Reading section in this chapter.

Further Reading

Berger, E. H. (2004). *Parents as partners in education: Families and schools working together* (6th ed.). Englewood Cliffs, N.J.: Merrill/Prentice-Hall.

This is a useful handbook for understanding important aspects of home–school relations. It provides a comprehensive look at parent–school partnerships and offers practical suggestions to aid collaboration between teachers and parents. It includes topics such as diverse families, the exceptional child, programs to enrich parent–school involvement, and communication necessary for partnerships.

Hill, C. E., & O'Brien, K. M. (1999). *Helping skills: Facilitating exploration, insight, and action.* Washington, D.C.: American Psychological Association.

This textbook outlines a three-stage model of helping and presents basic skills used at each stage, emphasizing the role of affect, cognition, and behavior in the change process.

Kottler, J. A., (2002). S*tudents who drive you crazy: Succeeding with resistant, unmotivated, and otherwise difficult young people.* Thousand Oaks, Calif.: Sage (Corwin Press).

The book blends theory and research with examples from practicing teachers, counselors, school administrators, and students. It offers tools for dealing with frustrating, hostile interactions.

www.wglasser.com

This is the website for the William Glasser Institute. Click on "Skits" for examples of ways for students to learn choice theory.

www.state.ky.us/agencies/behave/homepage.html

The Behavior Homepage is an interactive website that is working to make a difference for children with challenging behavior.

www.air.org/cecp

This is the website for the Center for Effective Collaboration and Practice whose goal is improving services for children and youth with emotional behavioral problems.

 ## Suggested Activities

ACTIVITY 8.1: DEVELOPING ASSERTIVENESS SKILLS

This activity provides situations for practicing assertiveness skills. For each situation described, prepare an assertive response. Use the following sequence of steps with each situation until you are comfortable with the approach. Then combine the steps so you have the experience of responding to situations.

> **STEP 1:** Write out a statement that describes the problem clearly or that insists your rights be respected. Compare and discuss your statements with a partner. Revise your statement if you wish.

> **STEP 2:** Use role playing to portray the situation, with you as the teacher and someone else as the student. During the role play, try to use appropriate body language (including eye contact and facial expression) to support your intervention.

> **STEP 3:** Get feedback from observers regarding your use of assertiveness skills. Use the Assertiveness Assessment Scales at the end of this chapter to assess your own behavior, and check out your perceptions by comparing your self-ratings to those of observers. Be sure to discuss any discrepancies and any problems you experienced in enacting an assertive role. Repeat Step 2 until you feel comfortable with your handling of the situation.

It is not necessary to continue the role play to a complete resolution of the situation. The purpose is only to provide experience in enacting assertive behaviors. The person playing the student role should respond as naturally as possible.

- *Situation A.* Scott has been sliding by lately, doing the minimum and barely passing. At the end of class today, he asks you whether it would be all right to turn in his project a few days late. He knows that you have already given similar permission to two other students who had difficulty obtaining needed materials.
- *Situation B.* Alyson and Maria are supposed to put the equipment away, but they have left much of it strewn about the gym. Now they are heading for the door in anticipation of the end-of-recess bell.
- *Situation C.* Victor has not been working on his assignment. You caught his eye but he looked away, and he has continued to talk to nearby students. As you move around the room checking other students' progress, he begins to make a paper airplane.

- *Situation D.* As you walk down the hallway, you hear two students trading insults ("Your mama . . . !"). The students are not angry yet, just fooling around, but several other students are gathering, and you think they may encourage the two students to fight.
- *Situation E.* As you begin class, you observe Daphne eating a Twinkie, in violation of the rule prohibiting food in the room. When she sees that you notice her, she stuffs the Twinkie into her mouth and gets another one out of the package.
- *Situation F.* During your current events discussion, Susan and Kris trade notes and laugh noisily. You sense that other students' attention is being captured by the duo's antics, and you begin to be annoyed by having to compete for the class's attention.
- *Situation G.* When you were absent yesterday, your fourth-grade class gave the substitute teacher a difficult time. According to the note she left for you (with a copy sent to the principal!), many students refused to work at all, four or five students left for the restroom and didn't return until lunchtime, and a paper and spitwad fight raged most of the afternoon. As the morning bell rings, you enter the room to greet your class.

ACTIVITY 8.2: RECOGNIZING LISTENING RESPONSES

Each of the following dialogues depicts a statement and a variety of teacher responses. In each case, decide which one is closest to a listening response; that is, which one invites further discussion or best reflects the idea or feeling? Check your accuracy against the key in the Appendix.

1. STUDENT: School stinks.

   a. Don't use that type of language.
   b. You seem upset about school.
   c. Come on, things aren't that bad.
   d. That attitude will get you nowhere.

2. STUDENT: I can't understand fractions. Why do we have to learn this stuff?

   a. You'll need it to get into college.
   b. Just keep at it. It'll make sense after a while.
   c. Something isn't making sense to you?
   d. Would you like to come in for extra help after school?

3. STUDENT: I don't want to sit near those boys anymore.

   a. Sorry, but seats have been assigned.
   b. If they're bothering you, I can move you.
   c. Can you handle this on your own?
   d. What is the situation?

4. PARENT: My child is very upset and needs more help or she won't be able to pass. She says she doesn't understand anything.

   a. Please go on. I'd like to hear more about this.
   b. She needs to pay closer attention in class.

c. She's very anxious, but actually she'll do just fine. She only needs to review more before tests.

d. Most students find my explanations to be quite clear. Perhaps she isn't listening.

5. TEACHER NEXT DOOR: My class is going to drive me up a wall. They have been impossible lately!

a. Have you ever considered being more assertive with them?

b. I know, everyone in this wing can hear them.

c. They are really a handful!

d. You think they're bad, you should have my group.

ACTIVITY 8.3: PRODUCING EMPATHIC RESPONSES

You will have to work with a colleague during this activity. Take turns role playing the student and the teacher. The person role playing the teacher should practice empathic responding skills, and the student should try to behave as naturally as possible. It is assumed that the dialogue is occurring at a time and place that permit this type of interchange and that the teacher is interested in allowing the student to describe the problem. These assumptions will not always be true, of course. You could not deal with these issues in the middle of reading groups, for example, nor will you always have the time to deal in this way with every student problem. In this exercise, avoid giving solutions for the student's problem; instead, concentrate on using listening and processing skills to encourage the student to talk about the situation and think through the problem.

- *Situation A.* Teresa is an ESL student who is doing well in math and science. However, she has displayed difficulty with writing skills. With tears in her eyes, she approaches you after class with a writing assignment that you have given an unsatisfactory grade. "I thought I did okay on this."
- *Situation B.* David, a bright student, offers you some advice: "This class would be a lot more interesting if we didn't have to do all these worksheets. Couldn't we choose our own work sometime?"
- *Situation C.* While the rest of the class is at work on an assignment, Barry closes his book, throws away his assignment sheet, and slides down in his seat disgustedly.
- *Situation D.* For the second time this week, SueAnn has not turned in an assignment. Last week she "forgot" to bring her homework twice. Later, you remind SueAnn that assignments are important. "I don't care," she responds.
- *Situation E.* Armand, a new student, has been having trouble making friends. Lately he has been getting into arguments with some of the more popular boys, and he has been teasing a few girls, apparently to gain attention. However, he has not succeeded in breaking into the social scene. After class one day he says to you, "I wish I could go back to my old school."

ACTIVITY 8.4: PROBLEM-SOLVING EXERCISES

Use role playing to practice the problem-solving steps (identify the problem and its consequences, identify and select a solution, obtain a commitment to try it out) with the following situations. In situations in which the student is the one primarily experiencing the problem, assume that the teacher's initial listening response is received positively by the student so there is a basis for continuing the discussion and for the teacher to assist the student in thinking through a solution. In cases in which the student's behavior is affecting the teacher's ability to teach or is interfering with other students' rights, the student may initially be reluctant to participate in this type of discussion, and the teacher will have to use assertiveness skills to overcome this resistance. In addition to these situations, you can use some of the situations presented in Activities 8.1 and 8.3 for additional practice.

- *Situation A.* Bob and Ray are noisy and distracting when they clown around and vie for other students' attention. Reminders and penalties have only fleeting effects on their behavior. Therefore, you decide to have them come in for a conference.
- *Situation B.* David is good-natured as long as no demands are placed on him. However, when reminded that class time is for learning and for working on assignments, he becomes defiant and insists that it is his right to do whatever he wishes, as long as he "don't hurt no one."
- *Situation C.* Lucy is a bright student but often turns work in late; frequently it is incomplete. She is able to pass your tests, however, and she could easily be a top student if she were prompt and better organized. Recently, you sent her parents a progress report because of missing assignments, and Lucy and her mother have come in for a conference to discuss the situation. Her mother wonders whether you will allow Lucy to make up the missing work to avoid making failing grades.

ACTIVITY 8.5: DIALOGUE ANALYSIS

Discuss the following three vignettes. To what extent did the teachers use the problem-solving steps as well as constructive assertiveness and empathic responding? Were they appropriately used? What other approaches might the teachers have tried for dealing with these problems? What are their advantages and disadvantages?

 Vignettes

These three examples illustrate the use of a problem-solving conference for problem situations described earlier in this chapter.

Dialogue 8.1: Brad

TEACHER: Brad, I asked you to stay to talk with me because of a problem we've been having during discussions. Often, when I ask a

	question, you call out the answer without waiting to be called on. Do you agree that this is happening?
BRAD:	I guess so.
TEACHER:	Can you tell me why this is a problem?
BRAD:	I suppose it doesn't give others a chance.
TEACHER:	That's absolutely right. I have to be able to find out whether other boys and girls understand what we are discussing.
BRAD:	What if they don't know?
TEACHER:	You mean, if nobody raises a hand or tries to answer?
BRAD:	Yeah, then can I answer?
TEACHER:	Do you suppose that some people might need more time to think about what they are going to say?
BRAD:	I guess so. But it's boring to just sit and wait for someone to think if I already know it.
TEACHER:	It is difficult to wait and be patient. But I must be able to teach the whole class and to conduct the discussions for everybody. Can you think of any way that we could handle this so that I can call on others when I want to and you can still have your fair turn?
BRAD:	I suppose I could raise my hand.
TEACHER:	That would be a big help. I would really appreciate that. I think you have some good ideas and should have plenty of chances to answer. Brad, how often would you like to speak during our discussions?
BRAD:	I don't know. (*Pauses.*) Three or four times, I guess.
TEACHER:	That would be fine. How about if I guarantee you four times during each discussion? You keep track of the times you answer, and I'll call on you when your hand is raised. If I don't call on you some time, you know you'll get your chances later.
BRAD:	Okay.
TEACHER:	How about our trying this for the rest of the week, and then we'll talk again and see whether it solves our problem?
BRAD:	Okay.

Dialogue 8.2: Alice and Alicia

TEACHER:	Girls, I asked you to stay for this conference because I've been having to take more and more of my time to get you to clean up and to keep work areas neat. I wonder what you both think about this problem.
ALICE:	I don't know.
ALICIA:	I don't think we're so bad about it.
TEACHER:	It has become very frustrating to me. Do you remember that I had to remind you and wait for the jobs to be done?
GIRLS:	Yes.
TEACHER:	Whose job is it to pick up materials and put things away?

GIRLS:	Ours.
TEACHER:	Do you think we can find a way for those jobs to get done? Do you have any suggestions?
ALICIA:	I could just do it without being asked.
TEACHER:	Okay. That is a good idea. Do you have any other suggestions?
ALICE:	We could ask someone to help us.
TEACHER:	That is an interesting idea. Do you know someone who wants to clean up your things?
ALICE:	I don't know. Probably.
TEACHER:	Would you like to help someone else clean up or put things away?
ALICIA:	Sure, it'd be fun.
TEACHER:	How about you, Alice?
ALICE:	Okay.
TEACHER:	Well, then I have an idea. How about if I let you both be my room helpers this next week. As soon as you finish your own cleanup, you can help me with jobs that I need to have done. How would that be?
GIRLS:	Yeah!
TEACHER:	Okay. Let's try this out. Tomorrow, when you have cleaned up, let me know. Then I'll tell you what you can do to help me. How does that sound?
GIRLS:	Sure! Okay.
TEACHER:	I'm glad we had a chance to plan this, because now I have two room helpers and we will have our problem solved.

Dialogue 8.3: Terrence

TEACHER:	I have noticed that you did not turn in the last three arithmetic assignments. What seems to be the matter?
STUDENT:	That work is too hard!
TEACHER:	You weren't able to do the work.
STUDENT:	No. I can't do it.
TEACHER:	When I was going around the room during seatwork, I noticed that you were able to do some of the problems, but then you stopped working.
STUDENT:	That's 'cause I couldn't do them anymore!
TEACHER:	I see. That's pretty frustrating. Do you know, that happens to other people, too. (*Student shrugs.*) Even teachers. Did you know that even teachers sometimes don't know what to do next?
STUDENT:	No.
TEACHER:	Even me. (*Student smiles.*) Do you know what I do when I can't figure out how to do something?
STUDENT:	You ask somebody?
TEACHER:	Right! Does that give you any ideas about what to do when you don't know what to do?

STUDENT: Ask somebody.
TEACHER: Sure. If you get stuck, ask. Do you know who you can ask?
STUDENT: You.
TEACHER: That's right. And you can also ask anyone at your table if I am busy and you need help right away.
STUDENT: Okay.
TEACHER: Did you finish your arithmetic problems today?
STUDENT: No. I need some help.
TEACHER: Why don't you get your paper from your desk and let's see what the problem is. . . .

Assertiveness Assessment Scales

When using the following scales, note that a midrange rating represents an appropriate degree of assertiveness. When rating your own or another teacher's behavior as either nonassertive or hostile, circle the descriptive term that best reflects the basis for your judgment, or write a note on the scale if the descriptors don't adequately capture your perception.

	Unassertive	Assertive	Hostile
	1 ———— 2 ————	3 ———— 4 ———— 5	
Eye contact	Teacher avoids looking at student.	Teacher maintains eye contact with student.	Teacher glares at student; stares student down.
	1 ———— 2 ————	3 ———— 4 ———— 5	
Body language	Teacher turns away, gestures nervously, trembles.	Teacher faces student; alert posture but not threatening. Gestures support statements.	Teacher crowds student, points, shakes fist threateningly.
	1 ———— 2 ————	3 ———— 4 ———— 5	
Message	Obsequious, self-denigrating; excuses student behavior; pleads with student.	Clearly states the problem or insists that the behavior stop. Makes own feelings known, may use humor to relieve tension.	Name calling, labeling, blaming, threatening, being sarcastic, preaching, lecturing.
	1 ———— 2 ————	3 ———— 4 ———— 5	
Voice features	Tremulous, whiny, hesitant, broken, or too soft.	Appropriate volume, natural sounding, varied for emphasis.	Voice too loud; shouts, yells.
	1 ———— 2 ————	3 ———— 4 ———— 5	
Facial features	Smiles inappropriately; nervous twitches and tics.	Expression suits message.	Excessive affect; contorted, disgusted, enraged expression.

9

Managing Problem Behaviors

In this chapter, we describe strategies for dealing with some problem behaviors you may encounter. Although previous chapters described preventive measures as well as tactics for managing inappropriate behavior, it is helpful to consider a full range of approaches. We hope that you will not encounter problems, especially serious ones, in large numbers. However, as you work with students, you will undoubtedly face difficult situations that must be resolved to preserve the climate for learning or to assist a student in developing behaviors more compatible with group life and learning. The aim of this chapter is to pull together and organize a wide array of possible strategies from which you can select. By having a broad array of approaches to draw on, you will be better able to choose one that fits your specific conditions. Having some alternatives in mind is very useful too, in case your first plan doesn't work.

FOR REFLECTION

Teachers' reactions to the problem behaviors described in this chapter are often affected by the adult models they observed and the type of discipline they received as children, both at home and at school. Recall your early experiences in this area and consider their implications. To what extent do these earlier models provide a positive guide for managing problems of varying severity? Would the strategies that were effective for you be equally appropriate or effective for the varied kinds of students you may teach? Are there current behaviors or environmental problems that you did not experience (e.g., drug culture, poverty, single parent/guardian homes, bullying)? Where should you add to or modify your approach?

We hope this chapter's concern with behavior problems will not be taken as a grim comment on the teacher's role. In particular, this extensive list of strategies should be considered within the context of the other chapters in this book. We have advocated generally for a positive, supportive climate with heavy reliance on preventive measures. Within that framework, however, you must be ready to deal with problems when they arise. With a variety of strategies at hand, you can tailor your approach to fit the situation, keep interruptions to the instructional program to a minimum, and promote positive behavior.

This chapter's focus is on problem behaviors rather than problem students. Only a small percentage of students exhibit maladaptive behaviors with such consistency and to such a degree that they warrant being labeled emotionally disturbed or behaviorally disordered. With a few students you may have to "teach" acceptable behavior. Most students do, however, behave inappropriately on occasion; we think it is much more constructive in the long run to help students learn how to behave rather than impute internal causes for their behavior and assume the students are restricted in the capacity to make good choices.

On occasion, problem behaviors result from stressors (e.g., abuse, a death in the family, parental unemployment, serious illness, or divorce) the student is experiencing at home or elsewhere. If a student's behavior changes, or if inappropriate behavior persists after reasonable attempts to deal with it have been made, a discussion of the situation with a parent, guardian, school counselor, or social worker is in order. Sometimes the student's previous teacher can provide additional information. When you talk with the student about what is happening, use listening skills (see Chapter 8) to try to understand the situation. Be empathic, but help the child understand that acting out will not help the problem. By all means, follow up if you discover that a situation outside the classroom is affecting the child's behavior.

What Is Problem Behavior?

The concept of problem behavior is broad. Rather than enumerate all possible misbehaviors that might occur in classrooms, it is more manageable to think of categories.

Nonproblem

Brief inattention, some talk during a transition between activities, small periods of daydreaming, and a short pause while working on an assignment are examples of common behaviors that are not really problems for anyone because they are of brief duration and don't interfere with learning or instruction. Everyone is the better for their being ignored. To attempt to react to them would consume too much energy, interrupt lessons constantly, and detract from a positive classroom climate.

Minor Problem

This includes behaviors that run counter to class procedures or rules but that do not, when occurring infrequently, disrupt class activities or seriously interfere with learning. Examples are calling out or leaving seats without permission, reading or doing unrelated work during class time, passing notes, eating candy, scattering trash around, and talking excessively during independent work or group work. These behaviors are minor irritants as long as they are brief in duration and are limited to one or a few students. You would not give them much thought except for two reasons: Unattended, they might persist and spread; if the behaviors have an audience, not to respond might cause a perception of inconsistency and potentially undermine an important aspect of the overall management system. Also, if students engage in such behavior for an extended period of time, their learning is likely to be adversely affected.

Major Problem but Limited in Scope and Effects

This category includes behaviors that disrupt an activity or interfere with learning but whose occurrence is limited to a single student or perhaps to a few students not acting in concert. For example, a student may be chronically off-task. Another student may rarely complete assignments. A student may frequently fail to follow class rules for talk or movement around the room or may refuse to do any work. This category also includes a more serious but isolated violation of class or school rules, for example, an act of vandalism or hitting another student.

Escalating or Spreading Problem

This category includes any minor problem that has become commonplace and thus constitutes a threat to order and the learning environment. For example, when many students roam around the room at will and continually call out irrelevant comments, content development activities suffer; social talking that continues unabated even when the teacher repeatedly asks for quiet is distracting to others; and talking back and refusal to cooperate with the teacher are frustrating and may lead to a poor classroom climate. Frequent violations of behavioral guidelines cause the management and instructional system to break down and interfere with the momentum of class activities.

Goals for Managing Problem Behavior

In dealing with problem behavior, several types of goals must be considered. You have to judge the short- and long-term effects of any management strategy you choose. In the short term, the desired results are that the inappropriate behaviors cease and the students resume or begin appropriate behaviors. In the long run, it is important to prevent the problem from recurring. At the same time, you must be watchful for potential negative side effects and take steps to minimize them. Also, consider the effects on the individual student or students causing the problem as well as the effect on the whole class.

> Joel is talking and showing off to a group of students during independent work. The teacher could squelch Joel by using a sarcastic put-down or a strong desist but chooses instead to redirect Joel's behavior and stand close by until he is working on the assignment. The put-down or strong desist might get faster results in the short run, but it may lead to resentment or even conflict if Joel tries a rejoinder. Redirection and proximity control take a little more effort but do not have negative side effects. In addition, they offer more support for appropriate behavior.

The ideal strategy is one that maintains or restores order in the class immediately without adversely affecting the positive learning environment; in addition, an ideal strategy prevents a repetition of the problem and results in subsequent appropriate behavior in similar situations. In practice, classrooms are busy places, and you rarely have sufficient time to mull over the various options and their effects whenever a problem arises, especially in the midst of a crisis. If only there were a "pause" button on classroom events! The need for prompt reaction should not, however, deter us from evaluating the results of our efforts and from seeking alternative approaches, especially when our initial efforts do not meet with success.

It is, therefore, useful to have a repertoire of strategies to apply to various problem situations.

Management Strategies

This section includes useful strategies for dealing with a variety of classroom behavior problems. The first several strategies can be utilized without much difficulty, require little teacher time, and have the great virtue of being relatively unobtrusive. They have much to recommend them because they do not give undue attention to the misbehavior and do not interfere with the flow of instructional activity. As we move down the list, we encounter strategies that are more direct attempts to stop the behaviors and to do so quickly; however, the strategies have more negative features: they demand more of the teacher's time, they may have unintended consequences on students, or they interrupt class activities. A general principle helpful in selecting a strategy is to use an approach that is effective in stopping the inappropriate behavior promptly and that has the least negative impact. An implication is that minor problems should usually be dealt with by limited interventions. As problems become more serious, the limited interventions may be ineffective in quickly ending the disruptive behavior and thus a more time-consuming or intrusive intervention may be required. With every level of problem and strategy chosen, however, you must be consistent and fair with all students.

Most elementary schools have prescribed procedures for dealing with certain types of major problems and sometimes even minor ones. For example, teachers' responses to events such as fighting, obscene language, stealing, vandalism, and unexcused absence are likely to be directed by school (or district) policies. Therefore, a beginning teacher must learn what policies are in force and follow them. When no specific policy is established for particular problems or when teachers are given latitude in their responses, the alternatives listed later in the chapter can be helpful.

It is a given that preventive measures are more desirable than reactive ones. Thus, the earlier chapters have mainly been devoted to setting up the classroom environment to eliminate the need for frequent recourse to major interventions. Sometimes responsive strategies are still needed. However, when teachers find themselves frequently using major interventions to deal with minor problems, it is time to reevaluate expectations and the overall management and instructional plan and make needed modifications. To this end, reviewing suggestions for management presented in prior chapters and perhaps using the checklists to provide focus could result in changes that help reduce the problems. Teachers should also be aware that sometimes the source of the problem lies in frustration with content that the student does not grasp or with tasks that the student lacks skills to perform. When the problem is one of a poor fit between a student's capabilities and academic requirements, the source must also be addressed by developing more appropriate class activities and assignments or by giving the student more assistance.

If you have a special needs student whose behavior is causing a problem, you may find it helpful to discuss the situation with a special education teacher and ask for suggestions. In particular, find out whether the student has a special discipline program as part of an individualized education plan (IEP). Sometimes such a plan specifies particular ways to respond to the student or gives useful alternative strategies. Even if no specific discipline plan is included in the IEP, you may be able to obtain helpful ideas for working with the student.

In the pages that follow we describe classroom strategies that have a wide range of application, but the list is not exhaustive. Readers interested in additional ways of coping with behavior problems will find articles by Shukla-Mehta and Albin (2003) and Myles and Simpson (1994) helpful. Books that contain good descriptions of strategies for dealing with specific problems or with crisis management include Poland and McCormick (1999), Cohen and Fish (1993), and Stoner, Shinn, and Walker (1991). Many of the recommendations in these books are for school administrators or school psychologists, but there is much of value for teachers as well. Finally, the *Handbook of Classroom Management* (Evertson & Weinstein in press) has many excellent chapters that describe strategies for managing problems.

Minor Interventions

USE NONVERBAL CUES

Make eye contact with the student and give a signal such as a finger to the lips, a head shake, or a hand signal to issue a desist. Sometimes lightly touching a student on the arm or shoulder helps signal your presence and has a calming effect. Never touch a student when you are angry, though, and avoid touching students when they are angry. Touching in these cases is likely to escalate the situation.

GET THE ACTIVITY MOVING

Often student behavior deteriorates during transition times between activities or during "dead" time when no apparent focus for attention is present. Students leave their seats, talk, shuffle restlessly, and amuse themselves and each other while waiting for something to do. The remedy is obvious: move through the transition more quickly and reduce or eliminate the dead time. This entails planning activities so that all materials are ready and adhering to a well-conceived lesson plan. Trying to catch and correct inappropriate behaviors during such times is usually futile and misdirected. Just get the next activity under way and direct students to the desired behaviors.

USE PROXIMITY

Move closer to students. Combine proximity with nonverbal cues to stop inappropriate behavior without interrupting the instruction. Be sure to continue monitoring the students at least until they have begun an appropriate activity.

USE GROUP FOCUS

Use group alerting, accountability, or a higher-participation format (see Chapter 5) to draw students back into a lesson when attention has begun to wane or when students have been in a passive mode for too long and you observe off-task behavior spreading.

REDIRECT THE BEHAVIOR

When students are off-task, remind them of appropriate behavior: "Everyone should be writing answers to the chapter questions," "Be sure your group is discussing your project plan," "Everyone should be seated and quiet unless you have been given permission to leave your seat or talk." If only one or two students are engaged in inappropriate behavior, a private redirection will be less likely to interrupt the activity or to direct attention toward the incorrect behavior. A redirection strategy that works well with younger children is the use of group and individual public praise for appropriate behavior. For example, if several students are talking and inattentive at the beginning of a new activity, the teacher should identify students who are behaving correctly: "I see many students who are sitting quietly, ready to begin. . . . I really appreciate the boys and girls who are ready for our next activity. John is listening, Donica is being very quiet. Oh, good, Demetrius, Richard, and Corby are ready. . . ." In most cases, off-task students quickly come around.

PROVIDE NEEDED INSTRUCTION

Especially during individual work or group work, off-task behaviors may reflect poor comprehension of the task. Check the work or ask brief questions to assess understanding; give necessary assistance so students can work independently. If many students can't proceed, stop the activity and provide whole-class instruction. Next time, be sure to check comprehension before starting the independent work activity.

ISSUE A BRIEF DESIST

Tell the students to stop the undesirable behavior. Make direct eye contact and be assertive (see Chapter 8). Keep your comments brief, and monitor the situation until the student complies. Combine this strategy with redirection to encourage desirable behavior.

GIVE THE STUDENT A CHOICE

Tell the student that he or she has a choice: either to behave appropriately or to continue the problem behavior and receive a consequence. Be sure to describe the desired behavior. Telling a student to "behave appropriately" does not communicate clearly what the desired behavior should be. For example, suppose a student has refused to clean up properly after completing a project: "You may choose to clean up now; if not, you are choosing to stay in during recess until your area is clean." To a student who continues to distract nearby students: "You may choose to work quietly on your assignment at your seat, or you will have to sit in the time-out area to do your work." The purpose of stating the consequence as a choice is to emphasize the student's responsibility for his or her behavior. Also, making the consequence clear increases the chance that the student will choose to self-regulate.

Moderate Interventions

These strategies are more confrontational than the limited interventions described previously and thus have greater potential for eliciting resistance. In cases in which the student's behavior is not especially disruptive, it is desirable to use a minor intervention or to issue a warning to the student before using these interventions. Doing so permits the student to exercise self-control and may save the teacher time and effort.

WITHHOLD A PRIVILEGE OR DESIRED ACTIVITY

Students who abuse a privilege (e.g., being allowed to work together on a project, sitting near friends, or having the freedom to move around the classroom without permission) can lose the privilege and be required to earn it back with appropriate behavior. Sometimes teachers allow quiet talking during independent activities and removing this privilege can be an effective way to limit unproductive social behavior. Other teachers allow a class to choose a favorite activity or a short period of free time on one or more days each week as incentives. Time lost from such activities can then be a strong deterrent to inappropriate behavior at other times. Although withholding a privilege is a form of punishment, it usually has fewer side effects than punishment that requires directly applying an aversive consequence.

ISOLATE OR REMOVE STUDENTS

Students who disrupt an activity can be removed to another area of the room, away from other students. It is helpful to have a carrel with sides, or at least a desk at the back of the room facing away from other students, to discourage eye contact from the time-out area. If no suitable place is available, the student may have to have time-out in the hall outside the door, although not if your school has a policy prohibiting this because of the problem of adequately supervising the student.

Time-out is a variation on the preceding consequence in that it takes away the student's privilege of participating in the activity. It is a good idea to allow excluded students to return to the activity in a short time, as long as their behavior in time-out is acceptable. Some teachers prefer to let them retain some control over the return, using a direction such as, "You may come back in five minutes if you decide that you can follow our class rules." Other teachers prohibit the student from returning until the activity is completed or until they have a brief conference with the student.

A problem with time-out is that some students may find it rewarding. They receive attention when it is administered, and it allows them to avoid an activity they dislike. When this occurs, you should switch to another strategy. Another problem is that a student may refuse to go to the time-out area. Usually this is a temporary problem; if you are firm, ignoring the student's protests and continuing with the activity, the student will go eventually. One way to move a recalcitrant body is to offer a choice: "You can either take time-out or walk to the principal's office. It's your decision."

Time-out has another risk. Its use clearly identifies a student as someone who is excludable, and it may result in implicit labeling by the teacher, by other students, or by the excluded student. If used frequently with a particular student, it may cause resentment and anger. Therefore, be sure to provide opportunities for the student to resume full participation in the class and use other strategies to promote appropriate behavior at the same time.

USE A PENALTY

Sometimes a small amount of repetitious work is required as payment for inappropriate behavior. For example, in physical education students may be required to run an extra lap or do push-ups. In math, students may work extra problems. The advantage of this type of consequence is that it can usually be administered quickly with a minimum of the teacher's time and effort. A disadvantage is that the task is being defined as punishing, and therefore the student's attitude toward the content may be negatively affected. Another problem with the use of penalties is that their ease of use can lead to overuse, detracting from the overall climate.

ASSIGN DETENTION

Another penalty commonly used is to require that the student serve a detention, whether at lunch, during recess, or before or after school. Because of the logical relationship between the problem and the consequence, this penalty is often used for misbehaviors that involve time (e.g., extended goofing off and time wasting; behavior that interferes with instruction or work time). Other common uses of the penalty are for repeated rule violations and for frequent failure to complete assignments. You may have to supervise the detention in your room, or your school might have a detention hall with an assigned monitor. The time in detention need not be lengthy, especially for misbehaviors that are not severe or frequent; a ten- or fifteen-minute detention is often sufficient to make the point.

An advantage of detention as a penalty is that it is disliked by most students, and they want to avoid it; at the same time, it is administered away from other students in the class and thus does not give undue attention to the behavior. Also, it is a common punishment, so extensive explanations and unusual procedures aren't needed. Finally, the teacher can sometimes use a little of the detention time to hold a conference with the student and perhaps work out a plan for improving the situation.

A disadvantage of detention is that it does take the teacher's time, especially when he or she must supervise it. Even when the school has a D-Hall, the teacher must write a referral. Another disadvantage is that students might be able to avoid detention, at least in the short run, simply by not showing up. Thus, the teacher or the school must have a backup plan, such as doubling the time; moreover, records must be kept and often additional time is required to deal with such students.

USE A SCHOOL-BASED CONSEQUENCE

If your school has a prescribed consequence for particular problem behaviors and you are allowed some latitude in its administration, you should consider utilizing it after you have not had desired results with other strategies. For example, some schools have a system of referral to the principal, who then deals with the student. Often a first referral consequence is limited to detention or to a warning, with subsequent referrals resulting in a parent conference. It is necessary to apprise the administrator of the basis for the referral and to discuss what outcome is desirable. An advantage of this approach is that it does not require much of the teacher's time. A disadvantage is that the usefulness of this strategy is dependent on others for its effectiveness; also, extensive and frequent external support for handling in-class problems is not a realistic option in most schools.

More Extensive Interventions

When students do not respond to minor or moderate interventions and their behavior continues to disrupt classroom activities and to interfere with their own and others' learning, one or more of the following strategies can be helpful.

USE PROBLEM SOLVING

Problem solving was described extensively in Chapter 8, so it is not discussed in this chapter. However, the next three strategies, which share features with problem solving, are sufficiently difficult to warrant separate presentations.

Use a Five-Step Intervention Procedure

Jones and Jones (2001) recommend following five steps when dealing with disruptive student behavior.

> **STEP 1:** Use a nonverbal signal to cue the student to stop.
>
> **STEP 2:** If the behavior continues, ask the student to follow the desired rule.
>
> **STEP 3:** If the disruption continues, give the student a choice of stopping the behavior or choosing to develop a plan.
>
> **STEP 4:** If the student still does not stop, require that the student move to a designated area in the room to write a plan.
>
> **STEP 5:** If the student refuses to comply with Step 4, send the student to another location (e.g., the school office) to complete the plan.

The five-step intervention process requires students to complete a form for the plan (Figure 9.1). When the approach is introduced to students, preferably at the beginning of the year, the teacher explains its purpose and how to fill out the form. Role playing the use of the five steps is recommended, both to teach the procedures and to provide a positive model of their application. It is helpful to laminate a couple of examples of appropriate plans so students have models.

Figure 9.1 Problem-Solving Form

Choose to Be Responsible

Name _____ Date _____

Rules we agreed on:

1. Speak politely to others.

2. Treat each other kindly.

3. Follow teacher requests.

4. Be prepared for class.

5. Make a good effort at your work and request help if you need it.

6. Obey all school rules.

Please answer the following questions:

1. What rule did you violate? _____
   _____

2. What did you do that violated this rule? _____
   _____

3. What problem did this cause for you, your teacher, or classmates? _____
   _____

4. What plan can you develop that will help you be more responsible and follow this classroom rule? _____
   _____

5. How can the teacher or other students help you? _____
   _____

I, _____, will try my best to follow the plan I have written and to follow all
other rules and procedures that we created to make the classroom a good place to learn.

From Vernon F. Jones and Louise S. Jones, *Comprehensive Classroom Management: Creating Communities of Support and Solving Problems,* Sixth Edition. Copyright © 2001 by Allyn and Bacon. Reprinted/Adapted by permission.

Advantages of this approach include its emphasis on student responsibility and choice. Also, a graduated response to the problem allows the teacher to intervene nonpunitively at first and thus provides a means of settling the matter quickly, with a minimum of disturbance to the ongoing activity. The steps are simple and straightforward, which promotes consistency by the teacher; students, in turn, are aided by the structure and predictability of the approach.

A disadvantage of the system is that movement from Step 1 to Step 5 can occur very rapidly, and intermediate strategies may be necessary to avoid excessive reliance on sending students out of the classroom. In addition, some students, especially in early primary grades, have difficulty writing an acceptable plan by themselves. Finally, setting up the system and, later, meeting with students to discuss their plans and monitoring implementation require at least a moderate investment of time.

Use the "Think Time" Strategy

Designed to help students learn self-control and to prevent a reciprocally escalating sequence of student noncompliance–teacher warnings and reprimands, the Think Time strategy removes a noncompliant student to another teacher's classroom to provide time for the student to gain focus and reenter the classroom after making a commitment to change the behavior (Nelson & Carr 2000). Using the Think Time strategy requires the cooperation of another teacher whose classroom is in close proximity. The partner teacher reserves a location in the room that is not in a high-traffic area and that will minimize attention to the entering student. After arriving at the receiving classroom, the student waits quietly in the designated area and thinks about what happened. As soon as is practicable (e.g., three to five minutes), the receiving teacher makes contact with the student and gives him or her a debriefing form to fill out that asks "What was your behavior?" and "What behavior do you need to display when you go back to your classroom?" The student is asked if he or she can do it, or if a conference is needed with the teacher. If the student completes the form acceptably, the receiving teacher sends the student back to the original class.

If you use this strategy, you will need to partner with another teacher. After preparing a location in your rooms to receive think time students, you each need to teach your students about Think Time. Nelson recommends treating this task as you would any other complex procedure: explain the purpose of the strategy (e.g., to help students learn self-control and to minimize disruption to learning) and what behaviors might result in Think Time. You also need to describe the signal you will use to send someone to Think Time (e.g., hand them a pass card) and model how students will be expected to leave the room and enter the other teacher's room. The students should also be shown an example of the debriefing form with examples of appropriate responses. For high school applications, Nelson recommends having a back-up administrative sanction, such as an office referral, if a student becomes disruptive. Likewise, if a student is required to use Think Time more than once in a class period or after the third time in a semester, then an office referral or In School Suspension (ISS) assignment is used along with a parent contact.

Think Time gives the teacher a way to manage students who don't respond to simpler desist techniques, and at the same time it short circuits the reciprocal escalation of hostile interaction that can develop when a student resists a teacher's attempt to stop misbehavior. Another advantage is that Think Time provides a "ceasefire" opportunity in which students acknowledge their part in the problem and identify a solution. In this respect, it is similar to other problem-solving strategies. Limitations in the use of the strategy are that it takes the cooperation and commitment of another teacher, and it requires planning and systematic application to be successful. A training videotape is available through Sopris West (www.sopriswest.com).

Use the Reality Therapy Model

William Glasser's (1975, 1977) ideas about reality therapy have been widely applied in education. The essential features when working with an individual student include establishing a caring relationship with the student, focusing on present behaviors, getting the student to accept responsibility, developing a plan for change, obtaining a commitment to follow the plan, and following up. Glasser believes strongly that students choose behavior depending on their perceptions of its consequences. Most students choose appropriate behaviors when they believe these will lead to desirable outcomes, and they avoid behaviors they perceive will lead to undesirable consequences. Glasser's plan can be put into effect using the following steps.

STEP 1: Establish involvement with the students. If students believe the teacher cares for them and has their best interests in mind, they will be more likely to follow the teacher's guidance when evaluating and changing their behavior. Teachers can show commitment to and caring for students in numerous ways: commenting favorably to the students about their work; being friendly; and showing an interest in student activities, families, likes and dislikes, and hobbies. Teachers can also get involved by demonstrating school spirit, joking, being good listeners, and taking time to talk with students about their concerns. The best time to establish involvement is before a student becomes disruptive, but even if a student has begun to exhibit problem behavior, it is not too late to begin. When a teacher makes a special effort to have two or three friendly contacts a day with such a student, it can be helpful in creating a more positive climate for change.

STEP 2: Focus on behavior. When a problem has occurred, Glasser recommends that a brief conference be held with the student. The initial concern should be to determine what the problem is. To this end, the teacher should ask only questions about "what happened" or "what's going on" and avoid trying to fix blame. Even if the teacher knows exactly what the problem is, it is wise to obtain the student's perspective.

STEP 3: The student must accept responsibility for the behavior. This means the student acknowledges that he or she did engage in the behavior. No excuses are accepted. Admitting responsibility is difficult, especially when there are so many other handy things to blame, but in the end, it is a form of denial to try to assign responsibility elsewhere when it was the student who engaged in the behavior. Of course, it is possible that more than one individual is responsible for the problem, but that should not be an excuse for irresponsibility.

STEP 4: The student should evaluate the behavior. If students have difficulty perceiving their part or they minimize it, Glasser suggests asking, "Has the behavior helped or hurt you? Has it helped or hurt others?" The teacher may have to point out the negative consequences of continuing to misbehave. Unless the student sees that the behavior leads to negative consequences and that changing it will produce desirable consequences, there isn't much reason to expect a change.

STEP 5: Develop a plan. The teacher and student identify ways to prevent the problem from recurring and the new behaviors needed. The plan can be written as a contract.

STEP 6: The student must make a commitment to follow the plan. Progress will be limited at best if students do not seriously intend to make a change. It may help if the teacher makes clear the positive and negative consequences of following or not following the plan. The plan should be do-able in a reasonable time.

STEP 7: Follow up and follow through. If the plan doesn't work, it should be modified with the student; if a negative consequence was called for in the plan, it should be used. Glasser also proposes several additional steps beyond the classroom if a student continues to be a problem. For example, use of in-school suspension could be a consequence of continuing misbehavior; before the student is allowed to return to the classroom, an acceptable plan must be agreed on. Only after several failed attempts to obtain a change should the teacher refer the student to the principal.

The reality therapy approach to dealing with individual discipline problems has several positive aspects. It is a systematic way for teachers to deal with many kinds of individual problems, and it provides a simple, yet effective, process for getting right at the issues and avoiding being sidetracked by fault finding, conning, or excuse making. Research on the effects of this aspect of reality therapy is generally supportive for applications to individual students (Emmer & Aussiker 1990).

CONFER WITH A PARENT

Sometimes a telephone call or an e-mail to a parent can have a marked effect on a student's behavior, signaling to the child that accountability for behavior extends beyond the classroom. This assumes you have established with parents how they wish to be contacted. Parents react best if they don't feel they are being held responsible for their child's behavior in school (after all, they aren't there), so don't put the parent on the defensive. Describe the situation briefly and say that you would appreciate whatever support the parent can give in helping you understand and resolve the problem. Acknowledge the difficulty in rearing children as well as in teaching them. Be sure to use listening skills (see Chapter 8) during the conversation, and be alert for information that might help you determine an appropriate strategy for dealing with the student. Have your grade book handy so you can give the parent specific information about the student's progress if the information is requested or needed.

Rather than a phone conference, you might have to schedule a face-to-face conference with a parent. Sometimes, but by no means always, when such conferences are arranged, it is because a problem has become severe, and other school personnel (e.g., a counselor or principal) may have to be present. If you have initiated the meeting, brief the others and plan your approach ahead of time; inform parents of other staff members who will be attending the meeting.

The secret to successful parent-teacher conferences is planning. If you have back-to-back conferences, provide a place for the next arrivals to sit and wait. Arrange chairs for all participants in a circle, a semicircle, or around a table. Decide which issues need to be addressed with the parent. Bring documentation and a collection of the child's work over time to support those issues. Have the child's grades written on a separate piece of paper; showing the entire gradebook may infringe on another child's right to privacy.

Begin the conference by describing some of the child's strengths. During the meeting, avoid "teacher talk," acronyms, or technical terms the parents may not understand. Encourage comments and questions. If possible, include the child in all or part of the conference. Keep a written record of suggestions, concerns, and plans of action. End the conference by reiterating any responsibilities that have been assumed. Thank the parents for supporting their child's education.

The chief drawback to parent conferences is the time and energy they require. The effort is frequently worth it. Although not every conference is successful, many times the student's behavior improves. Another potential problem is identifying beforehand the strategy that is best to follow with the parent. Occasionally parents overreact and punish children excessively. As the year progresses, you will get to know parents better and be able to gauge the probable effects of your call or conference.

CREATE AN INDIVIDUAL CONTRACT WITH THE STUDENT

When a student's inappropriate behavior has become chronic or a problem is severe and must stop immediately, try an individual contract. You should discuss the nature of the problem with the student, including the student's perspective on it. Then you and the student can identify appropriate solutions and agree on which course of action to take. Typically, the contract specifies changes the student will make, but it might also call for the teacher to alter some behavior or activity. You should make clear the consequences that will occur if the plan is not followed, and you can also identify an incentive to encourage the student to follow through with the contract. The plan and consequences are written down and signed by the student. Contracts can also be used with other strategies (see the Five-Step Plan and Reality Therapy sections).

Special Problems

Children sometimes behave in ways that require stronger measures than those described in the preceding sections. These behaviors include rudeness, chronic avoidance of work, fighting, bullying, and defiance or hostility toward the teacher. Although these behaviors are not pleasant to contemplate, they are an inevitable result of close contact with up to thirty students for long periods of time. Fortunately, few teachers encounter these behaviors in large numbers. Regardless of their frequency, it is wise to be aware of ways to cope with them if they occur.

Before discussing each type of problem, general guidelines applicable to aggressive behaviors will be considered. Consider coping with these behaviors in two phases: the immediate response and a long-range strategy. At the time the behavior occurs, your immediate concern is to bring it to a halt with the least disruption possible. Because these behaviors are annoying and can arouse your anxiety or anger, be careful not to exacerbate the problem. By staying calm and avoiding overreaction, rather than becoming overbearing or dictatorial, you are more likely to bring the situation to a successful conclusion. You may tell the student how you feel, but by avoiding an argument or an emotional confrontation you will be in a better position to deal with the student and the problem. Thinking about ways to handle disruptive behavior ahead of time and consulting with more experienced teachers will help you to act rather than react.

Long-range goals are to prevent a recurrence of the behavior and to help the student learn a more constructive means of dealing with others. Preventing a recurrence of the behavior is best accomplished by (1) finding out what triggered the incident and resolving the cause if possible, and (2) having a predictable classroom environment with reasonable and consistently used rules, procedures, and consequences. Aggressive behavior rarely occurs in such classrooms. Helping these students acquire better behavior may require much individual attention from you over a period of time. The extent to which this goal is feasible is, of course, limited by many factors, including your time constraints and the severity of the student's problem. In dealing with students who have chronic problems, you may need consultation and assistance from the student's parents, the school counselor, a special education resource teacher, or the principal. Suggestions for handling specific types of behavior follow.

Bullying

Bullying is a pervasive problem in many schools and communities. It is unacceptable behavior characterized by harassment or intimidation of one student through a pattern of threats, teasing, or physical abuse by one or more other students. Bullying is typically learned from peer groups, the home, or the media. Because of its damaging effects on students' self-esteem, some schools have a "zero tolerance" policy for bullying.

Bullying is certainly contrary to the climate of respect you want to develop early in the year, and it can lead to serious and long-term emotional difficulties both for the bully and for the victim. Make sure your students understand from the first day that bullying is not acceptable and should be reported. Bullying is sometimes hard to detect because victims are reluctant to report it for fear of reprisals, and victimizers often intimidate onlookers as well. Most bullying occurs on the playground, in the cafeteria, in hallways, or on school buses; be alert to the possibility of these types of abusive incidents.

The most effective programs aimed at decreasing bullying are schoolwide programs (see Olweus, *Bullying Prevention Program* at www.stopbullyingnow.com) that create a climate in which bullying is considered by everyone to be unacceptable behavior. In your classroom, emphasize social skills training (see *Bully Busters or Steps to Respect* at www.cfchildren.org). Students also need to learn deflective responses for potential victims and positive roles for bystanders. Loss of peer support is a major deterrent to bullying. In addition to group discussions on bullying and recognizing feelings generated in both the victim and the victimizer, provide lessons on friendship skills, assertive behavior, and respectful problem solving.

If you encounter bullying, evaluate the seriousness of the behavior. For instance, teasing because of racial differences, physical disfigurement, home issues, or other unique aspects should never be allowed. After meeting with the individual students involved, determine whether to contact school administrators, school counselors, and parents. Stopping pervasive bullying will need coordinated efforts. Your ultimate goal is to prevent bullying from being seen as acceptable. Changing individual and group perceptions of the behavior is critical to the mental and emotional health of your students.

Tattling

Although tattling is often not disruptive, it can nevertheless become a problem when it becomes a common practice. Most teachers in the early grades develop standard practices for dealing with tattling and apply them when it happens. To prevent tattling from occurring in the first place, let students know what kinds of information they should and should not report to you. For example, you need to be told about situations in which students are hurt or in danger. This includes bullying as previously described. You do not need to be told when students are whispering in class or not doing their work. If you move around the classroom and monitor well, you will see behavior occur, and students will not have to call your attention to it.

If it appears that several of your students are tattling frequently, plan a brief lesson with the class to clarify the difference between tattling and being socially responsible. Provide examples of tattling, such as (1) trying to get someone else in trouble, (2) trying to get someone else to solve a problem you could handle, or (3) trying to get help for someone else who is actually capable of solving the problem alone. One way to illustrate the differences between social responsibility and tattling is to draw a chart on the board with these two headings and help students think of examples to write under each one. For example, under the Tattling heading would be such things as "Someone called me a name," "Someone squirted some water from the water fountain outside." Under the Social Responsibility heading you would include such things as "Someone pushed me down and hurt me, and my elbow is bleeding," "Someone is in the restroom crying and won't come out."

In deciding how you will handle tattling if it should occur, keep in mind that students who tattle are usually seeking attention from the teacher. If tattlers are successful in getting you to intervene with the alleged misbehavior, other students are likely to follow suit. It is usually sufficient to remind tattlers of what they are supposed to be doing at that moment and have them return to it.

Do be sensitive to situations in which the student may really need your support. If you discuss other options for the student to try, encourage the student to tell you how the other strategy worked if the situation recurs. Another response to the tattler may be, "I'm glad you know not to behave that way. I'll deal with Jimmy (or whoever the other student is) if I see him do that." Do not pull the other student in for a "you did too/no I didn't" confrontation with the tattler. And do not apply consequences to another child based on one student's report. It is also probably prudent for you to follow up and check out the situation for yourself. If other students report similar problems with the same student, you will need to monitor that student more closely.

Other interventions that may be useful for persistent tattlers include pointing out the natural consequences of tattling (peers are likely to shun a tattler); coaching the student in strategies for handling situations without tattling (e.g., walking away); and teaching specific problem-solving techniques (identify the problem, decide on a goal, develop a strategy and plan for action, carry out the plan).

Rudeness toward the Teacher

Rudeness may take the form of back talk, arguing, crude remarks, or gesturing. Although this kind of behavior may trigger your anger, it is best to maintain a low-key, respectful, and professional manner in your response. In this way, you can model the kind of behavior you expect from students, and you will be more effective in interacting with the student in question. Determine if the student knows this is unacceptable. Frequently, the student is using such behavior as a means of getting attention from you or from peers, or to avoid an assignment that she or he does not feel able to complete successfully.

Avoid sarcasm, overreacting, arguing, or being trapped in a power struggle. To some extent, your response will depend on the degree of rudeness and on how public it was. In borderline cases, the student may not even realize that a comment was offensive, or the student may be impulsively reacting to frustration with an instruction or task that may be unclear or too difficult. A reasonable first reaction is to inform the student that the behavior is not acceptable, possibly referring to a general classroom rule such as "respect others" or "be polite," followed by an offer to work with the student individually as soon as you have finished giving instruction to the class. If the incident is repeated or if the original comment was intentionally rude, conferring with the student to find out the reasons for this behavior or penalizing the student may be necessary. Should disrespectful behavior disrupt the class or persist, the student may have to be isolated from other students or sent to the school office and not allowed to return until he or she agrees to behave appropriately. Most schools have a standard policy for dealing with extreme cases, and you will be able to rely on whatever procedures have been established.

Chronic Avoidance of Work

You may have students who frequently do not complete assigned work. Sometimes they do not complete assignments early in the school year; more often, a student begins to skip assignments occasionally and then with increasing regularity until he or she is habitually not completing them. This behavior can be minimized by a carefully planned accountability system (review Chapter 3 for details). However, even in classrooms with a strong accountability system, some students may still avoid work.

It is much easier and better for the teacher to correct this problem before the student gets so far behind that failure is almost certain. To take early action, you must collect and check student work frequently and maintain good records. When a student has begun to miss assignments, talk with the student, seek information to help identify the problem, and then take corrective action. If the student is simply unable to do the assigned work, you should provide appropriate assistance or modify the assignments. If the student feels overwhelmed by the assignments, break them up into parts whenever possible. Have the student complete the first part of the assignment within a specific time (perhaps five or ten minutes); then check to see that it has been done. A bonus of a few minutes of free time at the end of the period can be offered for completion of the portion within the time limit or for working steadily without prodding. Sometimes you can provide a list of assignments for the student to check off. This can serve as a self-monitoring device and can provide a sense of accomplishment.

If ability is not the problem, the following procedures can be used in addition to talking with the student. Call the student's parents and discuss the situation with them. Often they can supply the extra support needed to help motivate the student. A simple penalty of requiring that the student remain after school until assignments have been completed can prove effective. If the student rides a bus, you won't be able to use the procedure, of course, without making special arrangements with the parents. Any time the child is likely to be detained for more than a few minutes, alert the parents ahead of time. Another procedure that can be used when the parents are cooperative is for the child to take home daily a list of incomplete assignments and all books or materials needed to complete the work. Be cautious about using this procedure lest the student waste time thinking all work may be done at home.

" . . . and suddenly there were teachers all over the place!"

© 1968 by Bill Knowlton. Reprinted from *Classroom Chuckles,* published by Scholastic Book Services, a Division of Scholastic, Inc., by permission of Bill Knowlton.

Be sure not to soften the negative consequences of repeated failure to complete work by giving students higher grades than they have earned. Doing so teaches them to avoid responsibility. Provide added incentives for good effort and completed work. Set up a reward system (see Chapter 7) that encourages students to do their best.

Fighting

Fighting is less likely to occur in classrooms than on the playground, in the cafeteria, or in some other area of the school. In the elementary grades, you can often stop a fight without undue risk of injury. (If for some reason you cannot intervene directly, alert other teachers and administrators so that action can be taken.) When you do intervene, first give a loud verbal command to stop. This alone may stop the fight; it at least alerts the combatants that a referee has arrived. Instruct a student in the group of onlookers to go immediately for help; be specific about where the student should go. If you feel it is safe for you to do so, separate the fighters; as you keep them separate, instruct the other students to leave, to return to their play, or to go to their classes. Without an audience before which the fighters need to save face, you are more likely to be able to keep them apart until help arrives or until you can get them to a different location.

Your school will undoubtedly have a procedure for dealing with fighting; you should carry it out. Students may be questioned by the principal, who may call the student's home, arrange a conference, and determine the next step.

If school policy leaves the teacher with the responsibility and wide discretion for following up on such incidents, decide on your procedures. Unless the fighting was very mild or stopped immediately, you will have to talk with the children's parents before the children go home. In any case, it is generally best to arrange a cooling-off period. If you cannot find someone to supervise your class, let the fighters wait in separate areas of your classroom or in the school office. Older children can cool off by writing their versions of how the fight started. If you do not know what started the fight, try to find out from uninvolved students. As soon as you have an opportunity, meet with the offenders and get each one's point of view. The conference should focus on the inappropriateness of fighting and the need to resolve problems in ways other than physical aggression, accusations, or personal criticism. Help each student understand the other's point of view so they have a basis for better communication. Finally, stress the importance and your expectations of cooperativeness and friendliness toward one another, or at the least, the need to stay away from each other for the time being.

During the next day or two, watch for any indications of residual hostility. If the issue seems not to have been resolved, follow up by contacting the children's parents, discussing the matter with your principal, or talking with the students again.

Power Struggles

Dealing effectively with power struggles requires understanding what motivates this behavior and using techniques that deescalate the anger. What drives people to attack others generally arises from needs for power, belonging, and respect. For students who act out hostile and aggressive feelings, one or more of these needs is unmet in their lives. Allen Mendler (1997) (*Power Struggles: Successful techniques for educators,* Rochester, NY: Discipline Associates) has a number of suggested strategies for handling this problem.

Defiance or hostility is understandably threatening to teachers. They feel, and rightfully so, that if students are allowed to get away with it, the behavior may continue, and other students will be more likely to react in the same way. A student who has provoked a confrontation, usually publicly, feels that backing down would cause a loss of face in front of peers. The best way to deal with such an event is to try to defuse it by keeping it private and handling it individually with the student.

If an incident occurs during a lesson and is not extreme, deal with it by trying to depersonalize the event and avoid a power struggle: "This is taking time away from the lesson. I will discuss it with you in a few minutes when I have time." If the student does not accept the opportunity you have provided and presses the confrontation further, instruct the student to leave the room and wait in the hall. After the student has had time to cool off, give your class something to do and discuss the problem with the student.

When discussing the incident, remain objective. Remember—act, don't react. Listen to the student's point of view and respond to it, but do not engage in an argument. Separate the student's reason or excuse from the behavior itself, and point out that the behavior was not acceptable. State the consequence clearly, and implement it. If you are not sure how to respond, give yourself time by saying that you will think about it and discuss it later. However, you should still administer the penalty.

In an extreme (and rare) case, the student may be totally uncooperative and refuse to keep quiet or leave the room. If this happens, you can escort the student from the room yourself or, when dealing with a student who is older or larger, call or send another student to the office for assistance. In most cases, however, as long as you stay calm and refuse to get into a power struggle with the student, the student will accept the opportunity to cool down.

Although large-scale school violence is still extremely rare, heightened concern over isolated events in recent years has led many districts and schools to develop emergency plans similar to those for fires or natural disasters. Of course, you will need to familiarize yourself with these plans, which probably include steps such as remaining calm, moving students quickly to a safe area, and contacting administration and emergency personnel.

A Final Reminder: Think and Act Positively

In this chapter, many of the strategies for dealing with problem behaviors involve some form of punishment. This is especially the case for the strategies in the moderate and extensive categories. A drawback to punishment is that, by itself, it doesn't teach the student what behaviors should be practiced, so it may not help them change their behavior in the way you intend. Consequently, it is important for teachers using one of these approaches also to communicate clearly about the desired behaviors. That is, the focus should remain on teaching appropriate behaviors. Furthermore, a classroom in which the main consequences are negative does not have a good climate. Thus, teachers using strategies in the moderate and extensive categories more than occasionally should try to incorporate additional incentives or a reward system into their overall classroom management to help mitigate the effects of using punishment. After correcting student behavior, a teacher who supplies a generous helping of warmth and affection, offers ways to earn back points, and so on, reassures them that all is not lost and that they have been restored to good grace.

Further Reading

Cutona, C., & Guerin, D. (1994). Confronting conflict peacefully: Peer mediation in schools. *Educational Horizons, 72*(2), 95–104.

Problem behavior that pits student against student can escalate to threaten schoolwide climate and safety. These behaviors often frustrate teachers and are difficult to resolve through adult intervention alone. This article describes the use of peer mediation to resolve conflicts. Examples of such programs are also presented, along with an analysis of their benefits.

Davis, Stan. (2004). *Schools where everyone belongs: Practical strategies for reducing bullying.* Wayne, Maine: Stop Bullying Now.

This book outlines research on effective bullying prevention and interventions and presents specific practices and skills that help schools implement that research.

Evertson, C. M., and Weinstein, C. S. (Eds) (in press). *Handbook on classroom management: Research, practice and contemporary issues.* Hillsdale, N.J.: Erlbaum.

Johnson, D. W., & Johnson, R. T. (1994a). Constructive conflict in the schools. *Journal of Social Issues, 50*(1), 117–137.

Learning how to handle conflict constructively is a major accomplishment that eludes many adolescents and children (not to mention adults). This article describes the peer mediation approach to handling conflict, along with championing the use of cooperative strategies and structured controversy. Procedures involved in classroom-based and schoolwide peer mediation programs are carefully described, along with their rationale and supporting research.

Martin, H., & Hayes, S. (1998). Overcoming obstacles: Approaches to dealing with problem pupils. *British Journal of Special Education, 25*(3), 135–139.

This study highlights the fact that the context within which behavior difficulties occur plays a role in their occurrence. Students with behavior difficulties are more engaged and better behaved when they enjoy the lesson and when they are able to quickly experience some level of success with the lesson. However, appropriate behavior does not always indicate student on-task involvement with a lesson.

McCarney, S. B., & McCain, B. R. (1995). *The behavior dimensions intervention manual.* Columbia, Mo.: Hawthorne Educational Services, Inc.

This book presents clearly described interventions to address the most common and disruptive behavior problems reported in schools. Some interventions may be used as a general approach for groups of students; others are quite specific and are to be used for an individual student.

Mendler, Allen. (1997). *Power struggles: Successful techniques for educators.* Rochester, N.Y.: Discipline Associates.

This short, easy-to-read book outlines specific steps teachers and other school staff can take to de-escalate the cycle of hostility that can occur when students are confrontational. It includes checklists and other aids to help identify causes of power struggles and other hostile behavior.

Myles, B. S., & Simpson, R. L. (1994). Prevention and management considerations for aggressive and violent children and youth. *Education and Treatment of Children, 17,* 370–384.

Aggression is typically preceded by warning signs and follows a sequence of stages. This article describes prevention and intervention strategies keyed to these stages. Many of the suggested strategies are also useful for nonaggressive inappropriate behaviors.

Shores, R. E., Gunter, P. L., & Jack, S. L. (1993). Classroom management strategies: Are they setting events for coercion? *Behavioral Disorders, 18*(2), 92–102.

In describing the difference between positive and coercive interactions between students, especially those with behavior difficulties, and teachers, the authors suggest that most often teachers have coercive interactions with their students. To counter this potential difficulty, the authors present the value of positive interactions and the likelihood that these types of interactions will increase student performance, enhance the classroom climate, and make classroom management more effective.

Sprick, R. (1995). *The teacher's encyclopedia of behavior management: 100 problems/500 plans.* Longmont, Colo.: Sopris West.

This book addresses individual and classwide problems common to schools. It includes model plans along with specific interventions.

www.state.ky.us/agencies/behave/homepage

Organized by the Kentucky Department of Education, it assists parents and teachers in gaining access to information and sharing effective practices regarding a full range of behavior problems.

www.cfchildren.org

Committee for Children is an international organization committed to social, emotional, and academic learning. Special topics include bullying, youth violence, and emergent literacy. "Steps to Respect" is an award-winning program to combat bullying.

www.stopbullyingnow.com

This site presents practical research-based strategies to reduce bullying in schools. The Power Point presentation summarizing the basics of bullying prevention is very informative.

Suggested Activities

1. Review the descriptions of problem types presented at the beginning of the chapter. Decide which interventions would be best suited for each type. Given several alternative interventions for any type of problem, how would you decide which to use?

2. Within each type of intervention—minor, moderate, or extensive—are there any strategies that you distinctly prefer? Do you reject any? Discuss your reasons for liking or disliking particular approaches.

3. In this list of problem behaviors, decide on a strategy for dealing with each and also an alternative response if your first approach does not produce good results. Indicate any assumptions you are making about the teaching context as you choose your strategy.

   ■ *Situation 1.* Ardyth and Melissa talk and pass notes as you conduct a class discussion. Several other students whisper or daydream.

   ■ *Situation 2.* Desi and Bryce talk constantly. They refuse to get to work, and they argue with you when you ask them to open their books.

   ■ *Situation 3.* Joe manages to get most of his work done, but in the process he is constantly disruptive. He teases the girls sitting around him, keeping them constantly laughing and competing for his attention. Joe makes wisecracks in response to almost anything you say. When confronted, he grins charmingly and responds with exaggerated courtesy, much to the delight of the rest of the class.

   ■ *Situation 4.* When someone bumped into Marc at the drinking fountain, he turned around and spit water at the other child. Later Marc ordered a boy who was standing near his desk to get away, and he then shoved the boy. On the way back from the cafeteria, Marc got into a name-calling contest with another boy.

4. Make a list of student behaviors including defiance, rudeness, aggression, and unresponsiveness that are the most likely to embarrass you or make you uncomfortable. Think in advance about how you might handle each one.

5. Find out if your school has a policy regarding bullying and how that policy is communicated to students and parents.

10

Managing Special Groups

Although the classroom management principles and guidelines discussed in previous chapters of this book apply to most classroom settings, classroom management is also affected by the characteristics of students making up the class. The ages, academic ability levels, goals, interests, and home backgrounds of students have an impact on their classroom behavior. Consequently, adjustments in management and instructional organization practices are sometimes needed to meet the needs of different groups. Among the students who frequently present special challenges are those who are working below or well above grade level, those who are academically or physically challenged, and those whose English language skills are limited. A classroom often includes all of these types of students, presenting a special challenge to the teacher. Being effective with students having such diverse needs and abilities requires special effort.

This chapter presents information and suggestions that, combined with the principles in previous chapters, will help you organize and manage classes with a range of student achievement or ability levels, groups of students with below-level skills, and students with special needs.

Assessing Entering Achievement

To identify the extent of differences in needs and ability levels (i.e., the degree of heterogeneity) in your classroom, you should use several sources of information. These sources include your tests, your own observation of each student, and indicators of performance available in each student's file, including assessments from prior teachers, samples of the student's work, and standardized achievement test information. Of course, if one of your students is identified as having special needs, you will consult with the resource teacher, but be cautious about forming a hasty impression of a student's abilities based on only one source of information. Forming low expectations of some students and communicating these to the students can cause them to achieve below their potential.

Because of the importance of reading, language arts, and mathematics skills in the elementary school curriculum, these subjects will be the major focus of your initial assessment. As you evaluate your students, be alert to study and work habits such as following directions and maintaining attention to a task. Children with poor work and study skills or who are highly distractible may require special consideration in your room arrangement, in planning for instructional activities, and in monitoring.

When obtaining information about entering reading and math skill levels, give special attention to students for whom you lack information. Typically, these are students who have transferred from another school district. You must also be careful about the assessment if existing information is not consistent. Assess such children individually by listening to them read, checking their vocabulary and word attack strategies, and testing to identify their math skills. Consult with other teachers, other professionals, or both for help in selecting suitable assessment procedures if you do not already have them.

"I'm an underachiever. . . . What's your racket?"

© 1968 by Bill Knowlton. Reprinted from *Classroom Chuckles,* published by Scholastic Book Services, a Division of Scholastic, Inc., by permission of Bill Knowlton.

It is best to delay individual student assessment until several days after the beginning of school. During such testing, it will be difficult to monitor your class, and you may also have to leave students too long in independent work. By delaying testing, you can observe the students first, and the students will become better acquainted and more comfortable with you before they are tested. If you do individual testing, plan enough work to keep your class busy. When several students must be assessed individually, space the testing over several days.

Identifying Special Groups

For the purpose of classroom instruction, it is important to determine the range of entering achievement in basic skill subjects, the degree to which individual students are unable to work effectively with the grade-level curriculum, and other special needs of your students. Other characteristics such as students' interests and backgrounds can also affect learning and instruction and should be considered whenever possible as you plan activities and set goals.

Information on student ability levels can be used to identify small groups for instruction, to pair students for peer tutoring, and to create cooperative groups for learning activities. Each of these types of activities requires special planning and management considerations.

Strategies for Individual Differences

In the next sections, we describe strategies frequently used to adjust for individual differences and examine management concerns associated with them.

Team Teaching

Teachers at the same grade level frequently form teams to deal with heterogeneous student populations. Students can then be reassigned to different teachers on the team for instruction in one or more subjects. This allows teachers to form relatively more homogeneous subgroups than would be possible using only students initially assigned to their individual classrooms. For example, two or three students whose entering reading skills are extremely low might be grouped for reading instruction with similar students from other classrooms. At the same time, students at the highest level in the classes might be combined into a single group and taught by another teacher on the team. This arrangement permits instruction for these students to be targeted closer to their skill levels than would be possible if they remained in their original classes. Still, it is important that these students participate in groups with mixed ability levels in other activities.

Team approaches to heterogeneity can be applied to a variety of subjects but are most common in reading and mathematics instruction. If ability grouping is used, teaming should be considered whenever the range of abilities is too great to be accommodated by three groups in reading and two groups in mathematics. Although extreme heterogeneity within a class could theoretically be accommodated by forming more groups, doing so is usually not practical because it would place excessive demands on teacher planning and would reduce the amount of time each group receives for instruction. Because teaming requires careful planning and cooperation, the following items are important to consider.

COORDINATION OF SCHEDULES

The teachers on the team must establish compatible schedules for the subjects being team taught. If teachers deviate from the schedule without warning, children from other classrooms may be kept waiting with nothing to do, and everyone will be thrown off schedule.

MOVEMENT

Because some students will be going from one room to another, they must be taught what procedures and behavior to use during transitions. A teacher should accompany children in transit between rooms, at least until they have learned the routine.

REMINDING STUDENTS WHAT THEY ARE SUPPOSED TO TAKE WITH THEM

Sometimes children have trouble remembering their materials. When they do not bring the appropriate materials, they may be sent back to their classrooms, losing valuable instructional time and sometimes disturbing students in both rooms. If students need different sets of materials on different days, all teachers involved should be notified so they can help students remember what is needed and when, perhaps by posting a list of materials to take or by reminding students as they prepare to leave the room.

RULES AND PROCEDURES

Students coming to you from another teacher's class will not know your expectations for their behavior. Therefore, discuss with them the rules for conduct in your room and the procedures needed for small-group work and seatwork. Do this when you first meet with your new students. Monitor them carefully until good behavior becomes established. If possible, plan rules and procedures with other members of the team to establish a common set of expectations. Consistency across settings simplifies the task of teaching students to behave correctly.

MAINTAINING RESPONSIBILITY FOR WORK

In addition to rules for conduct and procedures for behavior, care must be taken to keep students responsible for their work. This may be more difficult to do in a team-teaching situation than with the students in your regular class because the full range of incentives, penalties, and parental contact may be limited. Also, you will not be able to supervise the students at other times of the day when they might have an opportunity to work on assignments (and when, ideally, you would check work and provide supplementary instruction). For these reasons, several steps should be followed to keep students accountable:

1. When you meet with students each day, check their work before you dismiss them, and give students whatever feedback they need to complete the work successfully.
2. Be clear about your expectations for work, other requirements, and your grading criteria.
3. Return graded papers promptly. Don't let these materials accumulate.
4. Be certain that students, especially younger children, realize that you are responsible for checking their work and assigning a report card grade.
5. Contact parents if children begin to skip assignments in your class. Don't rely on the homeroom teacher to do this.

Modifying Whole-Class Instruction

In some subjects, the use of small groups for instruction is not feasible or even desirable. Limited time, the problem of ascertaining individual differences on relevant entering skills, and greater procedural complexity may make small-group instruction less efficient than whole-class instruction. When used for subjects such as science or social studies, whole-class instruction can be modified to accommodate extremes in abilities and interests. A number of simple modifications and cautions should be considered.

INTERACTIVE INSTRUCTION

Try to involve all students in presentations, discussions, and recitations. Do so by making a conscious effort to call on all students, not only those who are eager to respond. Students with a special ability or an obvious interest in a topic can be encouraged to complete special projects and to organize their ideas in oral reports to the class. These opportunities allow the students to advance their understanding and receive recognition.

SEATING ARRANGEMENTS

Students who need closer supervision or more than the usual amount of explanation should be seated near the front of the room (or wherever you usually conduct whole-class presentations). Their proximity to you will enable you to check for understanding more readily and make it easier to monitor their behavior and progress.

DIRECTIONS

Communicating instructions and directions to a highly diverse class requires care. Be certain you have all students' attention, and provide both oral and written directions when feasible. Some students have difficulty following a long series of verbal directions. Break directions into manageable chunks, and provide visual cues. The use of questions to verify comprehension and careful monitoring are also helpful. Be certain to check with students who frequently have problems following directions. If you have seated them near you, you will be able to provide them with added assistance as needed.

ASSIGNMENTS

If you give the same assignments to all the students in a highly heterogeneous class, the work may be much too easy for some students and much too difficult for others. Consider giving assignments in two parts: a basic assignment for all students to complete and a second, more difficult part that is assigned to some students or that can be completed for extra credit. When assignments are the same for everyone, the students complete them with different degrees of proficiency and speed. In such cases, use a grading or credit system that, at least in part, emphasizes individual progress rather than competition among students. Enrichment or extra-credit material for students who finish classwork early should be work related and should not distract other students. Avoid free-time activities that are so attractive that slower-working students feel deprived or attempt to quit or rush through their work. Set up a system for giving credit, feedback, or recognition for completion of enrichment activities. If you allow students to read when they finish their work, be sure to provide supplementary reading materials at a variety of reading levels.

Supplementary Instruction

Sometimes student needs in some subject areas cannot be well met in the regular education classroom. For example, a student's skills may be so deficient in reading or math that he or she cannot profit from small-group instruction; even the lowest group may be too far beyond the student's current level. Or a student may be so distracted by the stimulation of twenty-five or thirty students in a regular classroom that he or she cannot focus on assignments long enough to complete them. Such students may fall behind in their performance, even though they possess average or above-average ability. Students whose first language is not English may need intensive help that cannot be provided in the regular instructional program. Finally, some students may possess special talents that programs for the gifted can more fully develop. In all of these cases, supplementary programs may be available. The term *pull-out* is sometimes applied to these programs because the students are taken out of the regular classroom for part of the school day to receive special instruction. Check to see whether a student is enrolled in a pull-out program intended to supplement or to replace his or her regular classroom instruction. This will have important implications for your planning. Examples of pull-out programs include the following:

- **Special education:** This is usually available in a resource room. Students with learning disabilities and other conditions that interfere with learning or adjustment in a general classroom setting receive instruction (usually reading or math or both) for part of the day. These students return to the regular classroom for other instruction.
- **Title I programs:** These are special programs established in schools that serve students from lower-income families. Students with deficits in academic skills receive supplementary instruction from special teachers.
- **Enrichment programs:** Programs that provide enrichment in particular subjects are often established for students who have special talent in the area. These programs frequently use community resources, parents, or other volunteers as well as the regular teaching staff to provide programs during school hours or after hours.
- **English as a Second Language programs (ESL):** These programs assist students with limited English proficiency (LEP) in learning the English language and provide support for the students, their regular classroom teachers, and the students' families.

The aspect of supplementary programs that can have a major impact on your classroom management plan is the removal of students from your class during the time that regular instruction is proceeding. Thus, scheduling must be carefully planned so that the pull-out students do not miss essential instruction and so that the other students' instructional program is not interrupted. Transitions out of and back into your classroom can become a major headache if they are not handled well.

COORDINATING TIMES WITH OTHER TEACHERS

As soon as schoolwide schedules are set for lunch periods and activities such as music, art, and physical education classes, plan a schedule with the other teachers that will be as convenient as possible for everyone. If a number of students leave for special reading instruction, arrange with the reading teacher to have these students leave in a group at a time when you will be meeting with a reading group in your class. If several students are pulled out for special instruction in a subject such as mathematics, you will probably want to schedule your math instruction for the rest of the class at that time.

STAYING ON SCHEDULE

When class schedules involve pull-outs and drop-ins, it is especially important for teachers to stay on schedule so that students can be where they need to be at appropriate times. Have a large clock placed where everyone can see it. If you have trouble remembering to look at the clock, enlist the aid of the students in prompting you. Older students should eventually assume responsibility for their own schedules. You may want to post a list of times at which students are supposed to leave to remind both you and the students. You can also set a timer as a reminder.

HAVING SOMETHING FOR DROP-IN STUDENTS TO DO WHILE WAITING FOR INSTRUCTION

Sometimes a teacher is not quite through with one group when it is time for another group to meet. Students who are working at their desks in the teacher's room should have enough activities to keep them busy. However, drop-in students sometimes arrive early and have nowhere specific to sit other than in the small group. You will need a procedure for dealing with these students so that small groups and seatworkers are not distracted. Some teachers tell students to take an empty seat while waiting. Other teachers set aside a waiting area on a small rug or at a table. While there, students can get copies of their textbooks or workbooks and begin reading the next lesson or do other constructive activities.

GETTING RETURNING STUDENTS INVOLVED AGAIN

After receiving instruction outside the room, some pull-out students may tend to dawdle or seem confused about what they are supposed to do when they return to the room. The best way to avoid confusion is to establish routines so that students always know what to do when they return. It is a good idea to post assignments or give students a list of assignments to help them remember. If you are working with a small group when some students return, give the small group something to do and go to the returning students to be sure they get back on task. Student helpers can be given the responsibility for explaining the assignment or activity to individual returning students.

ACTIVITIES WHEN SUPPLEMENTARY INSTRUCTION IS NOT HELD

Sometimes the special teacher is absent or the special class is not conducted for some other reason. When this occurs, it is important to have something for these students to do while you carry on with regular instruction. In some cases, students may be included in regular class activities. In other cases, you must provide special activities. If possible, meet regularly with the other teachers so you will know what students are working on and be able to assign appropriate activities. Have free-time or enrichment activities set aside to accommodate varying levels of ability. It is important to monitor these students and give them something meaningful to do; otherwise, valuable learning time is lost and they may become bored or disruptive.

IN-CLASS AIDES

Sometimes teachers are fortunate enough to have parents or other adult volunteers, teacher aides, or university education students to help out in their classrooms. These aides may be assigned to help with a particular subject or be available to help with any subjects. Other aides may help with materials and administrative tasks and have little contact with the children. If you have one or more aides, there are several things you can do to promote smooth functioning in your classroom. You should be specific in informing the aide of his or her responsibilities for teaching or working with students and for disciplining students. You will probably want aides to enforce your rules consistently when they are in charge of students. If you must leave the room, inform students that the aide will be in charge of the class and will enforce the rules as you do. If the aide will be working with individual students or small groups, create a space that will not cause distractions for the rest of the class, particularly if you are instructing simultaneously. Students should be told whether and when they may go to the aide for help.

CONTENT MASTERY CLASSROOM

A special form of supplementary (pull-out) program that has become widely used is the Content Mastery Classroom. This program designates one or more teachers, at least one of whom is trained in special education, to work with students identified as needing supplemental instruction. The Content Mastery Classroom is one to which students may come from their own class for extra help on assignments, new material, and so forth, or to have extra time to spend on tests. In many school districts, both a general education and a special education teacher are available in the CMC to help students, but in some places this is solely a special education option. An advantage of the CMC, compared to a resource or self-contained class, is that it allows the integration of special education students in regular education classrooms but provides support for them when they need more help. Also, the regular education teacher, who may have thirty other students, does not have to provide as much supplemental instruction. Another advantage is that students may either be sent by the general education teacher or go at their own initiative when they feel the need for extra help.

It is important to coordinate with the CMC teachers about which students may go to the CMC and when and what kind of information and materials they will need to take with them. For example, for younger students, a laminated assignment card may be helpful, with your name and grade level printed on it; when a student is to go to the CMC, you might write on the card a brief description of the help the student needs, page numbers in the text the student will take, and the time the student leaves your room. It is also possible, however, that the CMC teacher will have routines for getting information about student assignments, and so on, and that you can use these.

When you have one or more special-needs students who use the CMC regularly, provide assignments ahead of time (e.g., weekly) so that appropriate planning may be done by the CMC teacher. When students take your tests in the

CMC, be sure you have discussed your expectations for assistance ahead of time. Because the CMC teacher works with your students individually, he or she may have suggestions for adapting instruction or management that will aid you in teaching the student. Similarly, because CMC teachers have had substantial training and experience in working with students with special needs, you may be able to benefit from their suggestions. The CMC teacher may be reluctant to give unsolicited advice, so be sure to ask if you have questions about how best to work with particular students.

INCLUSION

Inclusion programs for students with special needs provide support to enable them to participate in as many regular education activities as possible. Typically a special education teacher works with regular education teachers of designated students, both to help modify assignments and written material as specified on the students' Individual Education Plans (IEPs) and to provide assistance within the classroom itself. Scheduled planning meetings between the special education and the regular education teachers are crucial to the success of any inclusion program. Only by knowing exactly what activities are planned by the regular education teacher can the special education teacher know how to provide support for the student.

On some occasions, the special education teacher may be in the regular classroom, such as when students are working on assignments or class projects. At other times, the special education teacher may provide copies of modified assignments. Both the timing and nature of the special education teacher's participation in class, as well as the extent of lesson modifications, can be specified during planning sessions. Case Studies 10.1 and 10.2 at the end of this chapter illustrate how regular education teachers can accommodate students with special needs in the classroom.

Individualized Instruction

When each student receives instruction, is given assignments at a level established by a careful assessment of entering skills, and is encouraged to progress at whatever pace his or her abilities and motivation allow, the instructional program is said to be individualized. Some educators consider individualized instruction to be the best means of coping with heterogeneity because it offers, at least in principle, instruction tailored to the needs of each child. However, individualized instruction is difficult to implement. It requires (1) careful and continuous assessment of individuals' progress, (2) management of time so that all students receive adequate interactive instruction from the teacher, (3) sufficient resources, including materials suitable for all ability levels in the class, and (4) time for the teacher to plan and develop appropriate activities. The absence of one or more of these features makes it difficult to mount an effective instructional program. Also, teachers who wish to implement such programs should do so gradually, allowing themselves adequate time to develop the necessary resources. Because of these difficulties, we regard the first strategies for coping with heterogeneity and low-achieving students to be the modification of whole-class instruction, supplementary instruction, and team teaching. Only when these strategies are not adequate should individualized instruction be employed.

When individualization of instruction is used for one or more subjects, you should anticipate a number of management problems and take action to prevent them or at least minimize their impact.

TRANSITIONS

Students engaged in individual rather than group activities generally finish at different times. If the next activity is also an individual activity, many individual transitions will occur throughout the period of instruction. This can cause confusion and lost time. Some students may not know what to do; others may delay starting the next activity. More efficient transitions can be effected if the teacher is alert to help students who are between activities. Assignments must be posted or written somewhere so that students will know what to do next. The teacher can also have students bring completed work to be checked to provide structure during the transition and to be certain that students know how to get started on the next activity.

MONITORING BEHAVIOR

Different expectations for students in different activities, along with a variety of simultaneous activities, make monitoring student behavior during individualized instruction difficult. Also, the teacher often instructs individual students or performs other tasks associated with individualized instruction (such as assessment), thus adding to the complexity of monitoring. To overcome these problems, the following key behaviors should be practiced:

- Know what all students are supposed to be doing at any given time so that you can support their efforts and prevent problems.
- Be sure students know what they are expected to do and what conduct is appropriate in different activities.
- Be alert for students who are having difficulty getting started or completing an activity so that you can provide help. Don't get overly engrossed with helping one or a few students, and don't wait until students quit working or become disruptive before providing assistance.
- Circulate among the students and look at their work periodically. Scan the room frequently to detect early signs of frustration or task avoidance.
- Usually a few students require more supervision than others. When possible, be sure these students are seated where you can observe and assist them readily.

ENCOURAGING STUDENT RESPONSIBILITY FOR WORK

The use of an individualized instruction program does not guarantee that students will accept responsibility for completing assignments and participating in learning activities. In fact, some students take advantage of the more complex instructional arrangements and limitations on the teacher's monitoring capability to avoid responsibility and to expend minimal effort. To avoid these problems, give clear directions for assignments and other activities. Many teachers prefer to review directions with students at the beginning of the period devoted to the individualized instructional activities. A basic set of activities can often be listed on the board and reviewed, or students can be given activity or assignment folders that list what is to be done. Such a folder can also be used to check off completed work. This system helps both the teacher and the students keep track of progress. Setting time limits for work on one activity before proceeding to the next will help students pace their efforts.

Students should expect their work to be checked frequently. If they become accustomed to simply completing one activity and starting a new one without feedback, their performance will deteriorate. The teacher should develop monitoring procedures that include periodic progress checks and evaluation and feedback on completed assignments and other work. It is also important to review overall student progress and decide whether the pace and scope of work are adequate. Some teachers prefer weekly or biweekly reviews and a short conference with individual students for this purpose.

Sometimes the teacher's role in individualization diminishes to the point that almost all of the teacher's time is devoted to making assessments, giving assignments, keeping records, and checking. When this occurs, students receive little interactive instruction from the teacher and do little except complete worksheets. The teacher's diminished instructional role may be partly due to the incorrect perception that because instruction is individualized, the teacher can instruct only one student at a time. In fact, it is far more efficient if the teacher presents information and conducts recitations with groups of students, supplementing these group lessons with individual instruction for students who require extra help.

CONTRACTS

Contracts are often used with individual instruction. Contracts usually include a list of assignments or activities to be completed by a student during a fixed period of time, such as a day or a week. Contracts also may specify the goals or objectives, materials, and incentives associated with completing the contract. Use of a contract has a number of advantages: It is a good way to communicate assignments and objectives, it enables students to suggest modifications they would find helpful or interesting, and the student's signature on the contract can increase motivation for completion within the agreed-on time period.

Additional Strategies

STUDENT COOPERATION: HELP FROM PEERS

Another method for coping with extreme heterogeneity and for dealing with low achievers is to use students to help other students. Examples of such peer helping arrangements include the following:

- Students work in pairs, reading and listening to each other read. "Reading with a buddy" can be part of contract work.

- Certain students are assigned as monitors to help other students when the teacher is busy with group or individual instruction.
- When the teacher is busy with small-group instruction, students who need help are encouraged to get assistance from another student before interrupting the teacher.
- Group leaders are assigned to each learning station to answer questions and set up materials.
- A capable, mature student is assigned as a helper for another student who needs frequent assistance. The helper's responsibilities are to answer questions and explain directions.
- Students may be permitted to help or seek help from a neighbor on some seatwork activities.
- A student from an upper grade may tutor a younger student.

When using students as helpers, recognize the potential for excessive noise, poor attention to the task, or excessive reliance on the helper by the helpee. Also, not all students are amenable to this type of arrangement or work well together. These negative effects can be averted by communicating clearly what is and is not permitted and by monitoring the helping arrangements and relationships to be sure that no undesirable side effects develop. As is true for all of the variations from regular instruction patterns, gradual introduction of new arrangements gives the best opportunity for managing their implementation and for correcting problems.

COOPERATIVE GROUPS

For many activities, using small groups with mixed ability levels, diverse backgrounds, or both provides a good opportunity for all students to help and to learn from each other. Researchers such as Robert Slavin (1995) have shown that working in mixed-ability teams can benefit both higher- and lower-achieving students in many subject areas. Benefits of cooperative groups include increased achievement, positive race relations, mutual concern among students, and increased self-esteem. Refer to Chapter 6 for details on managing cooperative groups.

PEER TUTORING

Peer tutoring provides an opportunity for each student to have access to one-on-one assistance, particularly when the teacher is unavailable to provide assistance. This can be done during class by pairing students at similar levels to work together or by asking a student who has achieved a certain level or learned a concept to work with another student who has not. The student who receives assistance benefits from individualized instruction. The helper, or peer tutor, benefits from planning for and explaining the concept.

To use peer tutoring effectively, certain management issues must be addressed. You must decide when tutoring is and is not acceptable. There may be some subjects for which peer tutoring is not appropriate. For instance, you may not be assured that the potential peer tutors have sufficiently learned the concept to be able to provide assistance.

Decide where tutoring will occur. Some teachers provide a special location within the classroom where peer interactions are less likely to interrupt other classroom activities or disturb students who are working unassisted. Others may allow students to work quietly side by side at their desks.

If you use peer tutors, you must teach students to be peer tutors. Potential tutors should be shown how to model behaviors, instructed in how to ask questions to assess the other student's understanding, and counseled on interpersonal behaviors. For long-term peer tutors, you may want to provide a brief training during class or after school. Other directions can be given as part of the overall instructions for an activity.

Working with Students with Special Needs

This section deals with students who have special needs, either because they are physically or mentally challenged or because they have background characteristics such as language proficiency that affect their classroom performance.

Research on students with special needs because of physical, mental, or emotional disabilities has shown the benefits of providing instruction to these students in the least restrictive environment (LRE), meaning among their nondisabled peers to the extent that is reasonable. Further, it is legally mandated that special education students be served in the LRE. As a result, more and more students with special needs are being served in the general classroom with some outside help from specialized teachers. Meeting these students' needs presents special challenges to teachers with a classroom full of children. Fortunately, research has provided specific guidelines to help teachers work with these students in ways that promote their peer acceptance and their self-esteem as well as their academic achievement. Following are suggestions for planning instruction for students with different types of special needs.

Students with Learning Disabilities

Although there is still no consensus for a concise definition of learning disability, certain characteristics are commonly seen. A primary feature is more difficulty with and lower achievement in certain academic areas than would otherwise be expected based on these students' overall ability levels. Other common problems experienced by these students are disorganization and a disconcerting tendency to forget something they seemed to understand thoroughly just a short time earlier. Accompanying these difficulties is a natural sense of frustration and the risk of developing a generalized attitude of anger or hopelessness along with a negative view of themselves.

Students with learning disabilities generally respond well to a positive and structured approach with predictable routines. They may forget steps even in familiar routines, however, and require much patience and repetition. These students need more help than others in learning to identify and pay attention to relevant cues. Point out cues and relevant directions, and have students repeat directions out loud to be sure they understand what to do. Place a special emphasis on what is correct rather than on what they are doing wrong. Model the appropriate behavior or actions to ensure that they are transferring positive learning rather than reinforcing negative learning. Avoid trial-and-error activities in which students may spend too much time doing the wrong thing, thus adding to their confusion.

Overlearning is important for these students, especially because of their retention problems. Remember that it is more helpful to distribute numerous short practices of tasks over a period of time than to have fewer but longer practices. These students benefit from a wide range of multisensory experiences in learning concepts. These experiences help students with learning disabilities to overcome problems they have because of lack of experience with their environment. Be aware that although social praise may help motivate, it may also interfere with the development of independent decision-making skills. Use praise sparingly, gradually reducing it to enhance internal motivation and satisfaction.

Students with learning disabilities often develop behavior problems. They may benefit from keeping their own records of specific behaviors, including the completion of assignments. This helps them to build a sense of control over themselves and their environment.

Students with Emotional or Behavioral Problems

Remembering that students with a diagnosed emotional disturbance are often different from others merely in the degree of emotionality rather than in the types of feelings they have may relieve some potential anxiety in working with these students. Any psychological report available can be helpful (it must, of course, be treated confidentially), both in shedding light on why students are having such problems and in providing recommendations for working with them successfully. The school psychologist and special education teacher can also help you understand and support these students. It is likely that a behavior management plan has been developed through the special education services, so being familiar with this and clear on how to follow it may prevent problems from occurring. If behavior is a serious issue, it is advisable to overlook minor inappropriate behavior, reinforce acceptable behavior, and reduce known stressors. This may include adjusting your expectations if the student is having an especially bad day. A positive, supportive, structured, and predictable environment is of key importance to help the student feel safe and accepted.

If you have students who tend to have temper outbursts or become easily or violently frustrated and angry, reinforce all attempts they make toward self-control. Learn to recognize any behavioral cues that may precede an outburst so that you can anticipate and intervene to prevent their losing control. Maintain a balanced perspective, remembering that it is more important that they get through the day without an outburst than that they follow instructions exactly or complete assignments errorlessly. Sometimes, if you think problems are developing, but before they escalate, it is helpful to allow the students to change their activity momentarily to defuse the situation (e.g., "Would you be willing to take this note to the office for me?" or "Why don't you get a drink of water and then we'll work this out together?"). Offering structured choices can also be helpful, especially with students who have a strong need to control and who often appear noncompliant and oppositional (e.g., "Would you prefer to do the odd-numbered problems or the even-numbered?" or "Would it be helpful for you to work a while in the study carrel, or do you think you can concentrate well enough at your own desk?").

Work with your principal, counselor, other teachers, and the child's parent(s) to devise a plan to carry out if a student with emotional problems has a tantrum or explodes in your classroom. These students may have to be removed from the classroom to a safe time-out place; they should be supervised as they cool down. Students with emotional or behavioral problems often do not know why they lose control and are frequently embarrassed and remorseful afterward. These students generally do not understand how their feelings relate to what has happened and have not learned to discern the subtle changes in themselves that trigger such outbursts. Learning to anticipate and divert these feelings in an acceptable manner is often their greatest need.

After any kind of violent outburst, when both you and the student have regained your composure (and it may take longer for one than for the other), it is important that you reestablish your relationship with the student. Other than attempting to learn from each incident to prevent future occurrences, it is best to leave each incident behind and not focus on past failures.

One crucial reminder: When students lose rational control and are verbally or physically abusive or violent, it is rarely personally directed at you, even though it may sound and feel that way. If you have learned about the backgrounds and histories of these students, logic will tell you that you have merely been a handy target, not the root cause of their pain or rage. Logic and feelings do not always coincide, however. Having someone listen to you and give you support and feedback when dealing with extremely volatile students is essential to your ability to continue to be supportive for these students.

Students with Serious Social Deficits (Asperger's Syndrome)

Within the past few years, increasing numbers of students who have odd or severe social skills problems are being diagnosed as having Asperger's Syndrome, technically a mild form of autism (Hodgdon 1995). As very young children, many of these students appear to be especially bright because of their ability to learn, remember, and recite facts. As they grow older, however, it becomes apparent that they have limited understanding of these facts and cannot generalize or apply any of the things they relate so accurately. Another severe deficiency becomes apparent: Although highly verbal, they have extremely poor communication skills. They tend to stand too close, avoid eye contact, talk too long and loudly in a preaching or robotic manner, and talk in great detail about factual matters that do not interest their peers.

Further, they are quite rigid in their outlook and develop set ways of doing things. They escalate quickly into extreme and visible anxiety when a routine is changed or when their expectations are not met. They may also have an acute sensitivity to sounds, with loud noises causing pain to their ears. Frequently they have concomitant learning disabilities and poor gross and fine motor skills. When emotionally aroused, some individuals may engage in repetitive stereotyped movements such as hand flapping.

When students have had such problems to a severe degree, it is likely that they have been referred for special education services and that some attempt has been made to teach them adaptive ways to cope with their strong needs for regularity and predictability, as well as methods for preventing escalating behavior with anxious verbal or physical aggression. Because most of these students have at least average intellectual abilities, they can usually succeed in general education classes and thrive on that intellectual stimulation. However, their odd reactions and behavior, despite coping mechanisms they may have learned, require that teachers understand their difficulties and use strategies to help them tolerate situations they may find anxiety provoking (such as those involving change, movement, or noise). The following teaching strategies can help support these students in the regular classroom.

1. Because students with Asperger's Syndrome are visual, rather than verbal, learners, use visual cues and prompts; physically demonstrate how you want things done, and use manipulatives whenever possible.

2. Often these students cannot process visual and auditory input simultaneously; that is, they are unable to look and listen at the same time. If this is a problem, give them either a visual or an auditory task, not both together.

3. Make instructions brief. These students often have difficulty remembering sequences, especially in terms of how they are to apply instructions. Write instructions for them, or check to be sure they have written them correctly. Otherwise, give only one or two instructions at a time.

4. Remember that eye contact is extremely difficult and anxiety producing for them. Although you may insist on their attention, do not insist that they maintain direct eye contact.

5. The use of "social stories" or "social scripting" has been found to be a highly effective technique to help these students prepare for new events or experiences or for changes in routine. These are often used extensively in elementary school, but there are situations in which they may be helpful in middle or high school as well. Their purpose is to prevent an escalation of anxiety and facilitate a smooth transition through new experiences or changes in routine. The teacher may write out the story or work with the student to write it before the event. The student should then read it several times so it will become familiar before time for the change to occur. Example: "On Thursday, I am not going to math class from advisory. Instead I am going with my advisory class to an assembly in the auditorium. After the assembly I will go to math class."

6. These students may be skilled at computer work or drawing; or they may be fixated on a particular topic, such as maps, weather, trains, and so on. Capitalize on these strengths or interests: reward students for completing assignments, pro-

vide opportunities to contribute positively to the class, and develop their talents or knowledge and enhance self-esteem.

7. Students with Asperger's Syndrome do not readily learn social skills by observation, so be alert to awkward situations and be willing to give them specific feedback or step-by-step instruction. If you cannot provide needed instruction in social areas, discuss with the students' special education teacher or counselor any problems you see. When activities within your classroom require extensive peer interactions, consider using the social scripting technique to help such students.

Students with Attention Deficit and Hyperactivity

Broad characteristics of students with attention deficit and hyperactivity include distractibility, a short attention span, impulsiveness, an inability to organize, and a high level of physical movement. As distracting as these behaviors are, it is important to remember that they are not deliberate. Even for the most highly motivated children, it is difficult and takes a long time for them to learn ways to compensate for or control these problems. A low-key approach with much predictability and structure is almost essential to enable these students to function successfully. Frequent communication with parents, often daily, is necessary to ensure that school and home techniques and expectations are compatible.

Techniques that have been found to have the greatest degree of success in working with these children include the following:

- Be sure you have their attention before giving oral instructions.
- Give brief and clear instructions, preferably one step at a time.
- If instructions involve a series of steps, have these written in sequence; teach these students to complete one step before going on to the next. Having them mark off each step as they complete it helps them to keep track and see progress.
- Monitor them closely as they begin a new assignment or activity; be willing to explain directions again.
- Adjust the amount of work required within a time period compatible with their attention span. The amount may be increased gradually as their ability to concentrate increases.
- Remind them that accuracy is more important than speed and that they need not be the first to finish or to speak up. Reinforce neatness and accuracy; when feasible, do not penalize messiness or errors. When accuracy is an issue, reinforce effort.
- Collect completed assignments, because they often lose completed work before turning it in.
- Show them how to use window cards as frames to help focus attention on a specific area, problem, line of print, or paragraph. Teach them to use their fingers as pointers so that they stay focused on the page or line.
- Organize the daily schedule so that stimulating or exciting activities come after, rather than before, activities requiring concentration.

- Develop a plan for them to move around every few minutes; for example, by bringing up their papers after they have completed part of the assignment (e.g., a few math problems, a paragraph).
- Find a spot with few distractions, and offer the option of doing independent work there.
- Prepare several low-pressure, low-risk activities for times when they need to spend a few minutes regaining control or relaxing.
- Teach them relaxation techniques such as deep breathing, tensing and relaxing muscles, and so on, to relieve tension during long periods or tests.
- If students receive medication at school, establish a cue or routine to help them remember to go to the nurse at the proper time. Monitor this until they have assumed the responsibility successfully.
- Express your confidence in them and their ability to learn new concepts and skills.

Students Who Are Deaf or Hearing Impaired

Students with serious hearing loss may be able to function in regular classes if some crucial modifications are made. If you have one or more students who are deaf or hearing impaired, it will be helpful to consult regularly with a teacher specializing in auditory handicaps about students' needs and techniques that benefit. If assistive devices are available (e.g., FM auditory systems, caption decoders for videos), the specialist can show you how to use them.

It is usually best to seat these students near the center of the room and close to the front. It is always wise to face the students when speaking, using the overhead projector rather than the board so that students can see your face while you are writing. Have the room well-lighted so these students can see your lips and face to lip-read. Take care not to stand in front of windows or a bright doorway while talking; the glare behind you can make your face difficult to see.

These students often miss important information, being able to catch only portions of words or phrases. Because understanding is more complex than just hearing or responding to a name and because these students are often reluctant to ask you to repeat, be ready to repeat and rephrase important information or instructions. When possible, provide written backup as well. The amount of new content vocabulary introduced routinely may be overwhelming, so the support of the auditory specialist in introducing vocabulary may be necessary for these students to succeed in the regular classroom. Content Mastery, a special form of supplementary program described earlier in this chapter, may be utilized to reteach, especially for written language assignments.

During classroom discussions, these students need to have you restate other students' questions and responses because deaf or hearing impaired students are probably not able to lip-read these. It is also helpful to check for understanding frequently during guided practice. These students require close monitoring as they begin written work. If note taking is required, ask a student with legible handwriting to take notes, using carbon paper, or to provide a copy to students needing help. Students who are deaf or hearing impaired cannot take notes and lip-read at the same time. During films, the narration and placement of actors may make it impossible to lip-read at all. The specialist may be a helpful resource in locating captioned versions of the videos you plan to use. You might also assign a buddy to cue deaf or hearing impaired students when it is important to watch the teacher, to locate information in the text being discussed, and so on.

Increasingly, students who are deaf or hearing impaired are assigned interpreters to accompany them to regular classes. Again, a consultation with the specialist on your campus is helpful to make clear what the role of the interpreter is to be. Interpreters may assist with oral or sign language interpretation and provide a "communication bridge" between teacher and student. As such, they relay information both from the teacher to the student and vice versa, but they do not typically function as a teacher's assistant in the classroom. Their role is to devote their skills to supporting their assigned student to ensure this student's success.

Students Who Have Visual Impairments

Students who are blind or who have severe visual impairments may be able to function well in regular classes with your help. Suggestions for adaptations of teaching methods and materials should be available in the student's functional visual assessment, written by a teacher of these students. The following suggestions may provide direction in accommodating the needs of these students.

- Remember to read aloud anything that is written on the chalkboard, overhead projector, or chart paper.
- Allow students to use a tape recorder or to have fellow students make copies of their notes for parents to read aloud at home. Large type, dark print, and good contrast are easier to see.
- When possible, use tactile models and hands-on activities along with verbal descriptions to demonstrate concepts; these students often miss gestures, facial expressions, and details in demonstrations.
- Encourage students to ask for help; if in doubt about how you can help them, ask them directly and do not hesitate to discuss their vision problems with them.
- Remember that students with partial vision may tire more quickly, in part because of the concentration and effort required to perceive material close to their eyes. Frequent changes in the focus of activities may alleviate this.
- Seat these students with their backs to the windows. Glare on materials, on someone who is speaking, or on the chalkboard or other displays seriously impedes their ability to see at all.
- Allow these students to walk up to the chalkboard or other displays as needed.
- Students with visual impairments may have limited knowledge of spatial relationships and directionality and may miss social cues. Assist these students in peer interactions and personal adjustment.

Students with Limited English Proficiency

Many students in our schools have a first language other than English. Some of these students have acquired sufficient English language skills to perform successfully in English-only classes. Other students have not acquired a sufficient level of skill in speaking, understanding, reading, or writing English, and they need additional assistance to participate successfully in school activities.

Some students need bilingual classes in which content is presented in their native language, with a specified amount of time daily spent learning English. Other children know enough English to benefit from being in a class with a bilingual teacher; here, the content is presented in English, but the teacher is able to explain in the students' primary language when necessary. For many students, English learning occurs in conjunction with content learning in a regular classroom, ideally with the aid of an English-as-a-Second-Language (ESL) certified classroom teacher and with instruction in English for a portion of the day.

Although children who speak virtually no English probably have a bilingual or an ESL teacher for most of the day, they often attend such subjects as P.E., music, and art without support of the bilingual teacher. If you find that you have students who speak little or no English in your class, here are suggestions for communicating with them.

- Find out from the bilingual or ESL teacher which children understand some English and which ones understand none, so that your expectations will be fair and realistic. If there is no bilingual or ESL teacher on your campus, find out who the specialist is and how to contact that person to evaluate the student and make suggestions.
- Learn what the children prefer to be called and be sure to pronounce their names correctly.
- Learn key words in the children's native language, such as "listen," "yes," "no," "please," "good," "stop," "look," and "thank you."
- Help these students learn basic vocabulary words needed for your class. These include instructional words you use regularly, along with words needed to understand the content of your class. Provide the bilingual or ESL teacher with an ongoing list of these words to reinforce with the student.
- Rather than relying on someone to translate for you, use your creativity in communicating, speaking naturally, and using phrases, gestures, and drawings or pictures.
- Reinforce key points with visual aids and demonstration, when possible, and by repeating in clear and concise words.
- Because these children are not accustomed to processing English and they assume that they will not understand what is said, ask the bilingual or ESL teacher to encourage them to pay close attention when they are with you to see whether there are words or phrases they can understand or learn.
- Consider assigning peer "buddies," who are outgoing and warm, to communicate what you cannot and to let you know when the students need your help and are reluctant to ask.

- Keep in mind that a long receptive period, during which they respond with gestures or nods before they feel confident enough to speak any English words, is normal for students with limited English proficiency.
- Be careful not to ignore or marginalize these students; include them in class activities as much as possible. For example, assign them to cooperative small groups with their peers. They may not be able to participate fully at first, but the interactions with their peers are important.
- Provide opportunities for these students to share with the class information about their language and culture. Demonstrations of clothing or foods and the introduction of a few simple words can help to integrate these children into the life of the classroom.

Students Living in Extreme Poverty

Many schools have increasing numbers of students who live in significant poverty, which requires understanding and adjustments from school staff. A key to success for these children is a strong, trusting relationship with the teacher in an environment in which they can feel safe, not threatened or stressed. You will probably be the one who must help them understand how school can ultimately benefit them, and why it will be worth the trouble for them to come regularly and to work hard. You will also be the one to help them learn how to negotiate what, for them, are the "hidden" rules and expectations of the school, many of which are taken for granted.

When young children from an impoverished background come to school for the first time, they are unlikely to have the "going-to-school" skills that many children have. They may talk louder than other children or physically defend themselves against perceived threats. They are generally more sensitive to nonverbal than to verbal messages and often are not skilled at processing verbal explanations. Rather, they are tuned in to tone of voice, volume and inflections, gestures, and facial expressions. These children will need the most basic expectations demonstrated before they can adhere to your classroom rules and procedures.

In making explicit the school rules, explain that the school rules and the rules of their neighborhood may be different, just like rules in various games are different (e.g., no tackling in basketball, but it's expected in football; no hitting at school even when you're called a name, though it may occur in your neighborhood). You must make explicit each specific step; for example, what they are to do when they first arrive in the morning—where to go; to walk, not run in the hall; how to walk in line properly; whether or how they are to talk (e.g., quietly or in a whisper); what they may and may not bring to school; what to do with anything they do bring, and so on. They may have difficulty with the new requirements and will need to depend on you to be encouraging and supportive, even as you redirect, remind, and correct them.

In impoverished neighborhoods, great emphasis is placed on "saving face." When being disciplined, these children may try to imitate the adults they have observed; they may grin or laugh off your reprimand or correction. Take great care not to overreact or to humiliate these students, and whenever possible, discipline them in private. This protects their dignity, reduces their need for defiance, and shows your sensitivity to their well-being, even while requiring that they follow the rules.

Approaches to working with these students can be found in Payne (1998). Because such students are often "at-risk" for educational disadvantage, strategies suitable for this population (cf. Hargis 1997) are also applicable. The following strategies may be useful for work with students from impoverished backgrounds.

1. Have some extra supplies and materials on hand to use in case they don't have them. Determine whether the school or district has a fund for such items or whether there are community organizations that provide help.
2. Teach procedures step by step. Encourage self-talk that focuses on the steps.
3. Because these students need a guide to the basis for the school's expectations, use a three-step approach: (a) pointing out what they are supposed to do; (b) giving meaning (reasons why); and (c) providing a strategy (how to do it).
4. Because they are often preoccupied with problems at home, help them "bracket" their worries, to put off worrying about something until a specific later time. Obviously, you will not do this if the problem needs to be addressed immediately.
5. Assign them a peer "buddy" and encourage them to discuss problems and solutions together.
6. Emotions affect children's ability to learn, and fear is a common feeling for these children. Allow them to write a letter or make a drawing expressing strong feelings; offer to keep it in a safe place or even in a sealed envelope for them.
7. Encourage positive self-talk that will enhance their feelings of self-control: "I do the task for myself. Not for the teacher, not for my parents, but for myself."
8. Teach goal setting; have them write down a concrete plan for class today, and at the end of the day, see what goals were met.
9. Allow them to help another student with something they do well.
10. When you meet with a parent of the student, your ability to demonstrate your enjoyment of and caring for his or her child will go a long way toward establishing a cooperative and mutually supportive relationship. Even if the focus of the meeting is to discuss a problem, you should set a pleasant and cordial tone. Keep the focus on positive steps to be taken to address problems.

Teaching Lower-Achieving Students

Many teachers feel they need help in organizing instruction to successfully teach students who are on a low academic level. Whether you have a class with only a few low achievers or one with many students whose entering skills are far below grade level, give special attention to the instructional needs of these students. Techniques that are good instructional practices with all student populations are especially important when teaching low-achieving students.

Active Instruction

Research has shown that students at a low academic level make more progress in basic skills when their teachers provide structured classroom activities with close supervision and lots of active, teacher-led instruction. Large amounts of class time spent in unstructured or free-time activities should be avoided, as should situations calling for frequent self-direction and self-pacing. It is especially important for lower-achieving students to have many opportunities to interact with the teacher during instruction, and to answer the teacher's questions and receive feedback about their work. Low-achieving students should be seated where they can easily be monitored and given assistance.

Organizing and Pacing Instruction

When teaching lower-achieving students, you can encourage more learning and better classroom behavior if you break instruction into small segments or short activities with frequent assessments of understanding. Avoid activity plans that require students to attend to a presentation or to work for twenty-five or thirty minutes at a stretch on the same seatwork assignment. Instead, use two or more shorter cycles of content development and work samples in each lesson, as described in Chapter 5. There are two distinct advantages to using several cycles instead of one when teaching lower-ability students. One advantage is that it is easier to maintain student involvement. Also, by carefully monitoring the first independent work/classwork exercise, you can easily observe whether students are able to complete the assignments, which in turn makes it easier for you to pace instruction appropriately and give ample feedback to students.

In planning lessons, keep in mind that especially with lower-ability students, it is more effective to cover material very thoroughly than to cover a lot of material quickly. Plan for plenty of practice and repetition, and keep your lesson plans flexible enough to allow for reteaching. This does not mean, however, that assignments for lower-level students should be limited to routine, repetitious, and uninteresting work. On the contrary, assignments and class discussion should provide opportunities for all students to think, be creative, and organize and apply what they know. At least some of the questions lower-ability students encounter in written and oral work should give them practice with these higher-level operations.

Plan introductions of new content very carefully. Clear communication is important in all classes, but it is especially important for lower-achieving students. Careless, overly complex communication is likely to result in confusion, frustration, and misbehavior. Follow the guidelines for clarity discussed in Chapter 8, paying careful attention to the amount of information presented at one time, appropriate vocabulary, and the use of concrete or specific examples to illustrate new concepts. Check for student understanding frequently. Avoid overlapping many procedural directions. Get student attention, then present directions in a step-by-step fashion, waiting for students to complete each step before going on to the next.

Remedial Instruction

For learning to occur, all students (and especially lower-achieving students) must be provided with instructional materials and tasks at which they can succeed. Lower-achieving students often require remedial instruction. When beginning a new unit, you may find that some students do not have the prerequisite skills. Or after teaching a lesson, you may realize that several students have not mastered the new material. Both of these situations require that you provide remedial instruction. Two considerations are crucial: You must build time for remediation into your classroom activity plans, and you must get instructional materials that are appropriate for the students who need remediation. Talk with your instructional supervisor, a resource teacher, or other teachers to obtain instructional materials that your low-ability students will be able to complete successfully.

Building Positive Attitudes

Even in lower elementary grades, lower-achieving students are more likely to have developed a poor self-image or poor attitude toward school. By the upper elementary grades, lower academic level students have often fallen two or more grade levels below average for their grade and age group. Some may have failed one or more grades in previous years. Because of their frequent failure in school in the past, some of these students will have become very discouraged; they may react by giving up easily or by fighting back. These reactions may be evidenced in the extremes of apathy, shyness, belligerence, or clowning in class. Especially in earlier grades, these students may perceive classroom events as arbitrary or mysterious. They do not expect to understand or to succeed in schoolwork, and maintaining their attention for long periods of time may be difficult, particularly when they encounter demanding or frustrating tasks.

As a teacher of lower-achieving students, an important part of your task is to improve these students' self-images and expectations of accomplishment. There are several steps you can take. First, remember that it is important for these students to finish their work and not give up. This may require that you shorten assignments for some or provide students with extra time and encouragement to finish their work. Be careful, however, that the extra time lower-achieving students are given to finish assignments does not prevent them from participating in interesting and worthwhile activities with the rest of the class. Constantly being denied participation in show-and-tell, art activities, interest centers, and recess does not contribute to an improved self-image. A better approach is to provide materials and assignments that lower-achieving students are able to finish in the available time.

Create opportunities for all children to be successful. Some students who have difficulty with reading or mathematics are gifted in drawing, technology, or strategy. Vary your instruction in ways that bring these strengths to light.

Class discussions are opportunities for students to display their knowledge. Because teachers' questions and students' answers are heard by everyone, the teacher's handling of discussions often communicates expectations about student performance. The way lower-achieving students are treated during class discussions can affect their attitude and achievement. Staying with students until they answer a question, giving them time to answer without being interrupted, providing constructive feedback to wrong answers, and helping students improve their answers are all ways that you can help low-achieving students succeed.

A warm, supporting, and accepting classroom climate benefits lower-achieving students, but be thoughtful in your use of praise. Research suggests that praise is more helpful when it is specific and contingent on good work, good behavior, or both. Don't make the mistake of frequently rewarding lower-achieving students with vague or general praise, with praise for wrong answers, or for sloppy, incomplete work. This may confuse students or convey the message that you don't expect much from them. Be alert for opportunities to give slower students deserved and specific praise.

Teaching Higher-Achieving Students

Higher-ability students may present special challenges in heterogeneous classes. The need to keep these students productively involved in learning activities requires that they be challenged at the appropriate level and given sufficient activities to avoid boredom or disruption of the rest of the class.

Research has shown that higher-ability students learn more when they are challenged. The level of success on activities can sometimes be lower than that needed for students with less ability; that is, they may not become as frustrated if they do not perform with an extremely high level of success. Effective teachers of higher-ability students tend to work at a faster pace than normal with these students, and they introduce more variety in their teaching methods and materials.

It bears noting that not all of your high-ability students will function in your classroom in the same way. Some high-ability students are high achievers; these students are often a joy to work with. High achievers may be well-socialized, independent workers who have developed positive attitudes toward school and learning. Some high-ability students, however, appear very different. They may be highly creative, highly divergent, gifted thinkers who approach every problem you present in your classroom differently from their peers, or they may create behavior problems. You must be careful not to confuse compliant behavior with academic ability.

The ability, creativity, and divergence of students who are gifted should be nurtured and encouraged, but this may be difficult in a heterogeneous classroom. Classrooms with more open-ended assignments, where each student pursues a project or a problem to the extent of his or her ability, may provide more support for divergent thinkers and may help to avoid behavior problems that arise out of boredom or frustration with the limitations of highly structured assignments.

Have resource materials available for these students to use for bonus questions or extra projects. Develop a file box of index cards with a variety of ideas for projects. Include extra or bonus questions on all assignments and tests, and encourage these students to attempt them. If your classroom or school library has a computer, check out programs from your educational service center or public library that provide enrichment to areas you are covering in class. Involve these students in activities that can benefit others, such as peer tutoring, peer counseling, school improvement projects, and so on. Encourage your higher-ability students to keep up with current events (as appropriate for their age) and to write their questions or opinions to the newspaper or to people in the news.

Higher-ability students can contribute greatly to the learning environment in your classroom. Their contributions to class discussions and activities may encourage creativity and divergent thought in your other students. Your response to them, as well as to the other special groups that make up your class, signals to all students that their range of abilities, interests, and skills is welcomed and appreciated.

Further Reading

Buzzell, J. G., & Piazza, R. (1994). *Case studies for teaching special needs and at-risk students.* Albany, N.Y.: Delmar.

This book contains more than twenty cases written by teachers chronicling their experiences with teaching students with special needs. The cases cover the full range of physical, mental, and emotional disabilities and provide grounding for analysis and problem solving.

Hodgdon, L. A. (1995). *Visual strategies for improving communication: Practical supports for school and home* (Vol. 1). Troy, Mich.: Quirk Roberts.

This book contains practical hands-on suggestions for working with students of varying ages who have severe language and communication impairments. The interventions focus on students' comprehension of instructions and of their environment, as well as their expressive communication.

Kronberg, R., Jackson, L., Sheets, G., & Rogers-Connolly, T. (1995). A toolbox for supporting integrated education. *Teaching Exceptional Children, 27*(4), 54–58.

Including students with special needs in the regular education classroom requires that special educators, regular educators, and administrators work together to develop new conceptions about roles and responsibilities. This article suggests a framework for thinking about how all participants should cooperate, and it also describes numerous activities and strategies to further this goal.

Students with special needs [Special issue]. (1996). *Educational Leadership, 53*(5), 42–74.

This theme issue contains helpful articles about the challenges in educating students with special needs. The authors deal with such issues as preventing learning disabilities through early intervention programs (Slavin), teaching English language learners (Gersten), holistic approaches to teaching students with Attention Deficit Disorder (Armstrong), and identifying and developing special talents (Feldhusen).

Tomlinson, C. A. (1995). *How to differentiate instruction in mixed-ability classrooms.* Alexandria, Va.: ASCD.

This book is a helpful guide for teachers who want to accommodate student diversity in their classrooms. The author describes differentiated instruction, suggests how to plan for it and how to manage it, and provides guidelines for assessing progress. The appendix describes several strategies for accommodating diverse learners and gives rationales and guidelines for the use of each.

http://iris.peabody.vanderbilt.edu

The home site of the Iris Center for Faculty Enhancement was established by the U.S. Department of Education's Office of Special Education. It promotes better awareness and understanding of the needs of special learners. Course enhancement materials, interactive training modules, case studies, activities, and an extensive resource library are available at this site.

www.circleofinclusion.org

This website includes demonstrations and information about the effective practices of inclusive educational programs.

www.ccbd.net

This website of the Council for Children with Behavior Disorders includes up-to-date information concerning issues and research related to behavioral disorders.

www.nichcy.org/resources

Organized by the National Information Center for Children and Youth with Disabilities, this is a comprehensive site with in-depth coverage of issues including learning disorders and behavioral problems.

www.schoolpsychology.net

This is a special education resource site for parents and educators with a wide variety of special topics and links to information, ideas for accommodation, articles, research, stories, and more.

www.air.org/cecp

Supported by the Center for Effective Collaboration and Practice, this is an extensive collection of links to sites on cultural competence, school violence, child welfare, early intervention, and more.

www.uniquelygifted.org

This site is devoted to gifted children with special needs (e.g., ADD/HD, LD, and Asperger's Syndrome) and has links to research, curriculum sources, assistive technology, and so forth.

Suggested Activities

1. Read Case Studies 10.1 and 10.2 to see two teachers' strategies for working with students with special needs.

2. Problems 10.1 and 10.2 describe two situations that elementary teachers frequently encounter. Use ideas presented in this chapter to identify strategies that could be used in these situations. Check your ideas with the suggestions in the Appendix.

3. Read Case Study 10.3
   - What modifications does Mrs. Laskey make to meet the needs of her inclusion students? How would these modifications benefit the students involved?
   - Why do you think she has the class arranged in groups? What does this mean for her inclusion students?

CASE STUDY 10.1

ORGANIZING READING INSTRUCTION
FOR LOW-ACADEMIC-LEVEL STUDENTS

Mr. Bartolo is beginning his second year as a first-grade teacher in an urban elementary school that serves a predominantly Hispanic population. His twenty-six students present a variety of challenges: a wide range of reading levels, several students with limited English proficiency, students who receive supplemental instruction from the resource teacher, and one student who has been diagnosed with attention deficit hyperactivity disorder.

In his first year of teaching, Mr. Bartolo used the recommended reading basal series with small, homogeneous groups of students. He has followed this format for the first six weeks of his second year, but he is especially concerned with the progress of two students in the classroom. The first student, Jason, is one of four students in the highest reading group. Jason has above average academic abilities but has difficulty getting along with his classmates. The second student, Juan, is one of five students in the lowest reading group. Juan's family immigrated from Puerto Rico at the beginning of the school year, and he speaks limited English.

Mr. Bartolo is familiar with peer tutoring, and he knows that several of his colleagues utilize it in their classrooms. After discussing peer tutoring with a colleague and with the boys' parents, he decides to implement this strategy with Jason and Juan. Mr. Bartolo hopes that the tutoring arrangement can strengthen Jason's social skills and help Juan's reading.

Before the peer tutoring begins, Mr. Bartolo knows that he must work with Jason and Juan to teach them strategies for comprehension and decoding unknown words during their small-group reading instruction. Other skills necessary for peer tutoring, such as listening, sharing, and problem solving, have been emphasized during the first six weeks of school.

In addition to these skills, Mr. Bartolo schedules extra time to practice the peer tutoring with Jason and Juan. After several practice sessions, Jason and Juan begin the tutoring without Mr. Bartolo's assistance. He continues to monitor and intervene as necessary, and he sees signs of improvement in the boys.

Along with the small-group instruction and limited implementation of peer tutoring, Mr. Bartolo modifies student assignments as necessary. This includes making audiotapes of books, shortening assignments, providing one-on-one instruction, and designing literacy projects for heterogeneous cooperative groups. Mr. Bartolo is confident that his students' reading comprehension has improved this year. He is thinking of expanding the peer tutoring to include every student in his class next year. What things should he consider?

CASE STUDY 10.2

SUPPORTING STUDENTS WITH AUDITORY DISABILITIES IN THE CLASSROOM

Ms. Chin has a lively class of twenty-four second graders, two of whom have severe auditory impairments. Bobby wears hearing aids that require Ms. Chin to wear an FM power pack so he can hear what she is saying. Sally has a cochlear implant, but she has virtually no hearing. Both children use sign language; Bobby speaks to some extent. An interpreter follows them throughout the day, sitting or standing near the teacher during instruction and signing. The interpreter stays near them during independent work periods to translate and sign any instructions that may be out of the children's line of vision.

During the first week of school, and before Bobby and Sally began attending Ms. Chin's class full time, she explained hearing impairments to the class so that they would understand. A specialist for the auditorily impaired showed the students the FM equipment, let them hear through it, and played a tape to demonstrate what sounds were like for those with hearing loss. Ms. Chin also spoke with the class about the interpreter's role, emphasizing that all students were to look at the teacher, not the interpreter. She marked a place on the carpet with masking tape as "Sally's spot," because Sally needed to be at the front and center of the room to see the teacher and the interpreter during rug time.

Ms. Chin learned basic signs herself and began using them while speaking to the class. Above the alphabet letters at the top of the board, she posted hand signs for each letter. She found that several children quickly picked up signing and began communicating with Sally and Bobby with signs, words, and gestures. The school also has a "Sign Club," through which the entire student body learns five new signs a week.

During center time, Ms. Chin usually places the FM power pack in the middle of the table for Bobby. She has taken care to let both Bobby and Sally sit near children with whom they have made friends, because this eases their problems with communication. Many of the activities are already structured to be hands-on, a preferred means of learning for auditorily impaired students. Ms. Chin does not use phonics approaches with Sally and Bobby, because even with Bobby's partial hearing he misses distinctions among "ch," "sh," "th," and some other sounds. Ms. Chin works closely with the special education teacher, who also teaches Bobby and Sally for part of the day, to coordinate and reinforce what they are learning. Ms. Chin also communicates often with Bobby's and Sally's parents so that they, too, can reinforce what the children are learning in school.

The teacher keeps a signing manual in her classroom, and when she starts a new unit, she sends vocabulary words home along with the signs for any words that are unusual so that she, the interpreter, the special education teacher, and the parents will be consistent in using the same signs. Bobby and Sally learn vocabulary words both orally and through signs. Several other manipulatives are available to help these students learn, such as a number line, shapes, and puzzle boards.

CASE STUDY 10.3

TEACHING STUDENTS IN A THIRD-GRADE INCLUSION CLASS

Mrs. Laskey has twenty-two energetic third graders, including four who qualify for special education support. She has student desks arranged in groups of five or six, with only one special student in any one cluster. She does not single out the four students, but she does make sure to check with them frequently for understanding. During discussion periods, she calls on the four students often, sometimes just to have them repeat instructions; she says this helps her know they are keeping up and also provides them with easy success. When students are doing written work or taking tests, she makes sure to walk by the desks of these four students, helping them when she sees a problem, rather than waiting for them to raise their hands for help. Based on recommendations from the special education modification written for each child, Mrs. Laskey gives directions in small, distinct steps, shortens written assignments, clearly defines limits (physical/behavioral), extends time requirements, reads test to students, allows use of math manipulatives during math tests, and has students repeat directions. One of these students has a history of behavior problems, and she engages him frequently, allowing him some extra movement around the classroom when it will not be disruptive

During tests and during certain instructional periods, such as language arts, Ms. Bonner, the special education teacher, comes into Mrs. Laskey's classroom. Ms. Bonner is there specifically to work with the four students in the special education program, in accordance with their individual education plans; at times she may also help other students when those four seem to be understanding and working well. This way, the four students are provided the extra support they need but are not singled out. On occasion, especially just after a new concept has been introduced, Ms. Bonner may take one or more of the four students to a corner of the room for additional instruction.

When Mrs. Laskey has her class gather on the rug for story time or instruction, the four children sit among their peers, wherever they choose. The child who has difficulty with behavior often chooses to sit in back of the other students so he can stand up and move around. Mrs. Laskey may motion or speak to him if he is becoming too active. If his movement becomes disruptive, she gives him the choice of controlling his own behavior and becoming quieter in the back; she asks him whether he can do that or whether it would help him to sit next to her. His choice varies, and he seems to understand that she knows he must work harder than other students to control his behavior. When he does opt to move up next to her, she touches his shoulder now and then for additional support and reminders. This also helps him focus on the material she is presenting, because he is closer to her.

PROBLEM 10.1

TEAM TEACHING

Mr. Miller and two other fourth-grade teachers use team teaching for math instruction. Shortly after lunch each day, some students from the other teachers' classes come to Mr. Miller's room and some of his students go to the other two teachers' rooms. Mr. Miller has grown dissatisfied with the arrangement because he feels that too much of his teaching time is wasted while groups change rooms, get organized, and get ready to work. Sometimes early-arriving students disrupt lessons. At other times, stragglers hold up the rest of the class. Students frequently arrive without the materials they need for that day. While Mr. Miller answers questions and deals with problems, students begin chatting and wandering around. When Mr. Miller is ready to start the lesson, he has trouble getting students settled down to work. What can Mr. Miller do to make teaming work more smoothly?

PROBLEM 10.2

A HETEROGENEOUS CLASS

Ms. Ortiz feels that her class this year is more difficult to teach than any she has had in her four years of teaching third grade. Of twenty-six students in class, seven are beginning the school year functioning at first-grade level or below in reading. Five of these seven are also far behind in mathematics concepts; the other two are on grade level. Three students in the class have advanced reading and mathematics skills, whereas others are nearer to grade level. Ms. Ortiz is frustrated in her attempts to meet the needs of the slowest students while challenging the brighter students. She now conducts four reading groups. What strategies might Ms. Ortiz consider?

Answer Keys
for Chapter Activities

Chapter 1

ACTIVITY 1

The room arrangement shown in Figure 1.3 could contribute to classroom management problems in a number of ways:

- When the teacher presents information from the area near the main chalkboard, students on the other side of the room are quite distant from the chalkboard and the teacher. This makes it difficult for them to see the material written on the chalkboard, and it is more difficult for the teacher to monitor these students. At the same time, the teacher's range of movement is restricted to a relatively small area, and there is no place to store materials needed in whole-group presentations.
- Traffic lanes are clogged or blocked, especially near the bookshelves, computer, and en route to the bathrooms and the pencil sharpener.
- The small-group table in the center of the room is too near the student desks. Not only might the arrangement cause distractions for students seated at their desks, but there is no place at the table where the teacher can sit and easily see everybody in the room.
- The teacher should consider using a low bookcase to avoid blocking the view of the center. Because of the location of the bookcase, the center may be difficult to monitor.
- Some students have their backs to the chalkboard and to the main presentation area.
- When the teacher assists individual students at their desks, he or she will have difficulty seeing students in several places in the room.
- The isolated desk near the girls' restroom door is a source of potential problems. Not only does it block the path to the door and to the computer, but also a student seated at the desk would be distracted by and be a distraction to students coming and going from this area. Also, the location of the desk makes it difficult for the teacher to monitor a student seated there.
- The student sitting at the desk against the teacher's desk might be distracted if the teacher worked with other students at the desk. Also, this desk is far from the main instructional area.

■ The location of the computer workstation may be a distraction to students using the station as others move to and from the restroom. There also may be an electrical hazard from water from the restrooms or water fountain entering the computer workstation. However, consider that the location of the Internet connections limits the placement of the computer workstation.

Chapter 3

ACTIVITY 2

CASE STUDY 3.4

DIAGNOSIS

The continuing confusion of Mr. Ambrose's students about due dates, directions, and completion of work suggests that although he may have planned plenty of activities for the students, he may not be explaining requirements clearly or checking for understanding frequently enough. In addition, students are not receiving feedback about their progress or the quality of their work, nor are there any apparent rewards or penalties connected with work completion or lack of it. Having students hold papers until the next day may result in the misplacement of many of them and in further delay in receiving feedback about the correctness of the work.

SUGGESTIONS

Mr. Ambrose can begin to improve his situation by trying the following strategies:

■ Each assignment should be explained carefully and in detail in addition to being posted on the board. Students can be encouraged to keep an assignment book or some other record of daily assignments in particular subjects. In addition, Mr. Ambrose can keep a record of the assignments in a folder so that students can refer to it if needed or check on assignments they missed while they were absent. Keeping several days' assignments posted on the board may be confusing unless these are clearly marked.

■ While giving directions and explanations, Mr. Ambrose should be aware of signs of confusion or inattention. He should also be sure to go over sample questions, problems, or exercises with the class, use a standard format for headings on papers, and use routines whenever possible to avoid constantly having to re-explain or give new directions.

■ Mr. Ambrose should also have students begin assignments under his direction. He can do a small part of an assignment orally, then question students to check their understanding until he is sure they can work independently.

■ He should circulate around the class and monitor student progress rather than sit at his desk doing paperwork. He should allow students to come to his desk for help only after they have tried the assignment. Then he should allow only one student at a time to come up. When several students need help, he should circulate around the class again rather than encouraging "come-ups."

- Assignments should be checked and collected as they are completed. If they are too complex to be checked immediately, Mr. Ambrose should check for completeness and return incomplete work to the students to finish. It may be helpful to set aside one or two specific times each day to review each student's progress on assignments. That way, students will know they are accountable, and Mr. Ambrose can more easily identify problems that students are having with work. In addition, he will be able to identify students who are having difficulty and need extra help before they get too far behind. Students who fail to turn in assignments should be given assistance and direction promptly.

- Mr. Ambrose can encourage students to set goals by helping them keep records of their scores on assignments in particular subjects. He may be able to boost motivation by encouraging the students to set a class goal of improved completion rates or overall student averages and may then provide a treat or a special activity as a reward.

Chapter 5

ACTIVITY 2

PROBLEM 5.1

In organizing her students' day, Ms. Kendall must plan to accommodate both "school givens" of time and space and "pupil givens" of numbers and abilities. Before developing her daily schedule, Ms. Kendall must check the school's master schedule to learn what times have been assigned to her class for lunch, recess, music, art, physical education, and so on. In planning around these time constraints, she must consider how many students will be in the class, the range of their ability levels, and the size of the classroom. She must take into consideration both student attention patterns throughout the day and attention spans within the day. Because students tend to be more alert in the morning and less alert after lunch, she will want to schedule academic subjects accordingly. Also, she will have to provide a variety of activities, with none lasting too long. Room size, however, will determine the number of centers and individual study areas available.

On the first day of school, Ms. Kendall's plans should include the following: greet the students; give a brief introduction of herself and her class; explain the areas of the room and procedures needed for the first week; begin a presentation and discussion of class rules, procedures, and consequences; direct a student get-acquainted activity; provide whole-class, uncomplicated academic activities; allow time to complete administrative tasks; and have constructive "time fillers" ready for use if needed.

PROBLEM 5.2

The following suggestions for Mr. Hart could improve his students' performance during independent work.

- He should make sure that everyone understands instructions before starting groups. Explanation alone may not be sufficient; students should be questioned and should repeat key directions. Mr. Hart can also write the directions on the chalkboard. Students should be told what will be checked and when.
- If independent work includes silent reading, reading comprehension questions can be listed on the board so that students have a focus for their reading and know what they will be accountable for when they are called to the reading circle.
- Students may need help pacing themselves. The teacher can show them on the clock how much time the first assignment should take or set a timer to signal when they should be finished with a particular assignment.
- To have time to get the independent work group started, Mr. Hart can give the first reading group a getting-ready activity to complete before he joins them. This will enable him to monitor all out-of-group students at the beginning of the activity to be sure they have made a good start.
- After working with the reading group for a while, the teacher can give these students a short activity to do on their own while he checks on the progress of out-of-group students and answers their questions. When out-of-group students are wasting time and in danger of not completing other necessary activities, their papers can be marked to show each student's progress on the first assignment. They can then start on their next assignment, but they should be required to finish the first assignment at home or later in class.
- Students should not be allowed to interrupt the teacher with questions during small-group instruction. They should be told to skip troublesome parts until the teacher can talk to them, or student monitors can be assigned the responsibility of giving assistance to children who need it.
- A visual signal, such as a sign or a flag, can be used to inform students when they may approach the teacher with questions and when they may not.
- A "help" list for the class may be established. Children can sign the list if they want to talk to the teacher when he is busy. The teacher must be conscientious about checking the list and going to the children as soon as possible (e.g., between reading groups).
- Students need to know what they may and may not do after their assignments have been completed. They should be given free-time enrichment activities or provided with a good set of interesting materials for free reading.

PROBLEM 5.3

Apparently, this type of instruction is new for Ms. Jackson's class, so students will have to learn a new set of procedures. They may be accustomed to highly directed lessons, and they may not have had much science instruction. Ms. Jackson will have to explain the procedures for a discovery lesson, including how to work on your own and with a partner, and the purposes for this science lesson. She should make sure she has everyone's attention before beginning the explanation. She should start by introducing the lesson and its purposes and demonstrating appropriate uses of the cups. She must make clear at the beginning what uses of the cups she sees as inappropriate.

Ms. Jackson must consider how to create a balance between overdirecting students and leaving them too much on their own. She should work through questions like those in Checklist 5 to focus on her purposes for this lesson and which aspects of it are new to her students. For example, what kind of product does she expect from her students? Will they demonstrate their findings, write a lab report, apply their findings to another situation? If pairs or groups work independently, what will they do if they finish at different times?

Ms. Jackson has to develop a system for distributing and collecting materials to minimize the time the teacher is unavailable to circulate and provide assistance. For example, she might appoint one student from each group as "Materials Manager" and set up a central place for that student to pick up cups for the group.

ACTIVITY 3

PROBLEM 5.4

See how many examples of Kounin's concepts noted on page 101 you can find in the following description.

As he is about to begin class after lunch, Mr. Case makes eye contact with two students who are exchanging notes; the students quickly get out their class materials. (**Withitness**) "Let's begin by working some of the exercises at the end of the chapter; you will need a piece of paper with a heading." As students begin to get out their materials, Mr. Case calls out, "Oops, I forgot to tell you to bring money for tomorrow for the field trip. How many of you will be going?" (**Lack of smoothness**) After a brief discussion, students finish getting out their materials. Mr. Case says, "We'll go through these exercises orally, but I also want you to write the answers on your papers as part of today's classwork. I'll come around later and check your answers. (**High-participation format and accountability**) Now, who can answer the first question? Hands please. Tyrone?" Mr. Case conducts the lesson by calling on various students, some with hands up, others seemingly at random from the nonvolunteers. (**Group alerting**) About halfway through the exercises, a student enters the room and says that he is new to the school and has been assigned to the class. Mr. Case goes to his desk, sits down, and says, "OK, come here. I'll check out some of your books to you. (**Lack of overlapping**) I wish the school office wouldn't send children in the middle of the period. Where are you from anyway? That's a nice shirt you are wearing." (**Lack of smoothness**) After finishing with the student and sending him to a seat, Mr. Case leaves his desk and says to the class, "Now where were we? Oh, yes, question 7. Say, where did Kim and Lee go? I didn't give them permission to leave." (**Lack of withitness**) After several more minutes, Mr. Case calls a halt to the activity and says, "Now, I'd like us to discuss the test coming up this Thursday. Let's make sure that you are all clear on what will be on the exam and what you will need to get ready for it." After a pause, he adds, "I almost forgot. Get your questions from before and look at the next to the last one. We have to add an important point that was left out. . . ." After finishing the item, Mr. Case turns the topic back to the upcoming test. (**Lack of momentum**) "Now, where were we. Oh, yes. I want to show you some items that will be similar to those on the test. Here's one." He writes it on the board, then pauses: "Well, I don't want to give away the test, do I?" Without discussing the test further, he turns to another topic. (**Lack of smoothness**) "Just wait until you hear about the videotape we will be viewing tomorrow. I borrowed it from another teacher, and she said that her students thought it was one of the most interesting, exciting stories they had ever seen!" (**Group alerting**)

ACTIVITY 4

CASE STUDY 5.1

DIAGNOSIS

Although Ms. Lake has planned interesting presentations, her students seem to be floundering during the follow-up activities. A large part of Ms. Lake's problem lies with poor instructional clarity, poor sequencing of activities, and unclear directions. Students' poor showing on the five-item test suggests that related content from the previous week had not been understood. The twenty-minute presentation contains several indicators of poor clarity, including presenting information out of sequence, backtracking, inserting extraneous information, and moving from one topic to another without warning. In addition, the assignment does not support the content development activity. The assignment is made without checking for understanding, and the directions are vague and indefinite.

SUGGESTIONS

Ms. Lake would achieve more success with her class if she concentrated on the following items:

- Information should be presented systematically. Plan the lesson sequence and stick to it; state major goals and objectives; pace the lesson so that adequate time is available to cover major points; and avoid vagueness by being specific and using familiar words.
- Ms. Lake should review her procedures for keeping students responsible for work, especially in the areas of communicating work requirements and giving directions clearly. She should be sure that step-by-step

directions are given for complex assignments, and she should ask students to repeat directions if there is a possibility that they do not understand them.

- During content development activities, frequent work samples should be obtained and other checks on comprehension used. With this information, available instruction can be adjusted as needed.
- The amount of information being presented in any one lesson should be considered carefully. It might be better to present less information and leave sufficient time to check classwork before assigning homework.
- Complex lessons should be broken down into smaller parts, and later concepts should not be presented until primary ones are mastered.
- If some students still do not seem to understand after a presentation and discussion, the teacher can meet with them in a small group to review the presentation and answer questions. If one or two students consistently have difficulty, they can be seated near the teacher's desk so that it is easier to work with them.
- During the independent work portion of lessons, the teacher should circulate to check student progress and to make sure that assignment directions are being followed.

Chapter 7

ACTIVITY 1

PROBLEM 7.1

DIAGNOSIS

Ms. Greene has failed to communicate and reinforce her expectations for classroom behavior and to establish rules and procedures that deal with the problem areas in her classroom. She apparently did not stop inappropriate behavior when it first began occurring; as a result, what could have been a good start during the first weeks of school has deteriorated into a difficult situation. At this point, even the well-behaved students are misbehaving, and her only deterrent has lost its effect.

SUGGESTIONS

Ms. Greene should decide what kinds of behavior she expects of her students with regard to general conduct as well as procedures they should follow in particular activities. She should then develop new rules and procedures where they are needed and clarify and reteach those that were part of her original plan but are no longer effective. For example, she could set aside specific times for students to get drinks, use the restroom, sharpen pencils, or visit the class pets.

In addition, she should select a time—perhaps a Monday or the day after a school vacation—to introduce or to review and reteach the rules and procedures to her class. She should also explain to the students the rationales for the desired behaviors and perhaps rehearse complex ones so she can give students feedback about especially important behaviors. She will certainly want to remind the students about when they are allowed to whisper quietly. Because students have acquired poor classroom talk habits, they may need visual cues such as stop or go signs to remind them about when they must work quietly and when they may whisper or talk in classroom voices. She can also help students learn when it is appropriate to talk quietly and when it is not by alerting them about class noise levels and encouraging them to monitor it themselves.

Ms. Greene should review with the students the procedures for working in small groups. She may have to adopt the following practices:

- Use shorter independent work periods, breaking up activities in the groups more often.
- Help students pace themselves by setting a timer to signal when work should be completed.
- Tell students ahead of time what work will be checked and when. Remind them that they will be questioned about their assignment when they come to the reading circle.
- Make sure that students in the first group understand their assignment by having them do an example or two before calling for the second group.
- Monitor the out-of-group students for appropriate behavior while working with the reading group.
- After sending one group back to independent work, don't call the second group until the work of the other students has been checked and help has been given when needed.

After the rules and procedures are introduced—or reintroduced—to the class, Ms. Greene should do the following:

- Monitor the class with the goal of anticipating and preventing misbehavior before it occurs and noting appropriate behavior.
- Make sure students have enough work to do and that they understand and are able to complete activities. Students should also know what specific things they can do when they have finished their assigned work.
- Structure time for movement and activity.
- Make statements that pace students through their work, such as: "You should now be working on problems 2 through 5. No one should be talking," or "After I've checked your paper, you may go to the listening center."
- Reward academic performance and other desirable classroom behavior regularly, using stars, happy faces, displays of student work, pats on the back, smiles, and so on.
- Be certain that stated consequences for inappropriate behavior are related to the misbehavior and that they can be carried out consistently. Positive consequences as well as negative ones should be communicated to students.

Chapter 8

ACTIVITY 8.2

1. b; 2. c; 3. d; 4. a; 5. c.

Chapter 10

ACTIVITY 2

PROBLEM 10.1

The following approaches would help the team operate more smoothly:

- Strive for good cooperation and group planning among unit or team teachers. Each teacher must try to maintain the schedule. Have students watch the time. Post times for students to leave, and list the materials they should take with them. Use a timer if necessary.
- Use established routines as much as possible for beginning and ending lessons; monitor the class to be sure that students follow them.
- Teach students exactly what behaviors are expected during transitions; include expectations for voice level, use of the pencil sharpener, procedures for passing between classes, getting ready for the lesson, and so on.
- If early-arriving students are a problem, establish a "waiting area" where these students must wait quietly until the teacher can speak with them without interrupting the class.
- Use a short review activity with the group while waiting for stragglers to arrive.
- Make sure students know what they are supposed to do when they return to the class. If they return while the teacher is conducting a lesson, give the group or the class a brief activity to do while making sure that students coming in get settled.

PROBLEM 10.2

Following are specific suggestions for Ms. Ortiz:

- Each day, plan assignments that all students can complete, then provide supplementary assignments at different levels: enrichment and extension for faster students, review and practice assignments for slower students.
- Find out whether any students in the class qualify for special assistance (such as special education, resource room, or bilingual tutoring).
- Use some small-group instruction in both reading and (at least temporarily) mathematics. Be sure to keep groups flexible, changing membership according to achievement.
- Consider whether it might be possible to team with one or more teachers so that students on similar levels can be grouped for basic skills instruction.

- Consider the use of peer tutoring for certain activities and assignments.
- Share materials with other teachers to build a collection of supplementary materials above and below your grade level.
- Arrange student seating so that you have easy access to lower-ability students and can monitor and help them readily during whole-class instruction.
- Be sure to include all students in class discussions and recitations. Do not let faster students answer most of the questions.
- After giving assignment directions to the whole class, check the lower-ability students first to make sure that they understand directions and are beginning work. If more than two or three students need further directions, meet with them immediately as a small group.
- When instructing the lower-level students, break assignments and lessons into small segments and check frequently for understanding. Follow the suggestions for basic skill instruction presented in the section on teaching low-ability students in Chapter 10.
- Consider using heterogeneous cooperative groups for activities and long-term projects.
- Consider using supportive, remedial, or enrichment software programs.

References and Further Readings

Readers interested in other publications on classroom management by this book's authors and other writers in the field may choose from the following references.

Alberti, R. L. (Ed.) (1977). *Assertiveness: Innovations, applications, issues.* San Luis Obispo, Calif.: Impact.

Alvermann, D. E., O'Brien, D. G., & Dillon, D. R. (1990). What teachers do when they say they're having discussions of content area reading assignments: A qualitative analysis. *Reading Research Quarterly 25,* 296–322.

Baloche, L. (1998) *The cooperative classroom: Empowering learning.* Upper Saddle River, N.J.: Prentice-Hall.

Barton, J., & Collins, A. (Eds.) (1997). *Portfolio assessment: A handbook for educators.* Reading, Mass.: Addison-Wesley.

Battistich, V., Solomon, D., & Delucchi, K. (1993). Interaction processes and student outcomes in cooperative learning groups. *Elementary School Journal 94,* 19–32.

Berger, E. H. (2004). *Parents as partners in education: Families and schools working together* (6th ed.). Englewood Cliffs, N.J.: Merrill/Prentice-Hall.

Brophy, J. (1981). Teacher praise: A functional analysis. *Review of Educational Research 51,* 5–32.

Brophy, J. E. (2000). Teaching. In H. J. Walberg (Series Ed.) *Educational Practices.* Brussels, Belgium: International Academy of Education.

Brophy, J. E. (2004). *Motivating students to learn* (2nd ed.). Hillsdale, N.J.: Erlbaum.

Brophy, J. E., & Alleman, J. (1991). Activities as instructional tools: A framework for analysis and evaluation. *Educational Researcher 20* (4), 9–23.

Burden, P. R. (2000). *Powerful classroom management strategies: Motivating students to learn.* Thousand Oaks, Calif.: Corwin Press/Sage.

Burns, M. (1995). The 8 most important lessons I've learned about organizing my teaching year. *Instructor 105* (2), 86–88.

Butin, D. (2000). *Classrooms.* ERIC Report number ED446421. Washington, D.C.: National Center for Educational Facilities. Available at www.edfacilities.org/ir/irpubs.html.

Buzzell, J. G., & Piazza, R. (1994). *Case studies for teaching special needs and at-risk students.* Albany, N.Y.: Delmar.

Casey, M. B., & Tucker, E. C. (1994). Problem-centered classrooms: Creating lifelong learners. *Phi Delta Kappan* (October), 139–143.

Castle, K., & Rogers, K. (1994). Rule-creating in a constructivist classroom community. *Childhood Education 70* (2), 77–80.

Cohen, E. G. (1994a). *Designing groupwork: Strategies for the heterogeneous classroom* (2nd ed.). New York: Teachers College Press.

Cohen, E. G. (1994b). Restructuring the classroom: Conditions for productive small groups. *Review of Educational Research 64,* 1–36.

Cohen, E. G. (1998). Making cooperative learning equitable. *Educational Leadership 56,* 18–21.

Cohen, J. J., & Fish, M. C. (Eds.) (1993). *Handbook of school-based interventions.* San Francisco: Jossey-Bass.

Cutona, C., & Guerin, D. (1994). Confronting conflict peacefully: Peer mediation in schools. *Educational Horizons 72* (2), 95–104.

Davis, Stan. (2004). *Schools where everyone belongs: Practical strategies for reducing bullying.* Wayne, Maine: Stop Bullying Now.

Deci, E. L., Koestner, R., & Ryan, R. M. (1999). A meta-analytic review of experiments examining the effects of extrinsic rewards on intrinsic motivation. *Psychological Bulletin 125,* 627–668.

Deci, E. L., & Ryan, R. M. (1985). *Intrinsic motivation and self-determination in human behavior.* New York: Plenum Press.

Educational Research Service. (1989). *ERS information folio: Cooperative learning.* Arlington, Va.: Author.

Emmer, E. T. (1986). Academic activities and tasks in first-year teachers' classes. *Teaching and Teacher Education 2,* 229–244.

Emmer, E. T. (1988). Praise and the instructional process. *Journal of Classroom Interaction 23,* 32–39.

Emmer, E. T., & Aussiker, A. (1990). School and classroom discipline programs: How well do they work? In O. Moles (Ed.), *Student discipline strategies: Research and practice* (pp. 129–165). Albany, N.Y.: SUNY Press.

Emmer, E. T., Evertson, C. M., & Anderson, L. M. (1980). Effective classroom management at the beginning of the school year. *The Elementary School Journal 80* (5), 219–231.

Emmer, E. T., & Gerwels, M. C. (1998a). *Classroom management tasks in cooperative groups.* Paper presented at the annual meeting of the American Educational Research Association, San Diego, Calif.

Emmer, E. T., & Gerwels, M. C. (1998b). *Teachers' views and uses of cooperative learning.* Paper presented at the annual meeting of the American Educational Research Association, San Diego, Calif.

Emmer. E. T., & Gerwels, M. C. (2002). Cooperative learning in elementary classrooms: Teaching practices and lesson characteristics. *Elementary School Journal 103,* 75–91.

Erwin, J. C. (2003). Giving students what they need. *Educational Leadership 61* (1), 19–23.

Evertson, C. M. (1982). Differences in instructional activities in higher- and lower-achieving junior high English and math classes. *The Elementary School Journal 82,* 329–350.

Evertson, C. M. (1985). Training teachers in classroom management: An experimental study in secondary school classrooms. *Journal of Educational Research 79,* 51–58.

Evertson, C. M. (1987). Managing classrooms: A framework for teachers. In D. Berliner & B. Rosenshine (Eds.), *Talks to teachers* (pp. 54–74). New York: Random House.

Evertson, C. M. (1994). Classroom rules and routines. In T. Husen and T. N. Postlewaite (Eds.), *The international encyclopedia of education* (2nd ed., Vol. 2, pp. 816–820). Oxford: Pergamon Press.

Evertson, C. M., & Emmer, E. T. (1982). Effective management at the beginning of the school year in junior high classes. *Journal of Educational Psychology 74,* 485–498.

Evertson, C. M., Emmer, E. T., Sanford, J. P., & Clements, B. S. (1983). Improving classroom management: An experiment in elementary school classrooms. *Elementary School Journal 84* (2), 173–188.

Evertson, C. M., & Harris, A. H. (1992). What we know about managing classrooms. *Educational Leadership 47* (7), 74–78.

Evertson, C. M., & Harris, A. H. (2003). *Creating conditions for learning: A comprehensive program for creating an effective learning environment* (6th ed.). Nashville, Tenn.: Peabody College, Vanderbilt University.

Evertson, C. M., & Poole, I. R. (2004a). *Effective room arrangement.* IRIS Center for faculty enhancement. Nashville, Tenn.: Peabody College, Vanderbilt University.

Evertson, C. M., & Poole, I. R. (2004b). *Fostering student accountability for classroom work.* IRIS Center for faculty enhancement. Nashville, Tenn.: Peabody College, Vanderbilt University.

Evertson, C. M., & Poole, I. R. (2004c). *Norms and expectations.* IRIS Center for faculty enhancement. Nashville, Tenn.: Peabody College, Vanderbilt University.

Evertson, C. M., Sanford, J. P., & Emmer, E. T. (1981). Effects of class heterogeneity in junior high school. *American Educational Research Journal 18,* 219–232.

Evertson, C. M., & Weade, R. (1989). Classroom management and teaching style: Instructional stability and variability in two junior high English classrooms. *The Elementary School Journal 89,* 379–393.

Evertson, C. M., & Weinstein, C. S. (Eds.) (in press). *Handbook of classroom management: Research, practice, and contemporary issues.* Hillsdale, N.J.: Erlbaum.

Fraser, B. J., & Walberg, H. J. (Eds.) (1991). *Educational environments: Evaluation, antecedents and consequences.* Oxford: Pergamon.

Freiberg, H. J. (1996). From tourists to citizens in the classroom. *Educational Leadership 54,* 32–36.

Fuchs, D., Fuchs, L. S., Mathes, P. G., & Simmons, D. G. (1997). Peer-assisted learning strategies: Making classrooms more responsive to diversity. *American Educational Research Journal 34* (1), 174–206.

Glasser, W. (1975). *Reality therapy: A new approach to psychiatry.* New York: Harper & Row.

Glasser, W. (1977). 10 steps to good discipline. *Today's Education 66,* 60–63.

Glasser, W. (1986). *Control theory in the classroom.* New York: Harper & Row.

Good, T. L., & Brophy, J. E. (2003). *Looking in classrooms* (9th ed.). Boston: Allyn & Bacon.

Goodenough, W. (1971). *Culture, language, and society.* Reading, Mass.: Addison-Wesley.

Guskey, T. R. (Ed.) (1996). *Communicating student learning, ASCD yearbook, 1996.* Alexandria, Va.: Association for Supervision and Curriculum Development.

Hargis, C. H. (1997). *Teaching low achieving and disadvantaged students* (2nd ed.). Springfield, Ill.: Charles C. Thomas.

Hill, C. E., & O'Brien, K. M. (1999). *Helping skills: Facilitating exploration, insight, and action.* Washington, D.C.: American Psychological Association.

Hodgdon, L. A. (1995). *Visual strategies for improving communication: Practical supports for school and home* (Vol. 1). Troy, Mich.: Quirk Roberts.

Holubec, E. J. (1992). How do you get there from here? Getting started with Cooperative Learning. *Contemporary Education 63* (3), 181–184.

Hoy, A. W., & Weinstein, C. S. (in press). Students' and teachers' knowledge, beliefs, and perceptions about classroom management. In C. M. Evertson and C. S. Weinstein (Eds.), *Handbook of classroom management: Research, practice, and contemporary issues.* Hillsdale, N.J.: Erlbaum.

Johnson, D. W., & Johnson, R. T. (1994a). Constructive conflict in the schools. *Journal of Social Issues 50* (1), 117–137.

Johnson, D. W., & Johnson, R. T. (1994b). *Learning together and alone: Cooperative, competitive, and individualistic learning* (4th ed.). Boston: Allyn & Bacon.

Johnson, D. W., & Johnson, R. T. (1999). Making cooperative learning work. *Theory into Practice 38* (2), 67–73.

Jones, R. A. (1995). *The child-school interface: Environment and behavior.* London: Cassell.

Jones, V. F., & Jones, L. S. (2001). *Comprehensive classroom management: Creating communities of support and solving problems* (6th ed.), Boston, Mass.: Allyn & Bacon.

Kottler, J. A. (2002). *Students who drive you crazy: Succeeding with resistant, unmotivated, and otherwise difficult young people.* Thousand Oaks, Calif.: Sage Publications/Corwin Press.

Kounin, J. S. (1970). *Discipline and group management in classrooms.* New York: Holt, Rinehart & Winston.

Kounin, J. S., & Gump, P. (1974). Signal systems of lesson settings and the task related behavior of preschool children. *Journal of Educational Psychology 66,* 554–562.

Kronberg, R., Jackson, L., Sheets, G., & Rogers-Connolly, T. (1995). A toolbox for supporting integrated education. *Teaching Exceptional Children 27* (4), 54–58.

Leinhardt, G., Weidman, C., & Hammond, K. M. (1987). Introduction and integration of classroom routines by expert teachers. *Curriculum Inquiry 17* (2), 135–176.

Martin, H., & Hayes, S. (1998). Overcoming obstacles: Approaches to dealing with problem pupils. *British Journal of Special Education 25* (3), 135–139.

McCarney, S. B., & McCain, B. R. (1995). *The behavior dimensions intervention manual.* Columbia, Mo.: Hawthorne Educational Services, Inc.

Meager, J. (1996). Classroom design that works every time. *Instructor 106,* 70–73.

Mendler, Allen. (1997). *Power struggles: Successful techniques for educators.* Rochester, N.Y.: Discipline Associates.

Mueller, C. M., & Dweck, C. S. (1998). Praise for intelligence can undermine children's motivation for performance. *Journal of Personality and Social Psychology 75* (1), 33–52.

Myles, B. S., & Simpson, R. L. (1994). Prevention and management considerations for aggressive and violent children and youth. *Education and Treatment of Children 17,* 370–384.

Nastasi, B. K., & Clements, D. H. (1991). Research on cooperative learning: Implications for practice. *School Psychology Review 20,* 110–131.

Nattiv, A. (1994). Helping behaviors and math achievement gain of students using cooperative learning. *The Elementary School Journal 94,* 285–297.

Nelson, J. R., & Carr, B. A. (2000). *The think time strategy for schools.* Longmont, Colo.: Sopris West.

O'Connor, R. E., & Jenkins, J. R. (1996). Cooperative learning as an inclusion strategy: A closer look. *Exceptional Children 62,* 29–51.

Olweus, D. (1994). *Bullying at school: What we know and what we can do.* Malden, Maine: Blackwell.

Olweus, D. (2003). A profile of bullying at school. *Educational Leadership 60* (6), 12–17.

Payne, Ruby K. (1998). *A framework for understanding poverty.* Highlands, Tex.: RFT.

Poland, S., & McCormick, J. S. (1999). *Coping with crisis: lessons learned.* Longmont, Colo.: Sopris West.

Raffini, J. P. (1996). *150 ways to increase intrinsic motivation in the classroom.* Boston: Allyn & Bacon.

Randolph, C. H., & Evertson, C. M. (1995). Managing for learning: Rules, roles, and meanings in a writing class. *Journal of Classroom Interaction 30* (2), 17–25.

Reeve, J. (in press). Extrinsic rewards and inner motivation. In C. M. Evertson & C. S. Weinstein (Eds.), *Handbook of classroom management: Research, practice, and contemporary issues.* Hillsdale, N.J.: Erlbaum.

Reeve, J., Bolt, E., & Cai, Y. (1999). Autonomy-supportive teachers: How they teach and motivate students. *Journal of Educational Psychology 91,* 537–548.

Schwarz, S., & Pollishuke, M. (1991). *Creating the child-centered classroom.* Katonah, N.Y.: Richard Owen.

Shores, E., & Grace, C. (2000). *The portfolio book: A step-by-step guide for teachers.* Upper Saddle River, N.J.: Merrill/Prentice-Hall.

Shores, R. E., Gunter, P. L., & Jack, S. L. (1993). Classroom management strategies: Are they setting events for coercion? *Behavioral Disorders 18* (2) 92–102.

Short, K. G. (1998). Creating a community of learners. In K. Short & K. M. Pierce (Eds.), *Talking about books: Creating literate communities* (pp. 33–52). Portsmouth, N.H.: Heinemann.

Shukla-Mehta, S., & Albin, R. W. (2003). Twelve practical strategies to prevent behavioral escalation in classroom settings. *Preventing School Failure 47,* 156–172.

Slavin, R. (1995). *Cooperative learning: Theory, research, and practice* (2nd ed.). Boston: Allyn & Bacon.

Slavin, R., & Cooper, R. (1999). Improving intergroup relations: Lessons learned from cooperative learning programs. *Journal of Social Issues,* (Winter Issue, 7 pages).

Sprick, Randall. (1995). *The teacher's encyclopedia of behavior management: 100 problems/500 plans.* Longmont, Colo.: Sopris West.

Stoner, G., Shinn, M., & Walker, H. (1991). *Interventions for achievement and behavior problems.* Silver Spring, Md.: National Association of School Psychologists.

Strengthening Student Engagement [Special issue] (1995). *Educational Leadership 53* (1), 1–69.

Students with Special Needs [Special issue] (1996). *Educational Leadership 53* (5), 4–74.

Tomlinson, C. A. (1995). *How to differentiate instruction in mixed-ability classrooms.* Alexandria, Va.: Association for Supervision and Curriculum Development.

Tudge, J. R. H. (1992). Processes and consequences of peer collaboration: A Vygotskian analysis. *Child Development 63,* 1364–1379.

Wade, A., Abrami, P., Poulsen, C., & Chambers, B. (1995). *Current resources in cooperative learning.* Lanham, Md.: University Press of America.

Webb, N. M., & Farivar, S. (1994). Promoting helping behavior in cooperative small groups in middle school mathematics. *American Educational Research Journal 31,* 369–397.

Weinstein, C. S., & David, T. G. (Eds.) (1987). *Spaces for children: The built environment and child development.* New York: Plenum Press.

Wiske, M. S. (1994). How teaching for understanding changes the rules in the classroom. *Educational Leadership 51* (5), 19–21.

Zuker, E. (1983). *Mastering assertiveness skills: Power and positive influence at work.* New York: AMACON.

Index

Notes and Reminders

Needed Materials and Supplies

_____

_____

_____

_____

_____

_____

_____

_____

_____

_____

_____

_____

_____

_____

_____

_____

_____

_____

_____

_____

Ideas for Procedures and Routines